The 7 Initiatory Fires of Modern Manhood

THE 7 INITIATORY FIRES OF MODERN MANHOOD

Awaken Your Inner King,

Own Your Power &

Live a Legendary Life

HENDRIX BLACK

NEW YORK

LONDON • NASHVILLE • MELBOURNE • VANCOUVER

The 7 Initiatory Fires of Modern Manhood

Awaken Your Inner King, Own Your Power & Live a Legendary Life

Published in New York, New York, by Morgan James Publishing. Morgan James is a trademark of Morgan James, LLC. www.MorganJamesPublishing.com

Proudly distributed by Ingram Publisher Services.

A **FREE** ebook edition is available for you
or a friend with the purchase of this print book.

CLEARLY SIGN YOUR NAME ABOVE

Instructions to claim your free ebook edition:
1. Visit MorganJamesBOGO.com
2. Sign your name CLEARLY in the space above
3. Complete the form and submit a photo
   of this entire page
4. You or your friend can download the ebook
   to your preferred device

ISBN 9781636980386 paperback
ISBN 9781636980393 ebook
Library of Congress Control Number:
2022944392

Cover Design by:
Rachel Lopez
www.r2cdesign.com

Morgan James is a proud partner of Habitat for Humanity Peninsula
and Greater Williamsburg. Partners in building since 2006.

Get involved today! Visit MorganJamesPublishing.com/giving-back

For B

Disclaimer:

Neither the publisher nor the author is engaged in rendering professional advice or services to the reader. The ideas, suggestions, and procedures provided in this book are not intended as a substitute for seeking professional guidance. Further, the information presented is the author's opinion and does not constitute any health or medical advice. The content of this book is for informational purposes only and is not intended to diagnose, treat, cure, or prevent any condition or disease. Please seek advice from your healthcare provider for your personal health concerns prior to taking healthcare or wellness advice from this book. Neither the publisher nor the author shall be held liable or responsible for any loss or damage allegedly arising from any suggestion or information contained in this book.

CONTENTS

ACKNOWLEDGMENTS

I 'm a firm believer (and experiencer) in the notion that an author is a channel for a message that has chosen to express through him. Neither too humble nor too proud in the endeavor. In that sense, the greatest debt of gratitude goes to whichever force has chosen me to be the worthy messenger of this material. It is my prayer that I have served it well.

Beyond that sacred encounter, countless heads, hearts and hands have lent their deft skill and unending support to bring this work into the world. Heartfelt thanks go to Anna Powers, David Hancock, Jim Howard, Emily Madison, and the entire Morgan James publishing team. Special acknowledgment to my editor, Leandre Larouche, who maintained the integrity of the work while ensuring the words and style would be as timeless and enduring as the message intends to be. And of course, Philip "The Wizard" Powis, for being a trusted brother and business partner in the unfoldment of this mission.

Endless gratitude to my teachers, coaches, guides, elders, mentors, mirrors and muses; in all forms they've taken, known and unknown.

To Steven Lumiere, a masterful guide and trusted friend, who has helped illuminate and clarify many of the patterns (and subsequent revelations) that appear in this volume. Eternally grateful.

To the pioneers of this "space": C.G. Jung, Robert Bly, Sam Keen, James Hollis, Robert A. Johnson, Bill Plotkin, James Hillman, Joseph Campbell, Douglas Gillette and Robert Moore. The terrain mapped has largely correlated with my own inner adventures.

And some of its more recent torchbearers: David Deida, John Wineland, GS Youngblood, Robert Masters, Terry Real, Karen Brody, Shems Heartwell, Aubrey Marcus, Mark Manson, Angus Nelson, Philip Drolet, Ege Reynolds, Derek Singh, Malcolm Fraser, Male, Valhalla Farms, Sacred Sons, Man Kind Project, The Good Men Project, and the countless others devoted to enriching the lives of men and their loved ones through their unique insight and contribution. Even if we haven't met (and regardless of full alignment in stated principles), it would be foolish to presume this volume could exist without the "work" you've all so powerfully ushered.

Special thanks to my brothers on the path; whom through just a single spark; or a lifetime of sharing the flames, have helped light and sustain an inextinguishable fire for wholeness, truth and the fullest expression of it: Marc Angelo Coppola, Corey Sheikh, Christopher Stoikos, Chris Evans, Greg Hickman, Miles Schwartz, Daniel Fantus, Peter Katz, Andrew Katz, Dan Martell, Todd Herman, Adil Amarsi, Josh Shipp, Miles Hanson, Matt Brown, Chris Dufey, Miles Stutz, Cody Crockett, Noah Hammond Tyrell, Samuel Woods, Caley Crossman, Michael DiMarco, Garrett Adkins, Joseph Ghaleb, Andrew Lindy, Danny Iny, Jack Born, Taylor Welch, Kameron Snow, Jared Mcdonald, Joshua Pellicer, Mike Heiser, Bradley Rausch, Edward Zaydelman, Ryan Khoury, Kevin Visser, Roy Hadad, Dane Mohrmann, Jay Goncalves, Ben McLellan, Allen Mowers, Phil Stewart, Chris Creed, Pedram Dara, Seth Ellsworth, Daniel Sanchez, Francois Turgeon, Malek Ghaleb, Derek Smith, Chris Robinson, Matthew Coughlin, Allan Fink, Adrian Sule, Ian Rosa, Carmelo Plaitis, Martin Desmarais, Michael Lipkowitz, Timur Grigorchuk, Emmanuel Lavigne, Prashant Sojitra, Michael Margulis, Jamie Aaron, Scotty Evans, Pat Normand, Dan Normand, and Nick Ieraci just to name a few. Forgive any omissions. If we've shared presence and insight; you've been more instrumental than you know.

To my sister. All sisters. And the countless Queens without whom any co-ascent would be both insipid and incomplete.

To my mother. All mothers. And *The Mother*. The throb of life herself.

To my father. All fathers. And *The Father*. That which holds and sustains all.

Finally, to S who initiated me into Fire #2.

B who initiated me into Fire #4.

And my family and ancestors; without whom, no initiation would be possible.

Preface:
A FIRE, LIT.

As my one-year-old son—healthy, vibrant and full of life, was blowing out his single candle flame through a toothy grin, all I could think about was how the previous twelve months had nearly destroyed me. And in the most fundamental of ways, they did.

For twelve months, I oscillated between the extreme poles of ecstatic joy and utter collapse. A gut-clenching, schizophrenic thrill ride that would lead me to the front lines of my own existential war. Each day was marked by a silent battle. On one side, a strengthened will to show up and rise anew. On the other, a seductive impulse to retreat into selfish exile—or worse, succumb to total self-destruction. Warring impulses felt impossible to reconcile.

On one hand, I was called to expand my capacities as a man. To be a better provider, a more loving partner, a more successful business owner and a more daring visionary. On the other, feeling more under-resourced, underslept, and under-supported than ever.

I was constantly questioning my capacity to measure up to the impossible standards I had set for myself and my family. And in truth, the demands were indeed unreasonable. Constantly shifting goal posts with a deadly cocktail of guilt, blame, shame, victimhood and resentment after each inevitable miss.

It took a full twelve months to discover that this was *actually* the point. That it requires this level of intensity to coax out the old shadows. The stuff you could have sworn was gone. The stuff that, without this soul-deep shockwave, would remain buried deep within your bones, continuing to operate in clandestine, influencing your life in the subtlest of ways. The gnawing, visceral clench of guts rubbing against bone before being boiled down in a pot of red-hot, simmering blood. A painful inner alchemy I kept resisting.

I suffered to "keep things in order" and to meet the expectations I had placed on myself. I suffered because I kept trying to restore a version of myself that no longer existed. I suffered to regain "balance" and "control" over a situation that inherently demanded a certain degree of chaos, combustion, and catharsis.

In short, I suffered because I expended all my energy trying to resurrect an "old me" that had perished twelve months prior with a heroic push from Sue. Like desperately trying to shock a frozen cadaver back to life with a 1,000-volt defibrillator days after it's already been plunged underground, and the maggots have had their way.

It took twelve months to surrender to the most confronting of truths. To re-emerge from this dark cave utterly transformed, renewed, and ready to express myself in new, more powerfully aligned ways. And to humbly acknowledge that the painful, systemic deconstruction of my ego and sense of self was in fact a prerequisite for my growth and healing as a man. Such were the gifts presented within the initiatory fires of fatherhood.

Fatherhood was, and continues to be just one initiatory fire that fuels my evolutionary path. A fire that continues to light up my shadows and expose all that no longer serves.

Entrepreneurship, the pursuit of purpose, my intimate relationship, and thriving physically, mentally, emotionally, and spiritually in an unbalanced world that continuously challenges them all serve as the others.

As you'll find in this program, these initiatory fires are present in your life as well. Your transformation and accelerated growth of a man doesn't require a life-long commitment to "self-development" or "personal growth." It doesn't require you to endure the soul-numbing indignities of sitting in a seminar room or an overpacked stadium fist-bumping on cue.

Instead, it requires you to stand tall in the fires you've already been gifted in your own life. To invite the flames with a steady gaze and an open heart, and dare look at what they expose. Not with shame or self-contempt. But in the depths of your timeless power, in complete awe and reverence of what you *already* are.

For on the other side of each fire, stands a king ready to rise.

A throne ready to be claimed.

And a kingdom to be served.

May you be so bold,

Hendrix Black

Somewhere, sometime.

Introduction:

ABOUT THE 7 INITIATORY FIRES

This book isn't a personal memoir. It's not a repackaged punch list of self-help soundbites and flaccid platitudes. Nor does it feature the cherry-picked case studies of other men who've marched this path. Beyond the preface, the author vanishes into the background as you and your inner king take center stage within the theater of transformation that follows.

For this *is* a path. One walked with a guide who has navigated, chronicled and marked sizable portions of the terrain. A guide who has encountered many of the beasts that dwell and put a name to the deranged howls rippling through the dark, moonless night.

But even a blazed trail has infinite variability in the challenges that arise. And much like how every ascent up *Everest* is different, there will be the infinite space between each step that is colored by the characteristics and challenges of your individual ascent. Your sharpened awareness and ever-growing courage shall be relied upon throughout. The fruits claimed shall be the fruits cultivated. Each step, a reclamation of what was once lost. Each breath, the roar of the inner king, no longer in forced exile or selfish slumber.

Welcome to the foothills.

Before we begin, let's take a high-level view of the journey that follows.

The *7 Initiatory Fires of Modern Manhood* program is built upon two core themes.

Theme 1: That as a modern man, the grounds for deep and lasting transformation are already present in your life. Namely

1. Thriving physically and mentally in an unhealthy world
2. Your intimate relationship
3. Your pursuit of purpose
4. Fatherhood
5. Your business or livelihood
6. Thriving emotionally and spiritually in an unbalanced world
7. Expressing fully in a suppressed world

Theme 2: All of these "fires," when approached from a place of deep reverence, regenerative power and expansive possibility, provide the accelerated growth and awakening that true initiation has always entailed.

The "place" from which these seven fires must be approached is your "inner king." The decidedly masculine essence of your soul or being in its most matured and evolved form. You can call him an emanation of your "higher self" if you feel so inclined. Beyond semantics, what's most important is that you begin to routinely access and embody the virtues he represents. His virtues being

1. Uncompromisingly powerful and regenerative
2. Unconditionally accepting and forgiving
3. Unshackled from expectation and influence
4. Unconditionally loving and compassionate
5. Unceasing in his fullest expression of love and truth
6. Unconstrained in his access to wisdom and insight
7. Unbound by time and space

In an earlier iteration of this program, it was suggested that we must first awaken our *inner king* before being led into the "initiatory fires." The logic being that one must attain a degree of awareness, strength, compassion and personal capacity prior to being initiated within the more familiar fires that follow.

The building up of such internal virtues and capacities remains necessary. For when unconditional love and authentic power are infused into the fabric of our everyday lives, our sense of possibility expands exponentially. We gain access to previously latent potencies that accelerate the expression of our gifts and the deep peace and fulfillment we feel within that expression. So while this sequential outlook of first "awakening your inner king" prior to immersing in the fires isn't necessarily wrong, we must remain practical. Life is happening *now*. We're building businesses, raising families, and engaging in relationships *right now*.

While a professional MMA fighter would love to master his takedown defense before stepping into the octagon with a master wrestler, he knows that by the time the bell rings, he must use the tools and skills already available to him. Similarly, when it comes to the "fires" of our daily lives, the bell has already rung. We're already taking hits and grappling with our shadows. Yes, let's cultivate skill and virtue within the private practice hall of our hearts. But let's not forget about the arenas in which we've already been called to put our skillfulness on display. For in doing so, we also run the danger of being perpetually involved in the "inner work" as a justifiable delay from tending to the *very* real fires before us.

Self-help in isolation provides an illusion of progress. A monk in a cave will never know his true attainments until he steps down from the mountain and tests himself within the friction of his everyday life and relationships. You don't get to choose your "readiness" to confront life. When the fires call, you must answer. If you fail to heed the call; you are often thrust. Avoidance and delay are no longer sustainable strategies in a time of rapid evolution and awakening. As such, the perfect attainment of these seven inner skills and virtues is no longer the goal nor the starting point. Nor do we have time to cultivate each of these virtues in isolation on some indefinite timeline while our kingdoms beg for greater, more evolved stewardship.

In that spirit, rather than waiting for an arbitrarily "high level of attainment" across these seven virtues before entering the fires, we simply seek to activate them within our awareness to the highest initial degree possible—and then allow them to gradually gain greater degrees of momentum and skillfulness as we progress. It's my experience that even an "entry-level" degree of cultivation on each virtue will suffice before embarking into the more familiar fires.

Likewise, the cultivation of these virtues is not linear. We may certainly cultivate a high degree of compassion with intentional practice on that virtue. But consciously navigating the initiatory fire of "relationship" or "fatherhood" may be both more accessible *and* bear richer and more immediate fruit. This is akin to the MMA fighter who may master a new technique on the practice floor or within the sink-or-swim dynamic of combat. The battlefield, with all its immediacy and necessity, can at times, be the place of immense personal revelation and spiritual breakthrough. Meaning, the cultivation of these virtues becomes more circular and bidirectional than linear. On one hand, we awaken our inner king, and allow "him" to gain greater influence and presence across all aspects of our lives—our relationships, our families, our businesses, our bodies, and our place in the world. On the other hand, a daring and open-hearted immersion into the fires themselves will awaken and enliven our inner king.

The goal then becomes to dynamically bring the mystical to the mundane— and the mundane to the mystical. As above, so below. And in doing so, rapidly collapse the distance between how we currently experience our reality, and what's truly possible for us. So, although short, the preliminary practices in the *Awakening Your Inner King* chapter will be ground zero in your transformation—and the initiations through the fires that follow will continue to activate the virtues he represents. For any "self-development" built atop shaky, unstable ground is only bound to crumble.

As a final note, the awakening of your inner king is not an impossible, aspirational feat. It's accessible. And it *must* be accessed. For when your inner king and his virtues are bypassed for something more seemingly practical, you're bound to fail. But once you begin to experience life as the unbound, unconditionally loving, uncompromisingly powerful version of you, you invite an indescribable richness and depth to all you do. Your actions are guided by higher purpose. And it's only from this place that the greatest of kingdoms can be built.

I honor you for being on this journey.

I honor everything that's led you here.

I honor everything that shall unfold from this moment onwards.

And it's in that spirit that I say…

I see you, King.

If you're feeling called to embark on a deeper immersion
and cultivation of each virtue, you're invited to explore
the most current offerings of our signature,
Awakening Your Inner King program

www.iseeyouking.com/awaken

A Brief Note on the Word "King"

Let's acknowledge from the start that the word "king" can evoke a wide spectrum of reaction. For some, it can trigger discomfort. For others, it may ignite an inflated sense of weaponized power, self-importance and grandiosity—or the opposite, self-contracted shame and smallness in relation to some unattainable largesse.

The word may be colored by one's faith or religious orientation. Or for those more steeped in classical "men's work," the archetypal-based commentary of Douglas Gillette and Robert Moore may inform your understanding. For some, the word "king" is a charged one, packed with the transgressions of tyrants past. And for others, it's a clarion call towards a healthy and evolved masculine ideal of self-rulership.

In our work, the word "king" is used to signify this evolutionary pull towards sovereignty and self-leadership—and the aforementioned virtues that make such a daring ascent possible. Likewise, within this work, the word "king" seeks neither to self-aggrandize nor to self-diminish. It is not meant to bear within it the tales of monarchs past. Nor is it meant to be placeholder for religious connotations.

Rather, the word "king" is deeply personal. It's *you* in your fullest expression as a sovereign, powerful and virtuous being. Careful consideration was given to the use of the word. But to shirk away and self-contract from the threat of potential and (temporary) discomfort would be contradictory to the nature of initiation itself. We are called to confront the uncomfortable. And to compassionately yet powerfully endeavor towards the absolute pinnacle of who or what we may experience ourselves to be. The word "king" is both a lighthouse pointing towards such mighty ideals, and a reminder that those ideals are attainable to any man who dares venture towards them.

Venture, we shall.

Chapter 1:

THE ART OF
MODERN-DAY INITIATION

Where Did Men Go Wrong?

"*W*here did men go wrong?"

I personally cannot think of a more disempowering and fruitless inquiry. Yet in the past few years, it's become fashionable to talk about a so-called masculinity crisis. To wax philosophical over the political, social, and cultural factors that have led to the apparent "brokenness of man," while longing for a return to some loosely defined glory days where "men were men."

We blame divorce rates, absent fathers and over-nurturing mothers. We blame a school system that straightjackets our creativity and suppresses our fullest expression. We blame a hyper-competitive society and a dog-eat-dog corporate world that pits one man against the other, shattering any possibility of true brotherhood and cooperation. But most of all, experts find consensus in blaming our brokenness on the lack of initiation.

"*We've lost the art of initiation,*" they say.

"*We've lost the elders.*"

"*We've bi-passed the necessary rites of passage into manhood.*"

All of these statements contain some fragment of truth. Yet they do nothing but invite a helpless shoulder shrug as we collapse into victimhood and point to a defenseless scapegoat. Our kids deserve better. Our partners deserve better. Our communities deserve better. But most importantly, *we* deserve better.

Even if we choose to entertain the idea that "man is broken," we don't need a full autopsy report on his rotting corpse to give rise to the next. Nor do we need a detached anthropological view of where things went wrong. Such overreliance on limp-wristed intellectualism is part of the problem. We tend to feel safe and distanced in our sterile, scholarly approach. Like sitting behind the thick-paned glass while the caged animal inside us withers and fights for freedom. We see ourselves separate from the pain we're observing—and in doing so, resist the undercurrent pushing us forward. Simply put, conversation alone doesn't move us forward. Nor does reflexive action. Only the deep, fully embodied transformation that initiation entails—and the new, empowered actions that stem from it. And in truth...

Being a man in the modern world is an initiation in and of itself.

Contrary to popular belief, we haven't lost the art of initiation, we've simply misunderstood it. Anyone who's ever felt despair or isolation is indeed sitting in the dark cave of his own soul, searching frantically for the light. To that extent, being a man in the modern world *is* an initiation. One that demands a new paradigm of accelerated evolution—not an infantile longing for the ancient rites of yesteryear, nor the helpless collapse into apathy and exile. Men's groups and retreats have undoubtedly started a valuable and necessary conversation. But beating a drum in the forest and simulating a long-lost "rite of passage" has its limitations. A weekend retreat is like a flush of morphine. It can only numb the pain as you continue to bleed out from your battered heart. Likewise, longing to restore the archaic initiations and ceremonies of ancient cultures may make for interesting *Instagram* fodder, but provides little more than a short-lived balm that rubs off the moment you step back into the friction of your everyday life. The sacred remembrance, if there's one at all, is far too soon forgotten.

As richly primal and invigorating as these one-off experiences may be, they don't match the context of our everyday lives, nor do they penetrate the deepest layers of our longing. Moving forward, the grounds for awakening and accelerated growth will no longer be solely in the deep backwoods; but in the deepest recesses of our own hearts and the everyday contexts in which they beat. For a guttural scream into the ethers will only ever be the performative, dramatized, and surface-level display of a subterranean rumbling. So long as the tectonic plates continue to shift from within, initiation is ongoing and ever-present.

Likewise, initiations will no longer be caught up solely in the outer dressings of tribal tattoos and overgrown dreadlocks; but in the wildness unleashed from deep within our bones. For initiations aren't recovered or restored. They're not the archaic, fossilized remnants of a time and place none of us were born into. They're discovered and created within the contextual relevance of the culture they're present in. And in truth, we're already stewing in the intense initiatory fires of our lives—in our relationships, in our businesses, in our role as fathers. Initiation hasn't disappeared; it simply comes in different "packaging." Namely

Thriving physically and mentally in an unhealthy world
Your intimate relationship
Your pursuit of purpose
Fatherhood
Your business and livelihood
Thriving emotionally and spiritually in an unbalanced world
Expressing fully in a suppressed world

All of these fires are more challenging and even death-defying than ever before; they demand the qualifications of embodied courage, intense exertion and widened capacity. They also require confrontation with shadow, ego death, and rebirth of higher consciousness that true initiation has always entailed.

The crucible is no longer found in a weekend retreat or in the nostalgic longings for simpler times, but rather in the fabric of our everyday dealings and the unmatched pressures and stakes they carry. For the weight of expectation on modern man has never been so great. We expect ourselves to "crush it" in life, in business, as fathers and as partners—without recognizing that the mere attempt is unprecedented in the obstacles they encounter and the heroics they demand.

Lost in the fervent call for men to "be more" is the fact that man already *is* more than he's ever been. Almost *unreasonably* more.

This is the most fearless initiation in the history of man. These waters are indeed uncharted. *Terra Incognita.* Yet instead of honoring the sheer will and courage needed to even embark on the journey, men often feel shamed, slandered and abandoned as their sinking ships succumb to an intensity they were never trained to withstand. The respect and reverence they so desperately thirst for themselves is unjustly reserved for the mythical hero with only a fraction of the real-life challenges we so courageously bear.

Superman didn't have to soothe a teething infant and save the world on three hours sleep.

King Leonidas didn't have to bring money home in a crumbling, post-industrial economy.

Buddha discovered his true nature, but left a wife and son behind to do so.

Statues have been erected and movies made for men far less courageous than you *already* are. So crown yourself, king. For you're already doing the impossible.

The demands on modern men require an evolutionary leap in being—not an endless cycle of finger pointing, nor an exceedingly impotent commentary on where things went wrong. When the scholars outnumber the swordsmen, we may achieve a form of intellectual *nirvana*. Yet whatever insight is gained will fail to pierce through the veils of suffering and delusion.

Therefore, the goal is no longer to "start a conversation" around what is meaningful and necessary, but to fire up the engine that drives us to change. Anything short of a quantum leap simply won't do. The stakes are simply too high. Over 34,000 American men took their lives last year, and tens of thousands more will inevitably do the same again this year. All of them leaving behind lovers, children, friends, wives, partners, and parents. All passing down the implicit message that "life is not okay," which will continue to ripple and reverberate across the wounded hearts of their sons and daughters for generations to come.

And relatively speaking, they're not wrong. Life, as most men experience it, is *not* okay. And no amount of crisis hotlines, symposiums or scholarly debates will fix it. 34,000 men ate lead, ingested poison, hung from nooses, and jumped off bridges last year. Yet perhaps even more tragically, if that's even possible, are the tens of millions of men who are *currently* submitting to an advanced state of decomposition even before being dropped six feet underground. Self-canceling amidst a seemingly insurmountable ridge of desperation and despair. For it is true that digging a grave requires less courage and labor than clawing back towards higher ground. Yet endure we must.

For death doesn't need a head start. You don't get brownie points for doing nature's job or doing your best impersonation of a living cadaver. Instead, you're called to drum up the courage to live with complete awe and reverence of what you *truly* are—to dare court a destiny of unimaginable depth and glory—and to lead the urgently needed evolution of modern man one heartbeat at a time.

One initiatory fire at a time.

One courageous confrontation with shadow at a time.

One rebirth at a time.

It's time to stop asking the disempowering question of "where did men go wrong," and instead, start *living* the answer to:

How will men go right?

Man will go right by bringing sacredness, power, and radical self-love to his present struggle rather than shame and self-hatred—and by taking full ownership over its transformation into something greater.

Man will go right when he stops bypassing the blood trail of his own destruction. When he can take full responsibility for all he's done. When he can experience a cracking open of his heart and the inevitable heartache that comes from sensing where he's unknowingly caused harm to self or other.

Man will go right when he stops outsourcing his growth to an "elder" who isn't coming back. An "elder" who he himself must rise into for the sake of future generations and for those around him.

Man will go right when he stops trying to escape from the vice grips of modern manhood—and instead deeply recognizes that those vice grips themselves *are* the initiatory fires; possessing all the characteristics needed to lead you through the dark night the moment you stop bypassing them for something more superficially enthralling.

Man will go right when he favors self-actualization over self-preservation. When he can courageously step into the flames, knowing that what emerges on the other side will be greater than anything he can ever fathom.

For a life of courage isn't one where we avoid the flames. It's one where we throw ourselves headlong into them, knowing in our hearts that what re-emerges has no choice but to be a stronger, more evolved expression of ourselves. When we resist these fires, we resist ourselves. I can personally think of no greater waste of one man's life.

There's a popular saying that goes: "*When the student is ready, the teacher will appear.*"

The teacher has appeared.

She's your lover.

She's your child.

She's your bold-hearted pursuit for a life of purpose and meaning.

She's your mission.

She's your shadow.

She's your light.

She's your body, your heart, your soul.

Resist the selfish exile of retreat. Stop being MIA in your own life.

Brave the flames.

Forge your crown.

Emerge as a king.

The Need for Modern Day Initiation

Initiation is a loaded word. From ancient tribes whose initiatory rites required extreme tests of strength, bravery and capacity to endure pain, to the bloody and brutal initiations of a street gang, to the keg stand in the American frat house, initiations have *always* been shaped and confined to what was culturally valued and accepted in a man. But when you initiate a man into forced callousness and capacity for brutality, the culture—being largely a product of such a man's reign—becomes more callous and brutal as a result.

When you crown a false king by the merit of how much *Bud Light* he can stomach in a single sitting, you embrace a culture of overindulgence and glorified self-abuse. When you teach a boy that his ascent into manhood is dependent on enduring a dehumanizing act of pain or self-mutilation through detached stoicism, you in turn breed a battle-ready man who lacks the heart to reign with love.

In all these examples, tribe and subculture, with all their inherent shadows, fears and existential necessities, have placed a certain value judgment on their men.

That value has for the most part been linked to the role of their men to overcome external threat (real or perceived) and uphold the values and ethos of said culture. Whether or not those values are truly life-affirming, regenerative and a movement towards greater love, sovereignty, and compassionate power is another story. A story that often gets ignored in the auto-romanticism over our long-lost rites.

Yet in all these cases, two things become abundantly clear:

1. The initiation of men, being dictated by the value judgments of the tribe or subculture, rarely, if ever, favored individual sovereignty, free will and self-actualization.
2. The initiation of men was rarely, if ever, a movement towards the abundant, expansive evolution of humankind—but rather a primal, knee-jerk contraction away from fear and existential threat.

As a result, the "ascent" into manhood has rarely been marked by greater levels of love, personal power, and reverence for life. Indeed, in times of war and strife, an initiated warrior will be a skillful and vital asset towards facing injustice, overcoming oppression and ensuring the survival of a tribe. This is no time to diminish the role of the warrior. But without a fully integrated initiatory ascent, even a conquering warrior (whether on a real or metaphorical battlefield) can only himself become a vengeful warlord. And so, the cycle persists.

Historically, few can argue that masculinity has for the most part been traded in the currencies of detached brutality, extreme endurance, and willingness to channel strength and power for an external authority. Currencies, which in modern times, afford us nothing but suffering on an even wider and faster scale. Our starting point, therefore, is really one of personal sovereignty. It's in the willingness to ask if these are truly the qualities that will lead men to be more powerful, compassionate and fully expressed fathers, partners and visionaries in this modern era and beyond. The answer is quite likely no.

And this is partly why initiation has disappeared. Because the qualities that men have traditionally been "initiated" into are no longer supportive of an evolved, cooperative, and sovereign society. Yet to shun initiation wholesale is also a critical mistake. It's a willful betrayal of what drives us to evolve as men—and one that, at least temporarily, absolves us of the need to play a leading role in the world we wish to inhabit. That's why modern-day initiation is more necessary than ever. Because when done right, modern-day initiation is a catalyst to our next level of growth and evolution as men. It's not a linear, micro step away from our current reality—but rather a quantum leap into a new way of being. A way of being that's *always* clearly marked by greater levels of awareness, power and reverence for self and other.

Modern-day initiation is not the reinforcement of archaic, culturally held values, but an accelerated ascent towards freedom and wholeness. Not in some far off, mystical never land. But right here. Right now. The very second we drum up the courage to make the inner shift. A shift we're not only called to make, but totally and completely responsible for. For it's only by surrendering to this process that we can achieve accelerated growth and quantum leaps in our lives. It's only when we're fully willing to let the raging flames of these fires light up our shadows and burn away those old fragments of self that we can come out stronger, more powerful, and of greater service to those in our kingdom. The world doesn't need a dull blade. It needs a skillful swordsman. Modern-day initiation is where you sharpen your blade and learn how to swing it.

Modern-Day Initiation as a Means of Awakening Your Inner King

At its core, modern-day initiation implies entry into something new and mysterious. An unyielding crucible and forcing function to step into a more evolved expression of authentic power that's guided by love rather than fear, by peace rather than petty vengeance, and by radical intimacy with truth rather than willful ignorance and self-delusion.

By definition, this process must be physically, mentally, emotionally and spiritually challenging. For it must offer a strong enough shock to the status quo to trigger our defenses. It must trip up our internal alarm bells—the ones that threaten our sense of control. It must be threatening enough to our current sense of self to coax out the shadows—the resigned whimpers of the victim and the deranged howls of the fearful ego.

Initiation is cataclysmic. A subterranean explosion that shakes up the very foundation that your old "self" was supported by. What you're left with is not a simple rearranging of your inner architecture, but a complete restructuring of who and what you experience and perceive yourself to be. One where your inner victim vacates the throne and gives way to your inner king.

Modern-day initiation is experienced as an inner movement from:

1. Disempowerment to Empowerment
2. Victimhood to Radical Responsibility
3. Dependency to Self-Reliance
4. Scarcity to Abundance
5. Cowardice to Courage
6. Contraction to Expansion
7. Destruction to Regeneration
8. Apathy to Resilience
9. Resignation to Willfulness
10. Suppression to Full Expression.

Throughout this volume, we'll be making these shifts across the seven most present "fires" of our daily lives. The ones that currently occupy most of our focus and attention. In upgrading our experience across them all, the result will be nothing short of life-changing.

Two Elements of a Powerful and Permanent Initiation

The question now becomes:

What exactly is needed to make these evolutionary leaps as men?

How do we safely and practically traverse the chasm between our pain and suffering, and one where we claim our throne and trust our rule? These are critically important questions that have been ignored for far too long.

According to Robert Moore and Douglas Gillette in their seminal work, King, Warrior, Magician, Lover:

"Ritual process is contained by two things, the first is sacred space sealed off from the ordinary world—and the second is the elder who is completely trustworthy and can lead the initiate to the other side. They are released from the

sacred space only when they have successfully completed the ideal, and been reborn as men."

It's a fair assertion. Across just about every authentic tradition, initiation has always required the presence of both the elder and the sacred space. But where does that leave us today?

Aside from the cultural inconsistencies, another reason we've failed to re-establish the tradition of initiation is because those "ingredients," taken at face value, don't sync up with the practicalities of our modern lives. A tech founder can't be pulled away by a wise elder in the middle of the night and be thrown into a dark cave for an indefinite period of time. A shift worker with a young family can't afford to go on a 30-day dry fast in the Mojave and wait for his power animal to whisper guidance.

True initiation, and all that it entails, must be updated to our current context. And the transformation it promises must be made accessible right here, right now. Not just for the fortunate few. But for *all* men brave enough to heed the call. And in truth, we already have access to both these core initiatory elements.

The Elder is present. Perhaps not in flesh and bone, but in an even more reliable form that can be accessed within. Likewise, the sacred space need not be a literal dark cave, but an intense, single-minded focus and intimacy with what's present—all while being held in a container that encourages transformation. Put another way, your prolonged focused awareness, and ability to access higher aspects of self are all you truly require to make these transformational leaps.

Traditional Initiation	Modern-Day Initiation
The elder	Your inner king
The sacred space (cave of transformation)	Radical intimacy and intense focus (your throne room)

Before moving on, let's take a deeper look at how we'll be accessing these two critical elements of modern-day initiation.

Element #1 - Your Inner King (The Elder)

What you seek is what you are. Breathe. Let that sink in for a moment. Instead of waiting for a literal "elder" to show you the way, we're part of the first generation of men that must discover our elder from within and allow "him" to lead us. How invigorating. There is no passive waiting to be led. There is no abdication of responsibility. There is no renunciation of our inner throne or permission from an outside source to claim it. The throne is yours for the taking. And make no mistake, it must be claimed. This is the first step we'll be taking to let go of subtle dependencies, and awaken to radical self-authorship in your life.

If you've had a positive relationship with the elders in your life, you're a rare exception. A recent study showed that only 19% of men report having a strong, nurturing relationship with their own father. Yet paradoxically, most men slave away to meet the murky, ever-shifting expectations, and gain the approval of a father (or father figure) that deep down they've never fully trusted or aspired to be in the first place.

Likewise, most of the men I've worked with have already gained a level of freedom, wisdom and wide-spectrum success that their own fathers couldn't; while most present-day fathers I encounter are motivated to be more powerful, present and supportive than their own. Still, there's no reason to overgeneralize our elders nor to disparage them. For their own growth has been shaped and supported by the inner and outer resources available to them. We can, and must, find compassion and forgiveness in this. In judging our fathers, we in turn judge ourselves. In holding them to an impossible and unreasonable ideal, we in turn condemn ourselves to a lifetime of shame-infused insufficiency. We offer our apologies for our harsh judgments and impossible standards. Likewise, we learn to forgive all.

But for now, we're met with the radical responsibility of making use of the tools at our disposal, and being the first generation of men that endeavors to awaken the elder from within—and in doing so, sets a more solid, self-sustaining foundation for the next. Anything less is a passive, apathetic shoulder-shrug that only prolongs our suffering while stunting the evolution of men. Whereas the previous generation may have sat passively waiting for the elder to return, we'll be waking him up from his deep slumber. For the outer elder has always been a crutch for he who hasn't accessed his own inner king. The hidden gift of our time is that we no longer have the luxury of such external reliance. The outer elder, for the most part, is absent and not coming back. Instead "he" must be awakened and accessed from within. And he absolutely can be. For he resides within you. He *is* you. And his presence will expand with each heartbeat dedicated to higher purpose.

If the idea of an inner king or "higher version" of you that's ready to be accessed and expressed is too challenging for you to accept right now, I invite you to consider the following: Is it not true that there have been moments in your life where you've been inspired or instantly compelled to act with greater courage, love, power, compassion and capacity than you normally would have?

Perhaps those moments have been rare. Perhaps they've been clouded and diluted between far more moments rooted in anger, fear and despair. But is it not true that you've had at least a handful of moments where you've been called to act in ways that extend far beyond the ordinary? Even if you never acted on them, have you at least ever felt the fleeting impulse? A sudden surge of inspiration to express greater love, power and compassion. A soft opening of the heart while being deeply rooted in an endless reservoir of power and potentiality.

I don't expect you to accept the possibility of an inner king at face value. In fact, I greatly prefer you don't. You deserve the ecstasy of experiential and ever-unfolding confirmation. Personal contact, not dogma, shall be your primary teacher. Similarly, if the idea of an inner king challenges aspects of your faith, religion, or spiritual practice; I encourage a healthy level of discernment and openness. We're not seeking to deify, worship or evoke anything that isn't already present within you.

While non-dogmatic, the virtues being accessed will understandably be colored by and contextualized within your particular faith or practice. This is encouraged. And whether you call the conglomeration of these virtues your "inner king" or something more linguistically and psychologically palatable is entirely up to you. Resist getting tangled up in the web of semantics. Words and titles offer referential cohesion, but language is still a clumsy art. It's the grounded experience, experiential insight, and the transformations they yield which count most. In the next chapter, you'll engage in a series of practices and guided journeys that will bring you face to face with the presence and energetic qualities of your inner king. Together, we'll wake him up from his slumber and grant him greater providence over your day-to-day experience.

As a final note of caution, beyond cultural or religious associations, students and readers will sometimes experience an additional degree of resistance at this stage. The popular question being "does the inner king really exist... or am I simply imagining it?"

To answer the question, you must first define what "exists" truly means. Is it only in the immediately observable objective reality? Or in your subjective experience regardless of what others can confirm or validate? Is Buddha *real*? Is your identity as an entrepreneur, actor, athlete, visionary, or foreman *real*? Is the functionality of your kitchen table real?

The wisdom you may achieve here is that it is *you*, as an infinitely creative being, that invests and imparts energy, intent, cohesion, and therefore, "reality" to things. Ideas aren't real, until they are. Beliefs aren't real, until they are. Identities aren't *real*, until they are—and then once again, aren't. And while objects, beings, and archetypal forces may indeed have some form of "existence" prior to and independent of your acknowledgment or perception of them—their transformative power becomes *most* real, at least to you, the moment you form a relationship with them.

So the goal becomes to resist fruitless inquiries and relish in experiential insight. To favor efficacy and empirical realization over scientific scrutiny and folded-arm defiance. And ultimately, to take practical steps towards communion with higher aspects of self, rather than cold-hearted closure towards any such possibility. Be open and courageous—and allow yourself the gift of experiencing a reawakening and reunion that informs and enriches every step you take from here on out.

Tool #1 - The King's Log

The King's Log™ will be your journal throughout this process. When you write, bring a sense of reverence to the process. Find somewhere you can be alone. Don't rush it. Breathe deep and write as your highest self or inner king would write. This "inner posture" of deep reverence and intentionality requires no extra time, yet will invite unfathomable power, depth and richness to your inner exploration—and the discoveries it yields.

King's Log:

1. What are 3 moments you can recall where you've acted in ways you normally wouldn't? Moments where you were almost divinely guided to act with greater love, power, compassion, capacity and courage? Where did that inspiration come from? How did it feel? Can it be re-accessed? Or can you be made more accessible to it?

Record your reflections in a new journal or document.

Tool #2 - Embodied Inquiry

Your body contains a vast amount of wisdom far greater than your conscious mind can even begin to comprehend. The millions of bits of information it processes every second and the tens of millions of functions it performs in a single hour all point to a complex web of somatic-based intelligence that is no less "you" than the conscious aspect of your mind that you more closely identify with. *Embodied Inquiry* is a tool we'll be using throughout the program to quickly gain access to a deeper reservoir of wisdom than our thinking minds will often allow us to.

Instructions:

Ask the following questions, and simply listen or feel for a response. The response may come as a vision, an inner "yes," or it could be experienced as a sudden jolt or wave of energy, excitement and inner knowingness. *Embodied Inquiry* will also coax out various negative beliefs and corresponding identities or mental/emotional patterns, including your inner victim who may be in harsh resistance to a deeper or higher truth you're working to embody.

This is normal and welcomed. Whenever resistance arises, simply notice it, and gently question where it's coming from. If you can observe it, know that it's not the "real" you but a malleable, impermanent and non-solid "packet of information" that can be consciously witnessed, unraveled and transmuted.

The most important part is to dwell in the answer for a moment or two. If beyond the resistance it still feels expansive, exciting or joyful, simply relax into that feeling and let it saturate you as much as feels appropriate at this time.

Embodied Inquiry Questions:

1. Can I accept that there's a part of me that's more powerful, loving and compassionate than how I'm currently experiencing life?
2. Can I accept that no matter how much anger, fear, shame, smallness, guilt or victimhood I've experienced in my life, there's still an aspect of me that's infinitely powerful, confident and courageous?
3. Is it true that I can consciously cultivate and expand my awareness and connection to this aspect of myself? Will I?
4. Can I accept that in just a few short hours, days or weeks I can experience myself in profoundly new and empowering ways I've never even considered before? Will I?
5. Can I accept that my levels of joy, peace, love and power are in constant motion, and I can rediscover how to turn them up at will?

Tool #3 - The King's Word

Instructions:

The king's word is law. When he speaks, his constituents, advisors and partners instantly organize and reorient around his declaration.

While similar, there's a key difference between affirmations and the king's word. The king's word is spoken aloud from a place of ultimate authority. From the highest part of you that you can access at any given moment. You are not a lowly, desperate beggar pleading with a mighty and uncaring universe. You are the king, fully trusting, expecting, and grateful that his authority and rule is respected and honored by all those who hear it.

One of the hallmarks of your ascent into kingship is to bring sacredness to your word. To not be wasteful with what you say and intend—but to offer every word as prayer—every thought, intention and utterance as a contract etched into the very fabric of *all* that is.

Your sacred declaration, and the level of intent, reverence and certainty behind it are the lines of code that program your reality. Most men go through their lives turning this power against themselves. Cursing themselves with the subtle and stabbing declarations of defeat, disempowerment and limitation. They've allowed the inner victim (and persecutor) to hijack the inner voice; and therefore become a helpless passenger to whatever perilous course the victim has charted.

From this day onwards, you will reclaim the power of your declarations. Throughout the practices that follow, you will learn to honor this precious gift, consciously, and with an upward movement towards your highest calling.

The King's Word:

Repeat the following with total conviction and celebration. Feel the energy and intent behind your words. Declare them out loud with more reverence, sacredness and certainty than anything you've spoken before. As you speak it, it is claimed:

1. It is my will, my duty and my ultimate birthright to access, activate, and embody my inner king and all it represents to me.
2. I awaken my inner king and effortlessly express his highest virtues and capacities across every aspect of my life.
3. It is my highest will and intent to access and live from my inner king.

Let the energy build with each repetition. After a minute, simply pause and close your eyes, observe your state and turn all your senses inwards. Are there any clues of an inner king? Record your response in your *King's Log* before moving on.

Element #2 - The Throne Room (Sacred Space)

The second ingredient of any successful initiation is the sacred cave. The purpose of the cave, and shutting out the outer world, is to ensure that you look deeply at what's present for you. It's to overcome the distraction, the noise, and the socially-justifiable delays and avoidance in that confrontation with shadow. You're here. You have no choice. Face your stuff.

When we confront these fires, we're often met with an overwhelming urge to numb out or shirk away. But we must be courageous in resisting this urge. We must resist the urge to shield ourselves with distraction, entertainment or addiction of any kind (work, alcohol, food, self-help masquerading as self-mastery, etc.). And we must be even more mindful to not prematurely extract ourselves from the very fires that are here to serve our accelerated growth as men.

The sacred cave will be your **inner throne room.** A place where your inner king resides, with all the qualities that we'll be activating. A place where "he" can hold court for all aspects of self—past, present and future—and direct the transformation you seek.

But while we're using the throne room as a place of initiation, it isn't just a place where your deepest wounds and darkest shadows can be revealed and reconciled. It's also where your greatest dreams can be seeded. It's where you can seek knowledge, attain insight, and cultivate new ways of being. It's a space where you can consciously program your reality and coalesce the energies and unseen forces around that intent. If that sounds overly metaphysical for your liking, once again, I encourage you to verify these concepts within your own experience. To not "accept" any truth wholesale, but to confirm it as self-evident through your own practice.

In practicing with the inner throne room, you'll be encouraged to honor the unseen. To become familiar with the other side of the mirror, and become masterful at reengineering its components. As you'll soon experience, there's a malleability within your inner world that distinguishes it from your outer one. You can experience and feel anything you choose within your inner landscape. Sometimes with even greater clarity and vividness than your so-called observable reality. It's only an adopted belief that leads you into thinking that what you're experiencing on the inner side of the lens is any less "real."

With that said, your strong attention and focus will be required to uphold this visualization. If visualization is challenging for you, know that this skill can and will be harnessed with practice. For holding a visualization itself *is* a core practice of focused attention, which in turn is the foundation for any transformation you seek.

In the "wild," presence and focused attention are rapidly developed in the name of survival. Dropped in the desert, jungle or frozen tundra, every man becomes a tracker or hunter whose sharpened awareness and sensitivity become more-prized tools than the knife in his hand. Sensitivity, awareness and presence precede our physical tools. The same is true in confronting your shadows; and the beliefs, identities, and psycho-emotional patterns condensed into them. This is very much a game of predator and prey. Most men suffer the fate of the latter. It is the strength of your attention that enables you to stalk your shadows; catch their stealthy movements, and only once spotted, use the tools to rip free.

Beyond that, your prolonged focus and attention are the key ingredients for *everything* you'll ever create as a man. It's also a capacity that's been under siege in a day of well-documented dwindling attention spans and endless forms of distraction. No matter your starting point, you'd be well-served in committing to the reclamation of your focused attention. As you'd rightly suspect, the benefits of cultivating this increasingly rare capacity extend far beyond the purposes of these initiations.

The practice we'll be using to access your throne room is called Experiential Embodiment™. It's the core inner technology behind the *Crowned Process* which we'll be using to self-initiate within the seven fires in later chapters.

We'll be harnessing this skill as we go, gradually adding layers throughout this program. For now, simply know that you can absolutely do this—and that in cultivating this skill, you'll also be building your capacity to direct and sustain attention, and therefore energy, on any reality (manifest or potential) of your choosing.

On a final note, the guided journeys that you can access online intentionally use minimal audio production. If you're experienced with guided journeys or meditations, you might be familiar with highly produced recordings that include soaring soundscapes, binaural beats, streams or other sound effects.

While there's nothing inherently wrong with these tools, they place a ceiling on your skill development and inner resourcefulness. When a "stream" is introduced on an audio track, you're deprived of the ability to sense one within your inner world. Training wheels are fine when all you desire is a leisurely ride around the suburbs. But when your goal is to venture into the rough and jagged terrain of the modern male psyche, you'd be best served by developing and sharpening your internal capacities to do so.

The following guided journey introduces you to the foundational skills of *Experiential Embodiment* you'll be using throughout the program.

Experiential Embodiment™ - The Dreamer and the Dreamt

The term visualization is a misnomer. Visualization, in its most effective form, leverages all the senses. Not just the traditional five (touch, smell, sight, sound, taste), but also emotional and mental states—and inner orientations (beliefs, identities). In short, it includes everything your normal "physical" state would—minus the limits.

What we're really doing isn't "visualization" but *Experiential Embodiment*. In simpler terms, we're having an inner experience, that to our subconscious mind, is every bit as real, if not *more* so because of how present and focused we are to the experience. Being fully immersed, participative and present to a "visualized" reality is far more *real* than sleepwalking through a physical one. In truth, Experiential Embodiment™ *is* manifestation.

It's the immediate and limitless creation of a subjective inner reality—free of the delay and latency period that your physical reality requires. The immediate and limitless nature of your visualization is quite literally a superhuman trait that's to be celebrated and honored, not undermined and disparaged. Don't deprive yourself of this richness by condemning a visualized reality as any "less valuable" or "real" than your observed one. Doing so, greatly dilutes the potency of this most precious gift. For it's your steadfast conviction and reverence in the realness of your visualization that gives it its ultimate power and ferries it over into a more physical one.

At its core, Experiential Embodiment™ involves seven elements of experiencing:

1. Experiencing total conviction of the "realness" of your inner reality.
2. Experiencing the five bodily senses (sight, smell, touch, taste, hearing).
3. Experiencing proprioception (or kinesthetic awareness) of your visualized body.
4. Experiencing and self-generating emotional/feeling states (i.e., anticipation, gratitude, excitement, joy, peace, love, desire, awe, etc.)
5. Experiencing and self-generating mental states (i.e., knowing, certainty, trust, deservedness, confidence, etc.)

6. Experiencing oneness or overlap between your inner and outer reality (noticing how emotional and mental states seamlessly carry over from one into the other.)

7. Experiencing creation and manifestation within lesser-physical planes.

While tremendously potent, the practice is relatively simple, beginner-friendly and non-esoteric. All you need is a sincere willingness to follow the guidance provided. These are natural capacities that have been dulled and atrophied by less-natural forces.

While at the beginning, it may seem like you are trying to "hold" the visualization and fight to "maintain it," in truth, doing so would be like trying to hold water, or even air, between your hands. At some point, you simply release into it rather than try to "hold it." You know yourself as no different than this more ethereal "you" and traverse it no differently. Paradoxically, it's in a strengthened focused attention (and a bit of willfulness) that we arrive to a place where we can simply surrender and immerse.

Our introductory exercise is a complete practice in itself. Performed regularly, you'll access heightened states of pleasure, confidence, presence, love and reverence for self and other—while gently peeling back the layers of who and what you perceive yourself to be. In short, don't let the introductory nature of this practice fool you. It's one of the most powerful exercises you'll experience on this path, and one I invite you to commit to at least once a week through the duration of the program—committing to a deeper, more immersive level of concentration with each repetition.

As a final note, we made the decision not to include the written-out journeys within the text of the book. Not only would it be unnecessarily tenuous to read through a guided journey with your eyes closed, but it would fill this volume with tens of thousands of words of written instruction. I'm confident you'll agree that accessing the complimentary recordings of all essential practices is far more practical.

**To access your recording of
the "Dreamer & The Dreamt" practice, visit:**

www.iseeyouking.com/dreamer

King's Log:

1. What was whispered to you in your visualization? Write it down and contemplate what this means to you, and how you plan to honor this guidance.
2. Do you feel differently than how you felt before you started? How so?
3. Acknowledge that while you were physically "just sitting or lying down with your eyes closed," your perspective and experience has changed in profound and tangible ways. Appreciate and relish in your ability to do this—knowing it will only get stronger with each time you practice, with no limit to how invigorating this can feel.
4. Finally, ask:
5. Was this experience any more or less real than where you are right now?
6. What evidence do you have?
7. If you can't disprove the "unrealness," can you give yourself the privilege of acknowledging the possibility that your inner reality is just as valid as your physical?

Final Words Before Awakening Your Inner King

At this point, your conviction in an inner king isn't necessary—only a curious mind and a courageous heart to confirm or deny *his* presence for yourself. If you're ready for the transformational thrillride of a lifetime, the following pages await you with equal desire and anticipation.

On the other hand, you'd be forgiven for resisting this work. For finding it too strange, esoteric, or impractical. Remember, most men will resist or fail their initiations. Callings are missed and hero's journeys are bypassed with far greater frequency than they are heeded and followed. The reason being free will and agency. It's your greatest gift, and you're invited to use it now.

Will your highest will bring you face-to-face with the long-lost part of you ready to rise? Or will it be a faint-hearted ambassador of the status quo, collapsing you back into the cozy confines of sameness and complacency?

There are no wrong answers. There are no right answers.

Only the one you choose in this very moment.

With your choice etched into the fabric of the universe itself—and with your word as law—let us now become what we've always been.

I see you, King.

Chapter 2:
AWAKENING THE INNER KING

As we covered in the introduction, the inner king shall serve as your elder. While tempting to go straight into the *7 Initiatory Fires* themselves, doing so without first attaining a degree of awareness of your inner king will greatly limit your capacity to brave the flames, dissolve your shadows, and awaken to a higher way of being across every part of life.

Indeed, awakening your inner king is now our starting point. You'll have accessed and activated "him" when you can successfully tap into the aspect of you that is:

1. Uncompromisingly powerful and regenerative
2. Unconditionally accepting and forgiving
3. Unshackled from expectation
4. Unconditionally loving and compassionate
5. Unceasing in his fullest expression of love and truth
6. Unconstrained in his access to wisdom and insight
7. Unbound by time and space

If this sounds impossible and unattainable, I assure you it's not. For these qualities are innately yours. Not something to be created, but dormant powers and virtues to be awakened and accessed. The "un" prefixes are not accidental.

They point to the inherent nature of these virtues. Throughout our practice, we'll release the parts of ourselves that compromise, place conditions upon, and otherwise inhibit their fullest expression. No matter how unworthy you believe yourself to be, or how unlikely such an inheritance of virtues may seem, the gradual embodiment of your inner king can and shall be accomplished.

If you're still experiencing doubt, I invite you to take thirty seconds right now and ask yourself: *"who is it that doesn't believe I can awaken, embody and express these seven virtues?"* Better yet, write down or record your resistance, and then pierce deeper and ask, *"who is it that feels that way—and why?"*

Doing this quick exercise should at least create a small enough crack in your armor. A chasm through the thick bedrock of belief and identity that allows you to dive into the realm of greater possibility. A possibility where these qualities are not separate from you, but innately yours and ready to be claimed.

While an entire book can be written for each virtue, our main concern here isn't philosophy nor dogmatized drivel, but the embodied awakening and practical application of deeper truth and wisdom. Therefore, the emphasis will be placed on practice, and the personal revelations they reveal.

But I will propose this: The path to your inner king is both profound and simple. When you exercise the *exclusive* rights, privileges and capacities of the inner king, you act in alignment with him. The more you access and live in alignment with these virtues, the more your inner king begins to eclipse all previous limited identities and ideas of self. In time, your inner king achieves a tipping point of influence. One where your actions are guided by these higher virtues—and your reality reshaped by the newfound power that emerges from them.

In this sense, *Awakening Your Inner King* is a complete program in itself. Devoted practice of this series of exercises alone will yield life-changing transformation, which by default, will carry over to every other aspect of your life. The next part of this book, however, offers the conscious exploration of those containers—and the accelerated seeding of the king's qualities within the everyday contexts you currently inhabit. In short, your inner king is first awakened—he is then accessed with increasing frequency—and finally, he's activated and expressed across life's major pillars.

On a final note, it may seem awkward or out-of-order to place the more seemingly mystical of these teachings before the more familiar fires in which you find yourself. For some readers, there will be a felt readiness and excitement. For others, trepidation and resistance. For all, a perceptible enough call from your inner king to plunge forward into a portal of transformation and mystery. One marked by reunion and reclamation. Let that deep inner knowingness be an overflowing source of courage, power and perseverance as you come face to face with that which you've always truly been.

Your initiation into kingship awaits.

Let's begin.

Foundational Practice 1 - I See You, King

Time: Seconds

Frequency: Constantly

Description:

The *"I see you, King"* practice is the cornerstone of our foundational training. As an internal mantra, it acknowledges the inner king residing within. Each utterance provides a clarion call to continue waking him up from his deep slumber. It's a declaration of your readiness and willingness to ascend to higher truth and deeper purpose.

As a silent, externalized affirmation, it confirms the inner king that resides within other men. It overcomes the survival-based instinct to "size up" other men, and instead acknowledges them for who they truly are beyond the outer shell.

For in affirming the inner king in others, you affirm it in yourself. And when you approach the men in your life from a place of shared reverence and inclusivity, you invite cooperation and shared growth rather than fear-based competitiveness. You transcend an unquestioned biological imperative that was never rooted in virtue to begin with.

How to use it with yourself:

As often as you can, affirm with a sense of self-reverence and assuredness, *"I see you, King."* Say it out loud to yourself when you catch your reflection in a mirror.

Let it vibrate internally whenever you catch yourself in a moment of fear, victimhood, exhaustion or frustration.

As you affirm it, recognize that at your core, beyond the surface-level feeling which is ever-fleeting, you are a *king*—with irrevocable access to all the virtues he represents. Do not let moments of fear, limitation, anger, hostility, resentment or victimhood fester for more than a few moments before lifting yourself out of the muck through this sacred reminder.

Yes, allow space for emotional processing and for witnessing these denser emotions and patterns to arise. But resist the temptation to overindulge or dwell in them. Even a released emotional pattern creates a momentary vacuum that must be quickly filled with positive virtue. Otherwise, you risk defaulting back to more habitual patterns. The *"I see you, King"* mantra will fill that newfound space with the qualities it represents. Similarly, when strong negative patterns feel dense and inescapable, ask, *"what does my inner king feel or believe about this?... How would he respond?"*

In the chapter *Thriving Emotionally and Spiritually in an Unbalanced World*, we'll dive deeper into the concept of an "emotional refractory period." But the short version is this: the faster we can self-elevate out of dense and non-beneficial patterns, the quicker we can reclaim skillfulness in each situation and therefore a higher quality of life.

As this internal mantra of *"I see you, King"* gains momentum, you'll develop a reliable reminder of your true power and capacity—and therefore more readily shift states with less resistance between the internal gear shifts.

How to use it with others:

Only the king has the power to crown his fellow man. While the peasant spends his life trapped in a petty, zero-sum game of comparison and competitiveness, the king constantly seeks to elevate his fellow man.

As men, we're constantly sizing each other up. Like a rotting evolutionary residue left over from a time when competition was necessary to the game of survival. While healthy competition may still be a useful tool in calling us towards greater capacity; comparison remains an unwinnable ego-based game. It's judgment, first expressed outwards then turned inwards, and a precursor to fear, anxiety, self-hatred or hatred towards others.

When we find ourselves in a game of comparison, or a reflexive "sizing up" of our fellow man, we're playing out the survival instinct. We're sending an influx of signals that things aren't okay. That there's danger lurking. That resources are scarce. We then feel the inner contraction and tightening up of our bodies as the dam ruptures and our circulatory system gets flooded with a cocktail of stress hormones.

This unconscious "sizing up" happens in the bar, the boardroom, the news-feed, the Zoom call, at meet-the-teacher night. It restricts our creativity and resourcefulness. Slashes inspired action and spontaneous flow off the menu of available expressions. It short-circuits our power and renders it unavailable.

Free yourself from this mechanism by catching it in the act and then consciously bringing a more awakened and evolved energy to the exchange. That of deep empathy, acceptance, appreciation and cooperation. Use it with every man in your life—father, son, friend, foe or stranger. In offering this affirmation of their own inner king, you liberate yourself (and them) from any knee-jerk judgments or subtle ill-will, while restoring access to your own infinite flow of power.

Resist falling into judgment over their worthiness. It's not your prerogative to do so. You're not commending nor condoning unworthy or ignoble deeds. You're simply acknowledging the goodness and positive power beneath and beyond it all, no matter how latent those potentials and their appropriate expressions may presently be. Moreover, what you acknowledge, even silently, in them, becomes something you've trained yourself to both witness and appreciate in yourself.

If you feel threatened by a so-called competitor's "unstoppable" focus, drive and passion—the uninitiated man will regress into an interlaced pattern of envy and ill-will. Pointing out presumed flaws, finding other areas to self-elevate, and even wishing for the other man's demise in some act of competitive-based schadenfreude. All this is due to the perceived existential threat of another man who's displayed excellence in a core area we've yet to fully cultivate in ourselves. Yet the excellence of another no longer needs to be a threat. Rather, a lucid and unignorable display of what's possible for us. If you find yourself envious and bitter about another man's success—as a businessman, an investor, a father, a leader, an athlete—resist the knee-jerk reaction to condemn or sour his accolades. Rather, silently affirm and acknowledge the virtues that preceded them. For in affirming them in him, you affirm their attainability in yourself. In crowing him, you crown yourself. Such is the secret power behind this practice.

Foundational Practice 2 - Embodied Inquiry - Awakening the Inner King (Version 1)

Time: 10-15 minutes
Frequency: Daily

Description:

Use this short practice daily to gently activate all seven virtues of the inner king—and take them deep within your body and mind.

While the *Awakening Your Inner King* mentorship program goes deeper into defining and contextualizing the seven virtues, what's most important is that you reach for your own perception of them. Don't treat these terms as absolute and abstract. Truly *reach for* your genuine experience of them. There will always be more genuine power, compassion, forgiveness, wisdom and self-knowledge available to you.

These virtues exist on a spectrum. The victim has a dualistic "all or nothing" mentality, which incidentally prevents him from any upward movement. While the starving soul may want a five-course feast, the awakening king is wise to claim the simple fruit within arm's reach of his awareness. In doing so, he receives the sustenance and energy to keep reaching forward.

You may follow or record your own version
using the script below. Or access the guided practice
inside the full *Awakening Your Inner King* program at:

iseeyouking.com/awaken

Practice Instructions:

1. Feeling the solidity of the earth below you, and placing your full attention on your feet, legs, and base of the spine, ask:
   a. What does it feel like to be fully in my power? And ask again...

b. What does it feel like to be fully in my power? One more time…

c. What does it feel like to be fully in my power?

2. Feeling the watery flow of all the liquids and fluids in your body, and placing your full attention on your genital area and hips, ask:

a. What does it feel like to be totally accepting and forgiving? Ask again…

b. What does it feel like to be totally accepting and forgiving? One more time…

c. What does it feel like to be totally accepting and forgiving no matter what?

3. Feeling the heat and fire in your belly and digestive organs, and placing your full attention on your solar plexus, ask:

a. What does it feel like to express my full, authentic willpower? Again…

b. What does it feel like to express my full, authentic willpower? Last time…

c. What does it feel like to express my full, authentic willpower?

4. Feeling a gust of wind around your chest, and placing your attention deep into your heart region, ask:

a. What does it feel like to be unconditionally loving and compassionate?

b. What does it feel like to be unconditionally loving and compassionate?

c. What does it feel like to be unconditionally loving and compassionate?

5. Sensing the underlying power that animates you, your words and your actions into form and existence, place your attention on your throat, and ask

a. What does it feel like to live in my fullest expression of love and truth?

b. What does it feel like to live in my fullest expression of love and truth?

c. What does it feel like to live in my fullest expression of love and truth?

6. Appreciating the vast intelligence that your body and mind have access to at all times, place your attention at the center of your head, and ask:

a. What does it feel like to have total access to wisdom and insight?

b. What does it feel like to have total access to wisdom and insight?

c. What does it feel like to have total access to wisdom and insight?

7. Feeling your entire body—and BEYOND your body as far as you can stretch it—ask:

a. What does it feel like to know myself beyond time and space?

b. What does it feel like to know myself beyond time and space?

c. What does it feel like to know myself beyond time and space?

Foundational Practice 3 - Embodied Inquiry - Awakening the Inner King (Version 2):

Time: 15 minutes
Frequency: Daily

Description:

When you're ready for a slightly longer and more integrated version of the above practice, proceed to the instructions below.

> You may follow or record your own version
> using the script below. Or access the guided practice
> inside the full *Awakening Your Inner King* program at:
>
> iseeyouking.com/awaken

Practice Instructions:

1. Feeling the solidity of the earth below you, and placing your full attention on your feet, legs, and the base of your spine, ask:
   a. What would it be like to be fully in my power?
   b. What has it been like to be fully in my power?
   c. What is it like to be fully in my power?
   d. How did I become so fully in my power?

2. Feeling the watery flow of all the liquids and fluids in your body, and placing your full attention on your genital area and hips, ask:
   a. What would it feel like to be totally accepting and forgiving?
   b. What has it been like to be totally accepting and forgiving?
   c. What is it like to be totally accepting and forgiving?
   d. How did I become so accepting and forgiving?

3. Feeling the heat and fire in your belly, and placing your full attention on your solar plexus, ask:
   a. What would it feel like to experience total and complete freedom of my willpower?

b. What has it been like to experience total and complete freedom of my willpower?

c. What is it like to experience total and complete freedom of my willpower?

d. How did I become so totally and completely expressed in my willpower?

4. Feeling a gust of wind around your chest, and placing your attention deep into your heart region, ask:

a. What would it be like to be unconditionally loving and compassionate?

b. What has it been like to be unconditionally loving and compassionate?

c. What is it like to be unconditionally loving and compassionate?

d. How did I become so unconditionally loving and compassionate?

5. Sensing the underlying power that animates you, your words and your actions into form, place your attention on your throat, and ask:

a. What would it be like to live in my fullest expression of love and truth?

b. What has it been like to live in my fullest expression of love and truth?

c. What is it like to live in my fullest expression of love and truth?

d. How did I become so capable of living in my fullest expression of love and truth?

6. Appreciating the vast intelligence that your body and mind have access to at all times, place your attention at the center of your head, and ask:

a. What would it be like to have total access to wisdom and insight?

b. What has it been like to have total access to wisdom and insight?

c. What is it like to have total access to wisdom and insight?

d. How did I gain total access to wisdom and insight?

7. Feeling your entire body—and BEYOND your body as far as you can stretch it—ask:

a. What would it feel like to know myself beyond time and space?

b. What has it been like to know myself beyond time and space?

c. What is it like to know myself beyond time and space?

Foundational Practice 4 - The King's Gaze:

Time: A few minutes

Frequency: Daily

Description:

Your eyes (and how they're "postured" as a gaze) are your most immediate and direct sensory portal into the "outside world." They precede and inform the mental and emotional "reaction"—and therefore can be trained to imbue experience with a more virtuous stance.

Most men view and perceive the world (situations, events, spoken and written words) with a "posture" of intensity, defensiveness, fear, threat or hostility. Our contact point with "reality" in turn, becomes one of friction, harshness and contraction; even when the situation would warrant lightness, warmth, and openness. With intention alone, you can encode all information, phenomena and stimuli with higher virtue prior to knee-jerk reaction.

The practice is simple. Choose an object. It can be a picture, a person, a mountain, an animal, or even yourself through the mirror, etc. Practice viewing the object through the following filters, rotating between them every 30-60 seconds—and gradually including "more" objects on each subsequent set until everything within your gaze is included. As you do, notice how your entire body and mind respond.

1. See an object through the eyes of uncompromising power.
2. See an object through the eyes of forgiveness and acceptance.
3. See an object through the eyes of divine courage.
4. See an object through the eyes of unconditional love and compassion.
5. See an object through the eyes of energy itself.
6. See an object through the eyes of pure insight and wisdom.
7. See an object through the eyes of pure awareness.

Next...

1. See a situation or memory through the eyes of uncompromising power.
2. See a situation or memory the eyes of forgiveness and acceptance.
3. See a situation or memory through the eyes of divine courage.
4. See a situation or memory through the eyes of unconditional love and compassion.

5. See a situation or memory through the eyes of energy itself.
6. See a situation or memory through the eyes of pure insight and wisdom.
7. See a situation or memory through the eyes of pure awareness.
8. Now expand to your entire field:
9. See everything and everyone through the eyes of uncompromising power.
10. See everything and everyone through the eyes of forgiveness and acceptance.
11. See everything and everyone through the eyes of divine courage.
12. See everything and everyone through the eyes of unconditional love and compassion.
13. See everything and everyone through the eyes of energy itself.
14. See everything and everyone through the eyes of pure insight and wisdom.
15. See everything and everyone through the eyes of pure awareness.
16. And then reverse it onto yourself.
17. Let everything perceive you as uncompromising power.
18. Let everything perceive you through the eyes of forgiveness and acceptance.
19. Let everything perceive you as divine courage.
20. Let everything perceive you with unconditional love and compassion.
21. Let everything perceive you as energy itself.
22. Let yourself be perceived through insight and wisdom.
23. Let yourself be perceived as awareness by awareness.

In doing so, allow your gaze to be a mirror to the world—and the world a mirror to yourself. Notice how there's no essential difference between inside and outside. Love is love. Power is power. Compassion is compassion. It permeates through you, as you, and beyond you.

Foundational Practice 5 - Experiential Embodiment - The Power of the King:

Time: 35-45 minutes
Frequency: weekly

Description:

Few concepts are more perplexing to men than power.

We crave it.

We chase it.

We fear it.

We accumulate it.

We kill for it.

We die for it.

We try to attain more of it.

We try to take it from others.

We try to exert it on others while fearing how others are exerting it on us.

Our turbulent and flat-out maddening relationship with power comes down to the fact that it's been compromised and hijacked by fear. But to be *uncompromisingly* powerful is to understand that power isn't something to be gained or extracted.

It's not something you collect in the winner's circle of a zero-sum game, nor something you relinquish in so-called defeat. It's something that naturally *emerges* when your actions become less bent by egoic fear, and instead, expressed fully and authentically with focused intent and purpose. For you don't *own* power. Power is fluid. It flows through you. And it flows through you to the extent that you, yourself, are an open enough channel to both receive and direct it.

Think of each "fear" or ill-intentioned motive as a circuit breaker that diffuses the voltage running through you. By the time it moves towards outer expression, the power has been diluted and dispersed across conflicting motives, stories and fears. None of which have received enough power to become fully expressed into form.

Therefore, it's not about becoming more powerful. It's about your power becoming less compromised and diffused. It's further compromised with every well-conditioned declaration of limitation. The hypnotic impulse to slide into the realm of *"I can't," "I won't," and "this is too much."* Trance-like whimpers of the inner victim that reverberate through your being, and leave a toxic imprint on every endeavor.

Such statements, while seemingly excusable and justifiable in the moment of trigger, are a sharp and scathing denial of any deepening or expanding capacity. The victim would rather rot and decay within the toxic soil of defeat than receive warmth and power from the sun above. For the victim, as a low-intelligence and temporal life-form, only knows and craves defeat.

The only fight he knows is the one to maintain his sense of powerlessness. It's perhaps the greatest perversion of the human spirit. Initially, your power isn't reclaimed from some external foe. It's reclaimed primarily from an inner victim who refuses to be anything other than such.

The victim has a contracted view. A distorted lens that knows only self-degradation, despair and defeat. He knows only the process of succumbing. Of premature and premeditated collapse. The feeling of exhaustion and overwhelm. And the boiling agitation of powerlessness. He screams out for arduous circumstance to arise. Not so that he may test his capacity against it, but so that he can be cloaked within his calamitous machinations. He stands ever ready to collapse. Yet he is cunning. He won't fall on his own sword, but throw himself in front of oncoming arrows, no matter how errant. He allows a flesh wound to become fatal. And uses his dying breath to curse his poor fortune, which was almost entirely self-created yet projected on some so-called oppressor whom he's all-too eager to persecute.

The victim and his inner strategies are the inorganic insulators that block energy flow, and therefore must first be unwired to allow genuine power to flow through you. As this unwiring progresses, you come to understand that you can never *be* powerful—but you are, at your very core, a channel or conduit for as much power as you're capable of fully and authentically expressing. For power, in its purest form, is a magically creative and lovingly regenerative force—and comes from a source far beyond your wildest comprehension.

Take the example of childbirth. Your seed, all 525 billion of them that you'll produce over your lifetime, flows through you without any conscious effort. Yet just one of those seeds carries with it the potential for human life—a life, which in turn, becomes creative, powerful and regenerative in of itself.

Let this serve as a reminder that you are not the source of power, but the channel through which it gets expressed. The main limits to your power are the boundaries you impose on who and what you believe yourself to be. These are not simply beliefs, but rigid identities such as the victim, that must be loosened for you to realize and experience just how much power you're capable of channeling.

A rageful fist may be able to break through gyprock, but an open palm, channeling the limitless power of the universe itself, can bend steel. It's that continuous unimpeded expression, not the fear-based accumulation and hoarding, that allows for more power to flow through you. It's what signals to the universe that you're ready to be a steward of this mysterious "stuff" that sustains all life and creates new galaxies. You are powerless to this mystery—yet infinitely powerful once you align with it and accept yourself as intimately and inseparably involved with that ever-unfolding mystery.

For power is nothing but the capacity to bridge intention into creation. You are that *bridge*. And you imbue power with your unique codes of creation. You *are* at your core the blueprint that raw power molds itself to in order to birth new forms of genius into the world. Power is impersonal. It exists as pure potentiality—seeking a steward to imprint it with direction and intent. Therefore, the more you're attuned and committed to your authentic mission and purpose—and your willingness to express it, the greater power you can access. This responsibility is great.

It's why power always seeks a trustworthy and awakened king.

For when you act from your inner king, you announce your worthiness and your willingness to fully and positively express the power that flows through you. Moment by moment. Breath by breath. And your willingness is only made genuine and sincere when you no longer fear the consequences of its expression—for you trust in the love, wisdom and compassion that precedes it.

Therefore, the paradox of power gets immediately resolved in the presence of unconditional love and compassion. Likewise, to become unconditionally loving and compassionate requires a sense of personal power as well. It's nearly impossible to activate the other virtues of the inner king when you feel weak, powerless and vulnerable—especially in relation to others and the world around you. Indeed, compassion and cowardice are contraindicated.

Therefore, all seven virtues of the inner king are synergistic and self-reinforcing. And while your flow of power will increase with each subsequent initiation, tapping into the power you *currently* have access to is a vital starting point to energize the process.

Authentic power is ultimately our starting point and our ending point. However, by the time you've activated and embodied all seven virtues, you'll be gifted with a potent, balanced, and highly integrated power that's ready to build the most magnificent of kingdoms.

A quick look at how each virtue unlocks more power:

Virtue 1: Uncompromisingly powerful and regenerative: We simply commit to cultivating our fullest authentic power, and expressing it for the highest good of self and other. In this commitment, we pledge to awakening and integrating all seven virtues.

Virtue 2: Unconditionally accepting and forgiving: Holding onto anger, guilt, blame and resentment severely robs us of our power. It only satisfies and energizes a small, fearful and petty part of ourselves that has little capacity for a healthy and productive expression of power. When we activate the second virtue, we withdraw power from these lower aspects of self—and all its suboptimal (or straight up malicious) expressions.

Virtue 3: Unshackled from expectation: This virtue is the birthplace of authentic free will. Not the one you've been mercilessly sold since birth, but a *pure* will that has sobered up from a cocktail of external influence and expectation. In unshackling yourself from these expectations, many of which have masqueraded as your own, you allow more power to be reallocated to your truest callings and most authentic desires.

Virtue 4: Unconditionally loving and compassionate: When you begin awakening to unconditional love and compassion, you begin to recognize how necessary a "cap" on your power has been. You start to see how your power hasn't always been shaped by positive intent—and become aware that on a subtle level, you were perhaps aware of this and thus mistrusting in your own power. As you begin to trust your intent, you become less fearful in expressing the full depth of your available power. You realize how much you've held back in the past to avoid harming others, and how such self-restraint is no longer needed. When you become less disposed to feelings of resentment, reactivity and vengefulness, you become more available for healthy and regenerative expressions of power.

Virtue 5: Unceasing in his fullest expression of love and truth: The natural emergence of this newfound self-trust is the full expression of your power in the forms of love and truth. This is where you become the willing and consistent channel for the source of power, (however you define it) to flow through you. For power isn't meant to be hoarded. It's meant to flow and circulate. It's your unceasing allowance of this process that allows even greater levels to flow.

Virtue 6: Unconstrained in his access to wisdom and insight: Naturally, much of this is predicated on your capacity to receive wisdom and insight on how your power needs to be expressed moment by moment. Not only in the form of a grand, overarching "life mission," but with whatever life presents to you in any given moment. This, of course, requires both access and sensitivity to a deepened presence and perceptive awareness that extends beyond the typical, myopic lens through which the common man experiences his reality.

Virtue 7: Pure awareness, unbound by time and space: Across many ancient cultures, the king wasn't crowned by forcible claim or inherited namesake. Instead, he was chosen based on his intimate and undeniable connection to source—higher power—the universe. He was given a lifetime of responsibility to be the trusted channel between *all* there is—and all we can perceive. In our practice, you'll begin to cultivate the skill of pure awareness, unbound by time and space, and in doing so, become a trusted channel for the deepest insight and power possible.

The Power of the King is an *Experiential Embodiment* practice that will energize and infuse your entire being with balanced and fully integrated power. Creating further coherence and communication between all seven of the core virtues we've started to awaken.

You may access the recorded practice at

www.iseeyouking.com/power

Final Words Before the Fires

Awakening your inner king is fundamental to *everything* we'll be cultivating moving forward. In the coming chapters, we'll be accessing our inner king to lead us through each of the seven initiatory fires of our daily lives. Namely, your intimate relationship, fatherhood, your pursuit of purpose, your business or livelihood, thriving mentally, emotionally, physically and spiritually in an unbalanced world. And finally expressing yourself fully in a suppressed world.

As a modern man, chances are that an overwhelming majority of your time, energy and attention is spent stewing in these fires. Re-approaching them with the virtues we've begun to awaken will be nothing short of life-changing for you, your family, and all those who share a place in your kingdom.

For now, and ongoingly, it's recommended that you continue to make a daily practice of the exercises learnt in this chapter. Do not slip into the delusion that the work is "complete." Reading a chapter in itself is an admirable task. Yet not to be confused with "the work" itself. Rather, the "work" is in each step. In each breath. And in each wisdom-infused and heart-informed swinging of the sword. For as far as we've come, we've truly just begun.

Awakening earns you no reward, but the richness of opportunity that such lucidity and skillfulness shall bring. The fruits gained shall be the fruits earned. And you're now well equipped to prune the damaged leaves, purify the toxic soil, and re-wire the root system for true and lasting sustenance.

What you do with your newfound capacity and awareness remains what you choose. May you be well guided in each step, and may all those within your personal kingdom be equally blessed.

With deep love and respect…

I see you, king.

Chapter 3:

WELCOME TO THE FIRES

Welcome to the fires.

On a collective level, these *7 Initiatory Fires* are presented to help shape the next men's movement, sparking an accelerated evolutionary leap in how men show up in the world. On an individual level, the raging flames will shine light on your shadows and mercifully transmute those aspects that no longer serve your fullest expression.

Within each fire, you'll be called to reveal the subtle patterns of your inner victim, and awaken your inner king—while bringing sacredness and meaning to the mundane. Each fire will be the grounds for burning away old aspects of self and transmuting them into a more powerful and matured way of being. From this place, far greater possibilities will become available to you. Engaging fully in *any one* of these fires will produce life-changing growth, with each subsequent one compounding to create a truly exponential effect in a relatively short amount of time.

You'll be called to rise up in ways that will spark a completely new way of being—one that is more abundant, peaceful and powerfully expressed for the highest good of both yourself and all those privileged enough to share the gifts of your kingdom.

This is not to be taken lightly. It's worth repeating that the sincere undertaking of these initiations *may* shake up your life and relationships in ways that you can barely begin to fathom at this time. This isn't a typical "self-help" program that will gently guide you through a slow, self-paced journey where you get to hold onto the guardrails, and retreat the moment things feel too jarring and disorienting.

If you're reading these words, it's because you're no longer interested in the safe and sanitized. You're no longer willing to compromise your power by taking one micro-step at a time towards becoming the man you're destined to become. Most of all, you're no longer willing to selfishly delay such an ascent when so much is on the line. You're aware of the stakes. The forced prolongation of existential dread and its devastating consequences no longer aligns with your will. And beyond it all, the call towards realizing your fullest depth and potential as a husband, father, and man exercising his true will in this world is simply too deafening to tune out for one moment longer.

That sacred encounter is long overdue. And while you'd be right to have some trepidation before moving forward, the guttural clench of self-restraint has become too unbearable. The sharp nails of the status quo have dug themselves into your heart and soul for far too long. Blessed you are for being so sensitive and awake to that inner tug, for it's a call many will miss.

The time has come, king.

In the previous chapter, you've taken the foundational steps to begin awakening your inner king, while he, in turn, has awoken *you* from your dream. You're about to be pulled from your everyday world and submerged into the dark wilderness where the greatest of inner treasures shall be uncovered.

With brilliance, the fires call.

With courage, you answer.

Transformation vs. Tactics

These fires are not about rearranging your current experience. They're about restructuring the very foundation from which your experience is built upon. It's a dismantling, a deconstruction, and a demolition of the inner structures that perpetuate your suffering and victim-informed reactivity—and a corresponding restoration, rebuilding and re-birthing of the inner king within each.

While each fire certainly invites discussion over the most optimal tactics and strategies, the focus in this volume will be the underlying mental, emotional, psychological and spiritual structures that truly run the show. After all, "who you are" and "how you show up" are the precursors to all experience.

We have an imbalanced fixation on tactics and strategy for they provide the illusion of progress. Yet a victim will always find a reason to collapse in defeat. A beggar will always find a way to be helplessly unfulfilled. A pawn will always find a new false king to follow. A martyr will always chart a new path towards self-annihilation. Yet a king, no matter the circumstances, will *always* find a way to rise.

Without awakening to your highest virtues in each fire and releasing their corresponding shadows, no tactic or strategy will sustain. It's why a fifty-billion-dollar self-help industry keeps people on a cycle of brokenness. It's why you can have eighteen books on "conscious parenting" and still find yourself unable to hold your son or daughter in total love and compassion amidst a breakdown. It's why you can own every course or program on how to scale a business, but still find yourself on the brink of bankruptcy, unable to execute an escape plan.

Just like the world's sharpest sword is useless when placed in weak and trembling hands, no tactic or strategy can compensate for a man who's yet to step into his fullness. Strategy and tactics can only be effective in the hands of a king. In someone willing to fiercely apply them with composure, focus and heart-centered power.

The fires are concerned with *that* transformation.

In the resources section of our companion site (www.iseeyouking.com/resources), you'll be invited to explore other books, trainings and guides who generously share their well-earned wisdom on the more tactical side.

But for now, let's walk the path we've chosen with courage and commitment.

You're Not Meant to Survive These Fires

On a final note, I offer a critical mindset shift that will serve you well as you embark on this most sacred of journeys. The seven initiatory fires you're about to step into aren't meant to be survived.

There's a damaging and flat-out erroneous belief that you can "conquer" these fires. That you can battle your way through their flames and reach a climactic end point where your "work" is done. Where your intimate relationship, your family life, your business, your health, or your connection to purpose will reach some kind of harmonious endpoint. A place where you can finally lay down your arms and breathe a sigh of relief. Where you can look out from your ivory tower and say, *"I made it."*

The illusion of this "well-deserved" endpoint is a major source of suffering in the lives of men. In reality, the belief in a blissful end point is a false entitlement. An unrealistic expectation and childish insistence imposed onto universal law that creates an unnecessary and unavoidable sense of defeat and discontentment.

The only entitlement we have as men is our agency, our attention and our *will* to continue growing in our power and capacity to hold steady in these flames. To let the fires illuminate our shadows—and dissolve all contractions and resistance until we, in turn, merge with that light and become a source of growth, healing and inspiration to all those around us. These fires are inextinguishable. Ever burning. With their eternal flames inviting us back for deeper revelation and transformation each time we engage with them.

Just like with your body's biological functions, homeostasis isn't static. It's achieved millisecond by millisecond. Actively. There's no passive endpoint. The fires only burn more brightly, and you become more skillful in letting yourself be transformed by them. You don't extinguish the fire. You merge with it. You're its kindling. In this, you recognize these fires not as foe, but as indistinguishable from your own source of wisdom and transmutational power.

The illusion of an endpoint is what creates suffering. The moment you start believing that your relationship should be easy is the second you invite willful delusion, blindness and resistance to its flames. The moment you believe your pursuit of purpose has been fully accomplished is the moment you invite complacency to settle back in. It's the moment you dishonor your fluid, ever-evolving mission in life—and slowly allow your gifts of expression to coagulate around a new fixed image or idea.

There is no "end point" to this work. And that's why many men will resist it. We've been conditioned to seek conclusion. We feel uncomfortable with the open loops in our lives. But in reality, this work isn't a closed circle, but an infinite spiral. You'll return to these fires until your final breath. Becoming more skillful, powerful, and peaceful with each deeper revolution. In doing so, you'll experience greater bliss and personal triumph than a false, self-declared conclusion can ever provide.

For your soul knows better. It doesn't believe your lie of premature victory, and will not provide you the boon in the winner's circle that a less-matured version of you believes yourself entitled to. Afterall, a king without an inner and outer kingdom to continuously tend to, is no king at all.

So, the invitation is this:

Allow these fires to consume you over and over again.

Learn to dance in their flames.

Endeavor to seek them in every moment. To lean into their eternal flames, knowing in your heart, that only what is ready to be revealed, dissolved and transformed will.

Be bold yet patient. Courageous yet gentle.

And grow ever trusting in who you are—who you're in the process of becoming—and the positive power you're here to share with the world in your own uniquely brilliant way.

May your heart shine ever brighter. And your sword remain ever sharp.

The Structure of the Seven Fires

Most men aren't afraid of "doing the work." They're simply confused and overwhelmed around what the work entails. An explorer without a compass is a castaway. A soldier without true cause is a weak-handed mercenary who will flee when the first arrow whizzes by. And a hunter without intimate knowledge of the prey he dares stalk will starve and wither as his expedition meets cold end. Indeed, a nameless foe and vast uncharted land invites overwhelm and powerlessness.

But with a description of the foe you seek, and a map of the land in which he dwells, a man can re-channel his inner resource into the courage and power to confront it. Bravery is best conjured when our mission is well-defined. When we can follow "the plan" and trust in the fruits that it may bear. And power becomes more readily available when we have a cause to direct it towards.

As such, each fire has been meticulously crafted to offer the safest, most potent and lasting transformation possible. It's recommended that you approach these fires in the exact phases they've been mapped out for you. For with a blazed trail and a clear mission, you're liberated to use the fullest extent of your focus and power on the task at hand.

Phase 1: The Activation

In Phase 1, you'll read about the initiatory fire itself—the three main shadows it illuminates, and the corresponding gift or virtue that awakens once your initiation has been successfully integrated.

You won't consume this information passively. Rather, you'll allow each section to activate a stream of thoughts, reactions and sacred remembrances of your own experiences within each fire. You'll recall how the shadows have been present in your own life; taking note of any sensations, images, imprints, energy signatures, thought patterns, memories, or beliefs that come to mind.

Read slowly and mindfully. Not with your eyes, but with your entire being. Form a full-bodied relationship with the words before you. Do not miss the opportunity for a passage to pull the cover off of a long-hidden shadow or pattern. The words in the activation are the stadium lights. Brilliant bulbs that allow nothing beneath them to remain cast in darkness. But it's in your own willingness to patiently observe, without judgment or haste, that will truly dictate what gets revealed, and what remains free to operate beneath the surface.

Some may wonder how reading a passage can be effective in uncovering a long-hidden belief or pattern. The answer is simple:

Shadows remain hidden until called out by "name." The negative ego, limiting patterns, and immature identities (i.e., the victim) are elusive by design. Yet they contain a fatal flaw. An Achilles heel. They wish to take credit. These shadows are largely narcissistic. Much like an elusive criminal may be compelled to reveal himself in frustration when another man, falsely accused, takes "credit" for his work, our inner victim will claim ownership over the patterns that are called out.

Likewise, they're quick to react and rise in protest to empowering statements and higher possibilities that contradict the victim stance they insist on maintaining. They don't want resolution. They decry resourcefulness. And a glimpse of higher virtue (in the "what awakens" section) will often invite a mind stream of rebuttals and resistance. This is to be expected and appreciated. For these rebuttals themselves are what reveal these shadows for what they are. They give up their cover. And so long as you can maintain enough distance and awareness by perceiving from your inner king, you immediately gain a degree of liberation from them.

This is the activation we seek in reading these passages. The "credit taking" and the "rebuttals" are the reactions we seek and expect from the shadows, while simultaneously activating a sense of higher possibility and virtue that we come into initial communion with.

The Activation Contains 3 Sections:

1. An introduction to the fire
2. The 3 Shadows that must be revealed and confronted
3. The Awakening

Let's briefly take a quick look at each of these components.

1. Introduction to the Fire

These fires are where you invest the majority of your time, energy and presence. Yet rather than see them for the modern-day initiations they truly are, with all their inherent challenges, shadows, and opportunities for accelerated growth, men often stumble and sleepwalk through them, failing to ascribe the respect and reverence they deserve, and succumbing to guilt and self-shame when the initiation is inevitably missed or failed.

We'll therefore begin each initiatory fire with a careful examination of *what* exactly makes each one an "initiatory fire," and what it's ultimately here to show us once we become brave enough to look.

2. The 3 Shadows

Recalling that every initiation entails a symbolic death and rebirth, the shadows as presented here are the most common and damaging patterns, identities and conditioned beliefs that obstruct your ascent into kingship within that fire.

In each of these fires, we'll explore three corresponding "shadow" aspects. You may think of these shadows as the aspects of yourself that get most agitated, reactive or inflamed when stewing in that particular fire. Left unexamined, these shadows influence the way you react and respond to the demands of each fire— mostly dysfunctionally.

Much has been said and written about "shadow work" over the years. In our work, it's helpful to understand that the shadows described are not isolated emotions, beliefs or identities, but entire chained and interlinked networks of them. A destructive and dysfunctional gestalt that has been expanded and reinforced with every thought, action, imprint, belief or memory that falls within its core operating pattern. We'll be seeking to illuminate the core pattern or central thesis behind each shadow.

For the most part, these shadow patterns are automatic and unconscious. They're so deeply entrenched and encoded into our internal "operating system" that we fail to see them at play. In most cases, they've had decades of momentum and reinforcement behind them, which nearly fossilizes them into place. For some, they're so tightly fused to their entire subjective experience and perceptive lenses, that they barely have enough separation to notice it. In other words, they're both the most subtle and influential saboteurs that threaten the very kingdom we wish to build. That is, until we create a small enough chasm to awaken to the possibility that "they're not us."

On a deeper, more spiritual level, the transformation of these shadows will reveal a fluidity of self. As the apparent solidity of these shadows dissolves, what you're left with is an astonishing sense of spaciousness, wonder and curiosity over who (and what) you truly are.

You begin to understand that most of what you've considered to be "your personality" is little more than a glorified trauma response. Layer by layer, parts of your so-called personality slip off the bone, and you come into closer contact with your core being. In this sense, genuine shadow work isn't solely a psychological pursuit, but also a potent gateway towards deeper spiritual insight.

Our work will be to compassionately see these shadows for what they are, how they came to be, and where they're still claiming power and influence over our lives. Once exposed in the brightness of our inner awareness, we'll then be ready to transmute them in the fires of initiation.

That's not to say that your work will be completely "done." With a lifetime of momentum and energy behind them, certain emotions, beliefs, identities and behavioral patterns will continue to show up for you. There will be the well-conditioned responses, energetic residues and aftershocks that reverberate long after the core pattern has been exposed. The difference is, you'll have greatly reduced their power by dissolving or disarming core parts of the overarching system or pattern that supported them—while having awakened and energized the more illuminated, evolved and matured version of you.

The culmination of this program is essentially the dissolution and positive transformation of 21 core shadow patterns that severely limit and distort your expression of authentic love and power as a man.

3. The 7 Awakenings

An awakening, by definition, can only reveal what was alive within you before the corresponding shadows blocked its light and expression. As a king, these awakenings are innately *yours*. You can think of them as long, overdue inheritances. They're your birthright, yet paradoxically, these awakenings must be earned. There are no false crownings. Your rule can't be faked. These awakenings can only be inherited by the king who has gone through the process of initiation.

Once you do, what you're left with are seven powerful awakenings and paradigm shifts that gain precedence and influence in your life as you transcend their respective shadows, and integrate them into your day-to-day awareness.

Symbolically, you can think of all seven of these awakened archetypes as different facets or expressions of your inner king as they pertain to that specific aspect of your life. They're his trusted "ambassadors" to the outside world, and all the containers you operate within.

Phase 2: The Pre-Initiation Practices

Following the activation phase, you'll have developed a basic understanding of how and where the shadows operate in your life. Through deeper self-inquiry and sharper self-awareness, the pre-initiation stage will be your chance to refine your understandings, and become even more intimate with the influence they've had.

Using the tools introduced in the last chapter (King's Log, Embodied Inquiry, King's Word), you'll acknowledge, to the best of your ability, where these shadows have shown up, and the impact they've had on your life and the lives of others.

Before being whisked away into your core initiation, you'll be given the chance to make amends with your past. With deep compassion, you'll forgive yourself, offer your apology to those who've been harmed, and close your affairs in preparation for that long-standing shadow to fully dissolve.

You may experience a mix of grief, sorrow, guilt and shame or even the surge of ecstatic aliveness that comes from gaining distance and separation from that which has predominantly overlayed your experience, masking itself as you. All reactions are valid and can be met in the warm embrace of the self-compassion you've already begun awakening to.

Finally, you'll declare your readiness to your inner king by offering a statement of irrevocable intent. With your word as law, your initiation will begin.

Phase 3: The Crowned Process™

In each fire, you'll be engaging in a guided initiation called The Crowned Process™. This is an advanced form of the Experiential Embodiment practice that was introduced earlier. While there are several advanced inner technologies at play, reimagined from various wisdom and psychological traditions, all you need to succeed in this process is a sincere commitment to follow along with the guidance to the best of your ability.

The seven overlapping aspects of the *Crowned Process* are as follows:

1. Confrontation with shadow

You'll begin the process by experiencing yourself in your throne room. You'll contact your inner king, and together, begin to confront the three shadows of the particular initiatory fire. Once again, your inner king shall serve as your "elder." He won't let you shirk away. Instead, you'll lean on his virtues as you bear witness to your shadows. Addressing them with respect, compassion and acceptance, while acknowledging that their time has come and that their rulership must now end.

2. Radical intimacy with all that emerges

Here, you'll courageously allow yourself to become more intimate with these shadows, calling them forward to reveal themselves more fully.

Each shadow may be the doorway to dozens of sub-patterns, emotions, beliefs or identities. You'll start experiencing them within your body, within your memories or mental field, within yourself. No longer something external, but something deeply personal and intimate. In the presence of your inner king, you'll allow yourself to see all and feel all with courage and compassion.

The strength and steadiness of your compassion-infused awareness is what brightens the fire. And it's the intimate contact between this awareness and your shadow patterns that catalyze and support their transformation.

3. Ownership over everything you encounter within yourself

While remaining intimate with all that arises, you'll bravely take ownership over them all. They are, after all, occurring within your experience—your thoughts, memories, and feelings.

We have been well trained in the art of disowning, dissociating and detaching from our "stuff." Yet until you compassionately accept their presence, and completely *own* your role in having created, adopted, maintained, insisted on, and perpetuated them, you'll be unable to fully release them. After all, you can't let go of what you've yet to acknowledge as being held. This will be done with complete love, compassion and forgiveness towards yourself.

4. Witness them all from the place of the inner king

Once you've taken full ownership over everything you can, you'll shift your viewpoint and entire experiential reference point to that of your inner king. You'll feel and *be* his virtues, and accept them as your own. He represents the already healed, evolved and transformed version of "you." Already existing in a state of effortless perfection. A reminder of where you inevitably end up.

5. Neutralize and Negate

As the king, make the empowered decision that these shadows, and all their corresponding fragments, are no longer you. With your word as law, you'll make this declaration for them to be fully neutralized and transformed into higher virtue or power. Withdrawing all power and energy from them. Withdrawing any permission, implicit or explicit you've granted them to govern any part of your experience.

6. Elemental Initiation

With your declaration made, you'll call on all the elements around you—earth, water, fire, wind and ether to continue facilitating the transformation through their various properties.

7. Death and Deliverance

Finally, you'll experience the symbolic death of these old aspects of self, and experience deliverance into the rebirth and awakening on the other side of it. This is not a violent or vengeful process, but a natural and compassionate completion of a cycle.

The culmination is the overthrowing of the false king, and the proper crowning of the awakened state or more evolved archetype. One where "he" now has the authority to use your most precious resources of energy and attention and direct them toward aligned action.

Phase 4: Evolutionary Accelerators (Integration Practices)

Once the shadows have been dissolved and the awakening has been seeded, it's essential to follow it up with the real-world actions, stances and practices that support this new shift in being.

Remember, you're working against years or decades of actions rooted in shadow. While much of the inner transformation has already been accomplished, it's the aligned actions you perform from your new perspective that gives life and momentum to the new "you" that you're in the process of becoming. The act of constant remembrance and choosing to see and act through the lens of matured wisdom and evolved being is integral.

The major difference here is that "behavioral change" is no longer a practice of blunt force, but a more natural and effortless cultivation and expression of who you're already in the active process of becoming. Put another way, aligned action isn't an act of egoic will or forcefulness. It's a natural emergent from upgrading your identity, and gets reinforced with each investment of energy you put into it.

But it must be practiced with sincerity and consistency, knowing full well that the echoes of patterns past may yet still try to lull you back to sleep under its well-rehearsed spell. Integration therefore requires sharpened awareness and battle-tested courage. The set of integration practices you'll work with are called Evolutionary Accelerators™.

They're the actions you'll take in the real world—and where you get to gift your new way of being to those around you. Being witnessed and experienced by others, and most importantly, *yourself* in this new state is key. It's the public coronation; and the rejoicement of all those who will benefit from this new, more benevolent and evolved reign.

The Journey Ahead

I leave you now with the map of initiations that follow. It's recommended that you proceed in the order provided, but if a certain "fire" is raging in your present-day circumstance, you're invited to use your inner guidance and forge your own path.

Finally, it's recommended that you complete this program in 14-20 weeks, taking around two weeks for each initiation, and leaving space as needed to integrate.

While this program asks for a strong commitment for nearly 4-5 months, the fruits earned will enrich you for a lifetime. Proceed as such, and the rewards shall be yours.

Finally, there may be occasional opportunities for private or group mentorship through the fires. While mentorship is no replacement for the self-reliance you're being called to develop, additional guidance, coaching and accountability may be valuable allies on your path.

If feeling called, you're invited to review
and apply for such opportunities at:

www.iseeyouking.com/coaching

The 7 Initiatory Fires of Modern Manhood

Initiatory Fire	Shadows	What Awakens	Evolutionary Accelerators
1. Thriving Physically & Mentally in an Unhealthy World	1. Regression to the Norm 2. Consumption of the Creator 3. The Gluttony of Distraction	The Alchemist	1. Stalking Reality 2. Sense Play 3. Intentional Action 4. Be the Bridge 5. The King's Feast

2. Your Intimate Relationship	1. The Burden of Balance 2. The Denial of Interdependence 3. The Illusion of Ownership	The Fearless Lover	1. Make the first move 2. Pickup lines 3. Evoke. Evolve. 4. The King's Gaze 5. A Kingdom, shared.
3. Your Sense of Purpose	1. The Seduction of Safety 2. The Vacant & The Grandstander 3. The Willing Pawn	The Willful Warrior	1. Find purpose in everything 2. Unshackling from expectation
4. Fatherhood	1. The Rejection of a Mother's Love 2. The Man in Exile / The Martyr 3. The Rageful & The Resigned	The King	1. Forgive your father 2. Mend your mother wound 3. Claim your kingdom 4. Draw your empire lines 5. Duty and capacity
5. Your Business, Career & Livelihood	1. The Human Resource 2. The Resigned 3. The Rank Riser	The Steward	1. Asset Appreciation 2. Make the first move 3. Exponential Activity
6. Thriving Emotionally & Spiritually in an Unbalanced World	1. The Reactor 2. The Suppressed Stoic 3. The Illusion of Permanence	The Master	1. Prima Materia 2. Emotional Sensing 3. Emotional Sparring 4. Emotional Ascension

7. Expressing Fully in a Suppressed World	1. The Sheathed Swordsman 2. The Potential Paradox 3. Your Legacy	_____	

Chapter 4:

FIRE 1 - THRIVING PHYSICALLY & MENTALLY IN AN UNHEALTHY WORLD

What makes this an initiatory fire

Our first fire is one we've been stewing in our entire lives—and one we'll be burning in until the day our physical bodies are plunged underground. It's therefore our starting point, and where we'll be setting the foundation for all the fires that follow. Remember, most men will fail or flat-out miss their initiations. This is made no more obvious than in the mental and physical states of modern men.

By every account, man is not thriving. By the age of thirty, most men enter a state of controlled erosion—giving up all hope of enduring vitality, and settling for a more stabilized, slow-burning decay. Sure, we take pride in an ever-increasing life expectancy—and owe a debt of gratitude to the innovations that have prolonged our physical experience on earth, gifting us greater opportunity to recognize what it was all truly for. But let's not delude ourselves into falsely equating life extension with life itself. This is no different than confusing deep, heart-expanding love with the embittered couple who'll spend fifty years with clenched jaws and clamped hearts. The stench of bitter resentment rolling off each painful exchange. No, to truly thrive mentally and physically is *not* the norm.

It's not *normal* to be vital and thrive.

It's not *normal* to be a prolific creator.

It's not *normal* to be free of chronic pain and debilitating illness.

It's not *normal* to exhibit courage, confidence and resilience.

It's not *normal* to *not* be dependent on a cocktail of meds past the age of 75.

But most of all, it's not "normal" to strive for something greater and more life-affirming.

Rather than a daring progression towards the comparatively "supernatural," most men will succumb to a regression to the norm. A gluttony of distraction to drown out the faint murmurs of his dying spirit. It's this alone that makes thriving mentally and physically one of the most intense and immediate initiatory fires you'll ever walk through.

The great challenge and opportunity before us is how closely interlinked thriving physically and mentally truly is. They are utterly inseparable and reliant upon each other. Like two paddlers navigating the harsh rapids towards the shores of wellness. Anything you bridge into physical reality is preceded by the mental, which includes your thoughts, beliefs, identities and conscious or unconscious choice of where to focus your attention.

Yet this relationship isn't linear. It's circular. For your thoughts, beliefs, identities and choices, are in turn, shaped and reoriented by the actions you take, and the observable reality they produce. This circular relationship is what generates speed and momentum. The mental and the physical will always mirror and reinforce one another, creating an accelerated, and often unstoppable drive towards a predictable end

Unfortunately, for most men, this momentum is often experienced as a forceful and unrelenting undercurrent, mercilessly guiding them towards some harrowing, painful or destructive conclusion. An "end" they feel they had no control or influence over—yet were unavoidably implicit in creating.

No, we don't have absolute control or influence over our lives. Just like a skilled rower doesn't have complete control over the rapids beneath him. The difference is, most men see themselves as the helpless passenger going headlong into unavoidable peril, rather than the rower with both the mental and physical capacities to ride the current towards a more favorable end.

It's no wonder then that most men, when they get *really* quiet, feel a sense of unavoidable doom. A thick layer of anxiety and existential dread that's so closely fused to their perceptive reality that they accept it as their own. To survive this fire is to learn, experientially, that you are not helpless to this seemingly unstoppable current. You are, in fact, the skilled rower who gives your ship power and direction.

As you assume this power, you begin to relish in the intricate relationship between the mental and the physical. You use it as a playground for your greatest creation. As you do so, you come into contact with your inner *Alchemist*. One who consciously plays with the inputs around him and transmutes them into an even greater reality—which, in turn, inspires and provides the next set of inputs to play with. This is where self-trust and genuine confidence is birthed. It's where your capacity for rapid and directed change becomes experiential, observable and celebrated.

Your body is the most effective and immediate means of recognizing this relationship. The beautiful thing about the human body is how it's our most intimate link to the physical world—and most importantly, its malleability. Your body is a constant, inescapable reminder of how our seemingly physical world of fixed objects is actually highly malleable and ever-fluctuating. It's a personal laboratory for observing how the "result" or "outcome" you seek is preceded by more subtle mental energies and mechanisms like will, intent and focused thought.

On a micro level, nobody moves to the other side of the room without first having the thought, intention or impulse to "move to the other side of the room." On a grander scale, we can look at our body in the mirror three months after an intense workout program. The change is undeniable and highly satisfying. Yet rather than stop there, we can tune in and appreciate all the underlying mental energy that preceded its physical counterpart. The motivation and intent behind each workout. The information you consumed to direct your decisions—from what food to eat to the best exercise protocol for your specific goal. Any man who has experienced rapid physical change has, at least briefly, accessed his inner alchemist. This is where true confidence is born. Not in the eighteen-inch biceps, but in the capacity for positive transformation, and the king who had to awaken to direct it.

That's why, at its core, "looking good" isn't about vanity. It's about appreciating, exercising, and ultimately observing your power to create tangible, observable change. There's a myth that fit people are afforded more opportunities in the world. If this myth holds any merit, it's likely not because of a certain aesthetic, but because of what precedes it.

What precedes it is a certain level of power, discipline and care. The ability to delay certain base-level gratifications—and bask in a deeper glow of nourishment and wellbeing. What precedes it are tens of thousands of micro choices—from *what* we consume, to how we consciously utilize those inputs as the key building blocks for the reality we wish to experience.

Indeed, the more consciously aware of these flames you become, the quicker you can blaze a path towards accelerated growth in any direction of your choosing. These flames are menacing and uninviting only to he who has yet to wake up his inner alchemist. And as "he" awakens, you realize that the so-called unstoppable momentum towards some harrowing end is anything but.

You come to learn that you possess both a safety brake and an inner gear shift that can change course and speed with a single thought and decision. You've seen this time and time again. The man who suddenly "wakes up" and changes course. In some circles, this is called a "pattern interrupt." A pivotal, life-changing moment or "wake-up call" where you suddenly get imbued with newfound clarity and power. In many cases, this comes with seemingly destructive force. An accident or illness. A near-death experience. The devastating loss of a loved one or career you self-identified with for so long. All these events, while destructive, pull you out of a self-induced coma and shift you into greater perspective where you can realign and chart a new course. In our work, the pattern interrupt isn't illness or job loss but reverence and celebration for that which you truly are within this magnificent interplay.

For everything you desire out of life is birthed within the dynamic interplay of the mental and the physical. You've been dancing this dance since the day you were born. It's now time to master its steps.

Shadow 1: Regression to the Norm (& The Curse of Comparison)

We'll open this discussion with a sobering truth. In the eyes of many, you are a statistic. A lifeless data point, devoid of any meaning beyond the prebuilt narrative your dot of existence either reinforces or challenges.

From the day you were born and dropped onto a scale like a slab of raw meat, to the day your body's plunged underground, you're constantly being tracked, measured and charted in relation to others. This is done with your height and weight as an infant who doesn't yet have a voice to protest the indignity—to the child at school, parroting information, desperately trying to secure his spot within the bell curve.

Yet the bell curve isn't where we magically end up, it's a self-fulfilling prophecy. A lighthouse to which our mental and physical ships are steered by those we had little choice but to entrust.

This is the shadow of consensus and mediocrity. And as we unpack and illuminate its influence, we come to learn that it's not man, himself, who just happens to follow a predictable pattern, but the power of the pattern itself that magnetizes and arranges men within it. We learn that the "law" of normal distribution is not natural law, but one that's artificially enforced and maintained.

Put another way, the world around us sets a certain standard that gains power and influence as more people ascribe to it. The standard then becomes an invisible hand guiding your actions and thoughts in the subtlest of ways. Man gets reduced to a moth flocking around artificial light, which in the short term provides the illusion of warmth, safety and community, before being the source of his eventual doom. By its very definition, normalcy rarely gets questioned. It doesn't draw attention to itself. Yet it's far from benign, and will be an unquestioned saboteur across all your endeavors towards excellence.

Practically speaking, this plays out in how it's become normal to drink three beers on a Sunday afternoon while consuming countless pickup truck commercials and covert impressions of the so-called pinnacle of masculinity.

It plays out in how that same man will curse the impending Monday morning. His march from the front door to his car akin to cattle marching to the slaughter.

It plays out in how easily we justify the culturally celebrated Netflix bingefest. Or when we glance into a restaurant window and see a group of six friends at a dinner table, five on their phone before the sixth reluctantly gets sucked in.

It plays out in the standardized tests that box intelligence into a single valid expression while shaming all others into deathly submission.

It plays out in how quick we are to "normalize" disease and dysfunction. The solace we take in being "under the average BMI" while chugging down a can of well-branded, high-fructose corn syrup.

In all these cases, unquestioned normalization is the death punch to discernment and self-discretion, and is the very force that draws us into the pattern of gradual self-destruction.

When we succumb to this shadow, we default to someone else's standard of acceptability, and in turn, experience total destruction of authentic, self-directed willpower, and the dreams that would come into fruition through its proper expression.

The cost of this shadow becomes most evident and destructive when we allow it to dictate our capacity or potential. The most harrowing truth is that most men will never truly know, let alone experience, their true mental and physical capacities. They'll stop short. They'll be lulled by the status quo. They'll feel burdened and victimized by any situation or context that demands extraordinary effort or capacity. They'll succumb to the seductive whispers of the inner victim, who, on the basis of consensus, insists on a life of easeful decay.

It is not *normal* to test one's capacity.

It is not *normal* to strive for the extraordinary or the exemplary.

It is not *normal* to excel beyond the point of expectation, and thus, inner contention.

When regression to the norm reigns supreme, we put an artificial cap on what we may achieve, and who we may become in the process. For *true* capacity will only ever be achieved when we drop our culturally imposed and self-accepted limitations, and cease coddling premature collapse.

When we believe that life must be easeful and without challenge, we'll shirk away and collapse at the slightest pressure. Most men will never know their limits, let alone test them. Which is to say, most men will never know nor experience their own capacity for greatness. Their inner victim will revolt at first effort, and quote the doctrine of consensus as its rightful defense. The "extraordinary" has been put on trial by the status quo. You won't have to look far to know who's winning.

As you'll experience throughout this program, every shadow identity (or false king) has its own expectations, entitlements and insistences. With righteous fervor, it insists on the world (and those within it) being a certain way. It feels entitled to that insistence. And it feels victimized when the world doesn't match up to that expectation. Reread this passage until it sinks in. For in grasping it, you'll uncover one of the very roots of suffering itself.

This is neither theory nor poetry. It's easily observable across each fire. A new father who still has an immature (and normalized) view or identity that life should be easy and free of responsibility, will feel violently betrayed by a reality that suddenly demands increasing levels of strength, resilience and capacity. He'll not only be unwilling to explore the natural expansion of his capacity but be inflamed and agitated that such a demand even exists. He'll feel besieged by an unholy army of faceless foes that dare attack his sense of comfort and conformity. And left unchecked, as most men will do, he'll experience decades of simmering angst as he confronts challenge with deathly defiance and folded-arm refusal.

There is no excellence in conformity. In this shadow, we die on the sword of consensus consciousness, confusing social proof and safety-in-numbers with life-affirming sustenance. Even when we can easily see the mass dysfunction and mental and physical decline before us, we struggle to take the steps needed to break free from it. Such is the magnetic pull of this shadow. Over time, a regression to the norm cripples our potential and makes upward ascent a fleeting and impossible dream.

Yet any heart that still beats is a heart that can strive to be free.

The king frees himself from the grips of this shadow by breaking through the illusion that the consensus is something to be cherished and strived for. He saws off the rusty chains and invisible anchors of insistence and entitlement that pull him back down into the blood-soaked jaws of the status quo. A status quo, that in his most lucid moments, he rightly suspects as the death trap it is—but until now, has lacked the drive and skill to escape from.

How rare it is, the king who sets his own standard. Who competes solely against himself. Taking no solace in his triumphs over lesser men, nor self-condemning while measuring against the hard-earned victories of his fellow king.

How rare the king who calls others to rise with him—even when outnumbered by the groans of the woefully resigned.

How rare, the king.

King's Log

1. What activities, behaviors and patterns have you normalized or justified for no other reason that they're the "norm" (i.e., food addictions, laziness, bingefests, desire for comfort, being "exhausted," complaining, hating your "work," being burdened by fatherhood, etc.) and why?

2. Do you truly believe in the safety of the "norm"? Are you okay accepting the consequences you can perceive in remaining on that trajectory?

3. In justifying your actions, moods, states, and habits as "normal," are you more or less likely to know and experience your true potential?

4. What beliefs about health have gone totally unquestioned—accepted wholesale without a moment of contemplation? (i.e., the truth about illness and aging? What is a "natural" lifespan? How do you know? What evidence do you have?)

5. What beliefs around wealth and career have you allowed to go totally unquestioned?

6. What other "norms" do you default towards in your health? Your career? Your relationships? Your behavior with friends and family?

7. What mental norms (beliefs, entitlements and attitudes) do you justify through consensus? (i.e., life should be easy, I shouldn't have to strive, etc.)

8. On a scale of 1 to 10, how deeply have you tested, explored and sought to expand your capacity for excellence and the extraordinary? What's that "ceiling" composed of?

King's Word

1. I forgive myself totally and completely for succumbing to any influence of consensus consciousness or artificial normalization. I offer my

heartfelt apology to all those who've been affected by the rule of this false king.

2. It is my highest will and intent to reclaim total sovereignty over my own thoughts and beliefs.

3. It is my highest will and intent to let no limiting or negative thought or belief be accepted wholesale and unquestioned.

4. It is my highest will and intent to live up to the highest standards of capacity, vitality and ability that I was designed to embody and express.

5. It is my highest will and intent to cherish, and be in constant celebration of my ever-expanding capacities.

6. I am in constant enjoyment and expansion of my physical and mental capacities; receiving every new challenge as an invitation to continue expanding with power, focus and self-compassion.

Embodied Inquiry

1. What would it be like to effortlessly let go of any non-serving beliefs, no matter how widely adopted and accepted they may be?

2. Who is it that justifies his "limitations" by pointing to what's "normal" and why?

3. What would it feel like to be in deep communion with the truthfulness of my own capacities and abilities?

4. How did I become such a perfect embodiment of my highest physical and mental capacities and abilities at all times?

5. What would it feel like to be in celebration of my own excellence?

Shadow 2: Consumption of the Creator

Let's start by taking a quick audit of what you've consumed today. Start with the physical. What foods or supplements have you ingested? Can you list them all? Down to every ingredient that went into every meal.

Let's move on to the mental. What ideas have you consumed? What bits of information have you allowed to pass through the gates of your awareness unchecked?

That Facebook rant from an old high school friend that blasted into your consciousness amidst that mindless 2 PM newsfeed scroll. The victim-laced whimpers from your co-worker, talking about how the government, the company, his kids are all pecking away at what little energy and motivation he has left. The billions of bits of information that get consumed in a single, seemingly innocent Netflix bingefest. Chances are that this audit has already become impossibly overwhelming. And appropriately so.

This shadow will be one of the most challenging you encounter, for it runs counter to so many of the cultural conventions we hold so dear. We'll defend it tooth and nail, without realizing that the very force we're defending is ultimately the one that'll consume us.

Make no mistake, as a modern man, you're about to encounter and conquer one of your strongest foes. Fortunately, the rewards that await are always proportional to the force you overcome. The first stage in overcoming this shadow is to see it for what it is. To size it up. To understand its strengths and vulnerabilities. In doing so, the first thing we learn about this shadow is how it's a modern phenomenon. And therefore, one that can only be conquered with modern practice.

At no other point in human history has man been exposed to as much information as he is today. But while the amount of information he consumes has increased exponentially, his ability to safely process and integrate it hasn't. It's not just the sheer volume and frequency of information he's consuming that's the problem, but also the quality of information—and the actions, feelings, beliefs, expectations fears and behaviors that it's informing.

Man was *not* designed to mindlessly consume information. Information used to be subtle and naturally occurring. A hunter in the woods would have to process, interpret and act on a much smaller, less-refined data set. The direction of the wind. The temperature of the earth. The ghastly howl in the far distance. He relied upon his mental and instinctual faculties to process this information, and transmute it into the physical actions that he and his tribe would depend on for survival. He stalked his prey and attuned to his environment with a naturally occurring "mindfulness."

One of the major reasons that "mindfulness" has been relegated to a ten-minute side practice for the "spiritually inclined" is because our physical survival no longer depends on the heightened, moment-by-moment awareness. Street signs and flashing lights tell us where and when to go. Beer commercials tell us how to feel. Ads tell us what to buy. News anchors tell us what to fear. Whereas our hunter had to digest and discern the information available to him, modern man swallows it wholesale—with all its artificial filler and synthetic bloat. It's no longer clean and raw, but processed, refined and encoded with a specific command or belief.

The information we were built to receive was impersonal, free of agenda, and demanded heightened awareness and discernment to achieve actionable insight from. But whereas the information of the hunter was designed to "inform," modern day information is actually here to instruct.

Concealed within the golden age of information is the dark age of covert influence and command. Marketing messages and entertainment are engineered to make you feel something. A feeling, which in turn, influences your next action. Behind every bit of information you consume, there exists the intent of the person or organization broadcasting it—and the manipulation of belief and pre-baked narrative that underlies it.

Consumption is therefore never benign. Whether physical or mental, consumption was never meant to be an act of blind passivity. Yet this is what we've been trained to do, from the culturally celebrated Netflix bingefest to the classroom we sit in for twenty years, we're bred into a life of mindless consumption, believing that it's building us up, when the irony of it all is that it is *us* that is being consumed.

Zoning out and binge-watching have become socially acceptable ways of unplugging from our stressful lives. But we're not unplugging. We're actually plugging into streams of information while willfully relieving our internal gatekeeper of his duties. In actuality, "mindless entertainment" is mindless *entrainment*—in the sense that it trains further mindlessness and the evaporation of the mental faculties that would block a belief or command from being ingested wholesale.

What it entrains is an army of the mindless. In the hundreds of millions. All standing "in formation," in service of an idea, goal or agenda that runs counter to one's own true will. The heartbreaking endpoint of this process is the consumption of the creator itself.

It's the cannibalization of the life-giving faculties we rely on for our fullest, most authentic expression. It's where you eventually lose any will or capacity to consciously create your own reality or author your own thoughts. Where you become a parrot for a never-ending stream of secondhand ideas you've unconsciously fed off of—and a product of the actions and behaviors they instruct.

Let it be known that there is no such thing as a "consumer." Only the creator and the consumed. Your conscious attention being the key decider of which group you fall into.

Your attention *is* the most valuable resource you steward. More so than time. More so than energy. More so than your health. For your attention precedes all of these. Having a hundred years but no authority over your attention and where to direct it is no different than serving a life sentence. Your attention *is* the ink pad that your inner creator uses to stamp his will onto reality. Yet your attention has been bought. Literally. This very shadow is the broker in a parasitic transaction that keeps you in a helpless state of perceived overwhelm and inundation.

Your mindless and continuous scroll through the newsfeed has a dollar value to it. Hundreds of billions, to be exact. But here's what's missed in this. Your attention can't actually be bought. It can't be mined. It can't be stolen. It can only be given. And you will never *truly* be free until you've reclaimed complete authority over how this most sacred resource is allocated. We're quick to defend our physical property from theft. Yet offer unguarded access to a far more precious resource.

The work of this reclamation is twofold. Of course, be more conscious of your inputs. Don't allow any information to enter your awareness unchecked. Choose inputs that enrich and gently inform rather than toxify, exhaust and instruct. Cease any habits that promote mindlessness or "checking out" and instead cultivate the sharpened, moment-by-moment awareness of the hunter—skillfully evading the information that would *consume* you; while in turn, stalking the world around you for the life-giving sustenance, wisdom, and inspiration it has to offer.

But more than that, be the channel between input and output—not the storehouse. The king never consumes passively. He listens with intent and sharpened discernment, always using information as a data point to accept or reject, not a pre-built decision he gets to defer to. There is no abdication. No blind reliance. No wholesale consumption. For he is a transmuter. An alchemist. Taking what he ingests and turning it into something greater. Whether it's the food he puts in his body or the ideas he allows others to share with him—it's always done with the intent of using those raw materials to better his inner and outer kingdom.

In overcoming this shadow, the king becomes a master of his attention, a steward of his will, and the author of his life.

In overcoming this shadow, the king becomes unshackled from the invisible chains dragging him towards the inevitable slaughter of mind and spirit.

In overcoming this shadow, the king becomes free.

King's Log

1. Where, to what, and to whom do I give my unguarded attention to? Why?
2. In the moments prior to mindless consumption, what do I feel? What is the impulse that precedes "checking out"?
3. Where (or to who) would I be best served to completely and totally withdraw and revoke my attention from?
4. What activities (i.e., conversing with a certain person, scrolling Instagram, watching the news) do I immediately feel less vital, motivated and energized by?
5. Why do I feel others (friends, strangers, reporters, teachers, influencers, etc.) are entitled to my unguarded attention?

King's Word

1. I am the sole owner of my attention. It is directed only as I choose.
2. I recognize and acknowledge my attention as more precious and valuable than gold, guarding and investing it appropriately.
3. I completely forgive myself for allowing my attention to be freely given up to this point.
4. With heightened focus, will and intent, I direct and invest my attention *only* to where it will yield positive return.
5. I honor myself and my attention by offering it *only* to inputs I deem worthy.
6. Without guilt or apology, I automatically and effortlessly withdraw my attention from any and all sources that are unnourishing and uninspiring.
7. I receive greater power, energy and capacity as I reassert guardianship and stewardship of my attention.

Embodied Inquiry

1. What would it be like to fully honor and cherish my capacity for attention?
2. What would it feel like to fully liberate my attention from all non-serving inputs?
3. How did I become such a powerful and effective guardian and steward of my attention?
4. What would become possible for me with a greater capacity for focused attention?
5. What is now possible for me as the sole steward of focused attention?

Shadow 3: The Gluttony of Distraction (and the Illusion of Progress)

When you come into the direct realization that your most valuable asset is your attention, and your ability to focus and direct it, then you become aware of just how damaging the gluttony of distraction is.

As we've already discussed, attention and focus precede everything. Time, in of itself, holds little value. In a world of distraction, focus has become a rare superpower. For with intense focus, you can accomplish in one year what most men will do in ten. With intense focus, you can completely transform your body and mind in a matter of days or weeks. With intense focus, you become more effortlessly aware of the state of your lover, your children, your business and your community, and can respond with greater love, skill and leadership in kind.

Yes, with intense focus, you quite literally bend time and call in a more favorable reality of your choosing. But despite its life-changing power, most men will auction it off for a mere pittance. Of course, the inner victim will claim to be oppressed by an environment engineered to rob him of his focus and attention.

He'll point to the smartphone. The deluge of ads and messaging flooding him from every angle. The urgency of the 24/7 news cycle, and the career with the built-in expectation of constant connectivity. He'll blame the social pressure of having to respond to every beep, ping and buzz within seconds, lest he be harshly judged by the one claiming ownership over his attention.

Yet when you take a deeper look at this shadow, you come to realize that this monster is entirely self-created and maintained. The smartphone hasn't shaped the way we interact. In and of itself, it's benign. A pocket-sized device with no innate power to lay claim over your attention.

If you're helplessly seduced, it's only because you're helplessly seduce-able. A perfect pairing partner to its sultry whispers. In our work, we claim full responsibility for our role in this perilous dance of thoughts and thumbs. As such, this shadow concerns itself with the inner factors and dynamics that make us susceptible to the siren call of the smartphone, the endless newsfeed scroll, or the second helping of sweet potato fries when your stomach is already begging for mercy.

The gluttony of distraction is as it sounds. An uncontrollable drive towards the excess. A merciless pounding of body and mind with more stimulus than it can handle. All in a desperate attempt to drown out the inner murmurs begging for your attention.

At its core, this shadow thrives off our need for delay and avoidance. Avoidance of the stinging flutter of fear sitting in your chest. Avoidance of the thoughts and emotions pounding against the walls of your awareness, begging to be seen and heard.

A few years ago, I took part in a three-day dry fast. Even though food and social media were completely off limits, I still found myself opening the fridge or reaching for my phone dozens of times per day. As I caught myself, I quickly realized that each impulse for distraction was preceded by an uncomfortable thought or emotion. A difficult conversation I was resisting, an inner feeling of frustration or unease when a project wasn't going a certain way, a careless and hurtful comment from a friend, client or lover. Rather than allowing these things to simply rest in my field of awareness, there was an insatiable pull to flood my senses with something—*anything* that would create a thick enough layer to blanket the thing I was avoiding. We claim to want sunlight, but the moment its rays reveal something uncomfortable or unflattering, we blanket the sky with the dense clouds of distraction.

For distraction spares us the agony of facing what is alive and active in us. The newsfeed scroll provides you temporary solace from the anxious thoughts spinning in your head. The extra trip to the fridge frees you from the inner pangs of anger or discomfort.

Attention spans haven't shrunk because of the smartphone. They've evaporated in response to the terror we feel over life itself, and our unconscious refusal to face it. For the lesser man, the smartphone is a savior. Its flashing pixels and fleeting faces a soothing balm to cover up the silent screams and secret wounds from which he still bleeds out.

The reason we so readily sell-off our attention is because there's a great cost to its reclamation. The cost, of course, is seeing and feeling all that we've feared and resisted within ourselves. It's bought back in cultivating the willingness, compassion, and bravery to face our darkest shadows, moment-by-moment, without the false sense of safety that delay and distraction provide.

It's a price that so few are willing to pay. Yet it's an investment the king wisely makes, knowing with absolute certainty that the reclamation of his attention is the very first step in building his kingdom.

As a king, this sacred reclamation is now yours to make.

King's Log

1. What habits or activities do you use to distract or avoid?
2. What do you gain out of those activities? Do you feel better and more expansive? Or more contracted and limited?
3. What are the most common feelings or situations you avoid through the gluttony of distraction? (What immediately precedes the newsfeed scroll or extra trip to the kitchen?)
4. Why do you resist uncomfortable feelings or situations? What part of you believes yourself incapable or unwilling to meet them with bravery and skillfulness?
5. What are the imagined consequences of facing those situations head on?

King's Word

1. I am infinitely capable of standing tall and present to whatever situation arises before me.
2. I let go of all impulse or need to distract myself from my own inner experience.
3. I honor and appreciate my ever-growing capacity to offer presence and awareness to uncomfortable situations.
4. I forgive and relieve myself from the shame of any past avoidances.

5. I act swiftly and decisively, doing what must be done, free from delay or distraction.

6. I bring greater awareness to any remaining situations where I habitually numb my experience with delay or distraction.

7. With courage and power, I overcome any and all resistance to being present, skillful and intimate with my full experience.

Embodied Inquiry

1. What would it feel like to be infinitely courageous and capacitated to hold any inner or outer experience before me?

2. What would it feel like to effortlessly be present to any and all situations?

3. How did I become so courageous and capable?

4. How did I become so capable of taking skillful and immediate action?

5. With this newly accessed courage to face all that arises, free of all resistance, what is now possible for me?

Awakening The Alchemist

Birthed from the charred remains of these three shadows is the inner creator. *The Alchemist.*

Rather than succumbing to the gluttony of distraction, he feasts on his own power of transmutation and creation. He does so with deep reverence for *what* he is. Not a mindless storehouse of secondhand thought and belief, but a sacred channel between inspired thought and committed action.

It's not that he's cultivated so much will and discipline as to be able to resist distraction. It's that in his fullest expression, he's undistractable. He no longer fears his inner state, and as such, doesn't need to sedate his senses with a ceaseless shelling of inputs. He doesn't seek escape. Instead, he plunges deeper into his present experience and all it reveals.

Rather than self-anesthetize through the auctioning off of his attention to anyone or anything willing to claim it, the king honors his attention as the alchemical agent it is, capable of shifting one experience to another. In this simple realignment, he's no longer a helpless victim to the world around him, but a trusted steward of his own attention. Never passive. Never mindless.

Always intimately involved. Always the faithful agent of a greater reality of his choosing.

Whether it's the food he puts in his body, or the thoughts, impressions, ideas and influences he allows to enter his mind, he's discerning. He consumes mindfully. He digests, absorbs, and ultimately alchemizes his consumption into his creation.

When challenges arise, whether it's a screaming toddler, challenging client, or stabbing comment from a wife or partner, he resists the reactionary force of his well-rehearsed response. Likewise, he trusts in his ever-expanding capacity to bear witness to the entirety of the circumstance before him without avoidance or distraction. He gifts himself to the moment rather than feeling burdened or besieged by it, and relishes in his capacity to shift it towards a more favorable end with swift and skillful action.

The higher truth you recognize in this fire is that nothing comes from nothing. We are all alchemists, transmuting one situation into the next. Everything is in a transitory state. In motion. In vibration. The billion-dollar tech company begins as a culmination of insight and inspiration that gets alchemized and refined into a solid, actionable idea. The "million-dollar body" begins as a feeling of inner richness. Only allowing enriching foods and thoughts in kind to enter our body and mind.

This is our gift. Our privilege.

We are the magicians that turn the subtle and subjective into the solid and the observed. We transform food molecules into an observably fitter and more functional body. We turn a lyric from a song into a c-minor note which later becomes the seedling for a new clothing brand—or piece of art—or a timely whisper to a hurting lover.

All that's needed is discernment over our inputs, and the directed and sustained attention over its transmutation into something greater. It's a natural and effortless process, for our inner alchemist can never be defeated. He can only be temporarily caged. He's freed when our shadows of consumption, distraction and regression to the norm are compassionately released.

And oh, how he rejoices in his freedom.

Crowing The Alchemist

The guided initiation into *The Alchemist* is available to stream at:

iseeyouking.com/wellness

Evolutionary Accelerators

Evolutionary Accelerator #1: Stalking Reality

Practice Duration: 1 Hour

Practice Frequency: At least once per week

Description:

For an hour a week, I invite you to approach the world around you with the mindfulness of a more primitive hunter. Move mindfully through your environment. Attune to the sights, scents, tastes and sounds around you—and interpret their meaning in real-time. Do so with the focused intent of one whose survival depends on the fullest sensing, and most immediate and accurate interpretation of what's around him.

In conversation with a partner, hear the words while sensing their underlying intent and emotional energy. The subtext that often gets missed, yet informs far more than the words themselves. When you walk through a forest, effortlessly attune to the rich sensual data that's there to inform your next move.

As you pick up on "data," practice being an interpreter of reality. Taking it impersonally. Not allowing it to instruct you or "evoke" reactivity, but as a way of having a more intimate understanding of the person or situation before you, and giving you a chance to respond more skillfully in kind.

Evolutionary Accelerator #2: Sense Play

Practice Duration: At least 5 minutes per day

Practice Frequency: Once per day

Description:

Our capacities for "communing" with our environment have, for the most part, been severely blunted and atrophied. We experience our "senses" in straight lines. Particular functions for particular sense organs. We see with our eyes. We listen with our ears. We taste with our tongues. In short, we process wide-ranging data through a singular input or "processing center" rather than utilizing our fullest capacities of perception.

Moreover, the hours we spend interacting with screens (mostly visual and mental) have created a myopic and distorted perceptive field that limits the sensual data that may be available to us.

Indeed, our abilities to perceive and synthesize information are far greater than we know. But when our "innate tools" hang in the inner shed, they become rusty and dull.

This exercise will walk you through playful new ways of perceiving and experiencing reality around you. For most, reality is experienced through mental reactivity. The patterns have become so well-grooved and automatic that our life experience has become mostly reduced to a series of unconscious reactions.

Beginner Option: Singular Object While Sitting/Standing

Sit or stand still. Pick at an object before you. It can be a sunset, a lover, a picture, a coffee mug, a decorative object, a mountain, a deer, the moon, the sun, etc.

You'll then perceive it through the sense organs in the table below. But rather than limiting your observation to a singular sensing mechanism (i.e., smelling with your nose), you'll practice rotating different sensing mechanisms with different sensing organs.

This may feel like an act of imagination initially. But with just a bit of effort, your capacities for full spectrum "perceiving" will grow significantly in a very real way. Your senses will begin to work together to create a fuller, somatic-based perception of the word around you.

Sense Organ	Sensing Mechanism
Nose	Smell
Eyes	See

Ears	Hear
Hands / Skin / Energy Body	Touch / Feel
Mouth	Taste
Heart	Love
Entire Being	Know

Focus loosely on the object before you with the intention of *knowing* it fully, beyond outward appearance.

1. Feel it through your eyes.
2. See it through your nose.
3. Love it through your hands.
4. Hear it through your heart.
5. Taste it through your ears.
6. Smell it through your tongue.
7. Know it with your entire being.

8. Smell it through your eyes.
9. Hear it through your nose.
10. Taste it through your hands.
11. Feel it through your heart.
12. Love it through your ears.
13. See it through your tongue.
14. Know it with your entire being.

15. Love it through your eyes.
16. Feel it through your nose.
17. Smell it through your hands.
18. Hear it through your heart.
19. Taste it through your ears.
20. Know it through your tongue.
21. See it with your entire being.

Keep rotating dynamically, perceiving through any permutation or sequence from the table above. You may experience slight feelings of inner bliss as your perceptive field "opens" to include richer input.

Intermediate Practice: Full-Spectrum Perceiving of Mental/ Emotional States

When you're caught in a mental spin (recurring or obsessive thoughts) or a dense and reactive emotional pattern (i.e., anger, victimhood, sadness, grief, desperation, etc.), attempt to perceive it through your different senses.

This can be combined with the "King's Gaze" practice from Part 1.

- See your anger
- Touch and feel your sadness
- Smell your recurring fear-based thought
- Know your grief with the entirety of your being
- Taste your joy
- Love your sense of confidence or certainty

Advanced Practice:

After a week or so of dedicated "still" practice, begin making this practice dynamic and ongoing as you move through your day.

When you drink your coffee, see if you can taste it through your eyes. When you listen to inspiring music, endeavor to listen with your heart. When you're in the presence of a lover, smell or breathe her with your ears. Read this book with your heart. With your entire being.

Bring awareness to your emotions through touching or smelling them.

None of these actions should be an act of forced effort. Rather intend it and allow your body/mind to respond accordingly.

There are infinite permutations to this practice. The culmination of which is a form of sensual awakening that tunes you into deeper *knowing* and fuller awareness of the objects that surround you—as well as your inner thoughts and feelings. You'll process both faster and with greater skill. Intuition will sharpen.

Creativity will expand. And as a result, you'll bring greater wisdom, skillfulness and decisiveness to every situation.

Evolutionary Accelerator #3: Intentional Action

Practice Duration: Seconds
Practice Frequency: As often as possible

Description:

So many of our actions are impulsive, informed, and based in unconscious reactivity. We'd be well served to repair the bridge between intention and action. To experience the alchemy of intending a thought and acting it out in objective reality, as well as relishing in the sacred relationship between them, and our role within the interplay.

As often as you can remind yourself to do so, practice intending an action, performing it, and then intending the next action from the new set of options that the previous action made available to you.

As you do so, tune into who you are in this process. Bring focus and appreciation for this powerful but overlooked capacity. Amplify it. For this basic formula is the basis for all you would create.

Evolutionary Accelerator #4: Be the Bridge

Practice Duration: Ongoing
Practice Frequency: As often as possible

Description:

Information is not instructive.

A request is not a command.

So much of the "victimhood" and "overwhelm" we feel is when we allow information to enter "wholesale", and believe each instruction to be an imposition or command. We react as a servant, rather than process and respond as the king.

The king is not commanded. The unconscious verbal attack from a work "superior," lover, or stranger is benign in of itself. Information floating into the ethers. It may be "directed", but that doesn't mean it has any chance of a "direct hit" unless you allow it. You don't need to work to dodge or evade. You simply need to cease throwing your body in front of those arrows. This is what the victim does. He makes himself the target. He insists on being hit so he can express within the narrow range of emotional reactivity known to him. That of powerlessness, defeat, rage, resignation and resentment.

You have the power to accept or reject any statement or request. Overwhelm is no excuse to allow those commands to come in unquestioned. You have the right to deliberateness and skillfulness. To not "regress to the norm" of those around you who live their lives in a constant sense of overwhelm and victimhood. There is no victory to be gained in that game.

The practice then is to notice the gap between information and reactivity. To allow each verbal or physical response to be deliberate and informed—not reactionary and evoked. The quality of your responsiveness will raise dramatically; and as such your skillfulness in navigating the choppy tides of an at-times frantic world.

Evolutionary Accelerator #5: The King's Fast / The King's Feast

Practice Duration: 3-9 hours
Practice Frequency: As often as you feel called

Description:

Before you attempt this challenge, check with your health and medical practitioners to make sure it's safe and appropriate to do so. Practice discretion and assume your own risk. Suffice to say, this is not health or medical advice, and you and you alone, are responsible for your choices.

If you choose to participate, the goal is to experience the polarity between fasting and feasting.

If you consider yourself to be fairly distracted, start with just 3 hours. If you've already cultivated a high degree of discipline and/or meditative practice, endeavor for a full day from rising to sleep. For whichever practice duration you commit to, you'll fast on nearly all inputs:

1. No food consumption (with the exception of water and coffee if necessary to prevent withdrawal headaches).

2. No information consumption (television, conversation, social media, or music—other than minimal ambient or natural soundscapes).
3. No unnatural environmental consumption (i.e., don't go into a mall or busy street). If you do go outside, be in nature.

As you fast from all inputs, your senses may quite literally become more available than they have your entire adult life. Out of sheer habitual force, you may find that they grasp for an input.

When this impulse arises, become aware of it. Don't wrestle it or try to silence it into submission. Question it. Explore it. Observe it from all your senses. Observe it from your highest self. Observe it as your inner king. And try to gently pierce the very source of this impulse for distraction.

Ask:

1. Who or what wishes to flood my senses?
2. Who is it that's insisting on (eating, scrolling, talking, etc.)?
3. Why does it wish to bludgeon and coat my senses?
4. What is it trying to avoid? Protect itself from?

If the craving for distraction becomes extremely challenging and doesn't subside through questioning and observation alone, acknowledge and invoke the part of you that's beyond seducible with the mantra *"I see you, King."*

Every 30-45 minutes, consciously "feast."

Feast on:

1. Your raw innate power and capacity. Do so by exerting yourself fully through physical movement (i.e., max out on pushups, squats, shadowboxing, sprints, etc.) and feast on your own sense of capacity and power.
2. Your own creative power: Write, draw, sing, dance as an offering. Feast at the buffet of your own creative expression, and the source or wellspring it comes from.
3. Feast on the gratitude of your own beingness / sense of being alive.

For the duration that you choose, you'll oscillate between feasting and fasting. With practice, you'll expose and weaken the impulse towards all three shadows—and instead, feast on your most natural and cherished powers, virtues and capacities.

Chapter 5:

FIRE 2 - YOUR INTIMATE RELATIONSHIP

What makes this an initiatory fire?

Approached with reverence and awareness, there are few things as potent and immediate as your intimate relationship for illuminating your shadows, and pushing you towards growth.

Our intimate relationships offer a beautiful microcosm to our relationship with life itself. There's an inherent resistance in the interdependent energies of co-creation. There's a denial of the dynamic, ever-shifting nature that relationship presents. And there's a fear in opening up fully to the gifts that this fire is here to offer.

For men, especially, there's a seductive safety in solitude and artificially maintained independence. A fear of giving up a sense of perceived control and direction. In this, the simplicity of the single man is alluring. The zero-latency period between decision and inspired action is both compelling and seemingly more energetically expansive than the contraction of compromise that most relationships normalize and default towards. For when decisions become shared, or worse, filtered through layers of permission and compromise, it deadens the initial desire and disempowers our sense of mission and purpose.

This is the subtly emasculating experience of the common man. Asking for "permission" to join his brothers on a week-long hiking expedition. Going to the gym on a Sunday morning instead of spending time with a cup of oolong tea and furniture catalogue. Decisions become binary, deflating, and guilt laden.

Beyond the casual Sunday morning itinerary, being in relationship reconfigures the ascent into a more fulfilled life. Dreams are shared. Steps are co-created. And a subtle frustration simmers over the lack of control you have over a partner, who, in turn, carries a seemingly disproportionate influence over your life experience. It's what has many men sabotaging countless relationships for the better part of their adult lives. For these flames are fierce and utterly unaccommodating to any fragment of self that would insist on holding onto an artificial sense of total control.

Yet lost in this, is that she doesn't actually want or crave your compromise. These are merely cheap substitutes for what she truly yearns for. Rather, she desires and craves your uncompromising love and reverence which you've yet to put on full display. For when you continuously straddle the line between longing for the single life while "settling" for the soft comforts of a committed partnership, you've crept your way into a vapid, half-hearted affair.

The transience of a one-night stand can sometimes bring more reverence and sacredness than a so-called committed relationship. Yet culturally, we reward and value decades of fake smiles and suppressed pain more than the two-week tussle that expands our hearts beyond the safe borders we've spent our lives hiding behind. True relationship is a passport to this exhilarating, heart-pounding encounter with deeper truth and personal revelation. But like any wild adventure, there's very little room for a false sense of tranquility.

What must be understood is that relationships are almost *always* mutually supportive, yet rarely in the ways we'd expect or hope for. But even in their friction, they always spark a fire and shine a light on something worth examining. Relationships, like nothing else, will coax out our fears, attachments and insecurities, while providing us with the fertile ground for practicing genuine compassion, intimacy and connection.

A relationship can't be considered a "failure" when it reaches its conclusion. It can only be considered a failure when the chasm of your heart hasn't been filled with the inner learnings it was there to offer. Understand that all *relationships* end. Even if it's a lifetime, there is a natural conclusion, that of course, can be forcibly delayed. But when we measure the success of a relationship in "years spent" rather than "growth inspired," we foolishly miss the point.

Endurance, suppression of pain, and stunting of one's growth in the name of forced continuity may earn you a fiftieth anniversary party at your local banquet hall. But the trade-off is insurmountable. The true purpose of relationship isn't artificial harmony or self-masochistic suffering. Relationships, in their fullest expression, are powerful containers for healing, revelation, and awakening. This is what ultimately gets revealed once we confront and dissolve the shadows guarding this most precious gift.

Shadow 1: The Burden of Balance

There's perhaps no shadow more painfully destructive and limiting in modern relationships than the need for so-called balance. When we approach our intimate relationships with the need for "balance" we essentially doom it from the start. We set up an equation where there will *always* be someone underserved and undernourished. Someone taking too much and someone giving too little.

We invite a stingy game of scorekeeping where victory itself bleeds us dry and rewards us with the sting of resentment. A relationship that insists on achieving balance and homeostasis will always crumble. For there will always be indebtedness. There will always be a victim. Someone who was "sold too short", and someone who "took too much."

Yet the burden of balance has been a long persisting paradigm. In Steven Covey's (mostly) brilliant *Seven Habits*, he introduces the idea of an "emotional bank account." One that tracks deposits and withdrawals based on the actions of our partner. In Gary Chapman's *Love Languages*, he speaks of the different currencies of love we're able to give and receive.

Each model, while temporarily useful, keeps us locked in a paradigm of "balance" where love is reduced to a finite resource, and a currency that can be used in a dysfunctional game of give and take we call "relationship." But your relational books will never be "balanced." And if you make your happiness and willingness to love contingent upon it, you're going to suffer. You're going to water the seeds of resentment while atrophying your innate capacity to live as a constantly flowing expression of unimpeded love.

In the game of balance, we weaponize our love and affection. We reduce it to a constantly depreciating currency, and limit it further by turning it into a fixed "thing" that we can control. We withhold it when we're angry or when we feel the need to punish our partner. And in doing so, our love gets distorted and disfigured as it passes through the jagged lens of petty vengeance and selfish pride.

Likewise, we offer our love as a reward or as a bargaining chip. A means to a fruitless end. We dangle it like a rotting dog treat, offering to drop it only if our partner meets an ever-shifting set of conditions. Conditions that we ourselves remain mostly blind and unconscious to. In all these cases, we've taken the most powerful force of life herself and weaponized it in the name of "balance." An unbearably high price to pay for relational homeostasis.

Birthed from this need for balance is the fallacy of reciprocity. Where we wait to be seen, heard, appreciated or loved before we feel safe in reciprocating with the same gifts. So we each withhold. We hoard our love. We weaponize our inner or outer resources. We hold our own happiness and love hostage out of fearful pride—and feel victimized when our partner fails to provide these things.

Built into this fallacious equation are the well-woven power dynamics we've normalized and succumbed to. It's where we self-justify and "regress to the norm" within the relational sphere. A woman may use her love and affection as currency; while a man, feeling helplessly at the whims of his partner's openness or closure, will weaponize all he remains in control over. Withdrawing finances, and even silently inviting his own financial or physical collapse, lest she continue benefiting from either without the equal or balanced gifting of her own. Indeed, for many men, the rage around a partner's perceived entitlement and ingratitude is enough to call forth the energies of self-annihilation. Ultimately, "passive-aggressiveness" is anything but.

This shadow is not to be underestimated. It claims far more than just marriages. It claims businesses, families and even lives. The insistences within it are self-righteous and singularly-obsessed on balance no matter the cost. And its refusal to make the "first move" makes annihilation the more likely outcome.

For when we insist on the need for our partner to act first, we become kamikaze pilots steering our hearts into inevitable doom. On a subtle level, we communicate to ourselves and our partners that we'd rather crash and burn in needless destruction and heartache than pull up to gain higher perspective. We bring each other down for the sake of selfish pride. And it all runs counter to that which you truly are.

For you are not a beggar. You are a king.

Know the difference, but more importantly *live and act* the difference. If you're feeling unseen, unheard, unappreciated, unloved or uncared for, you're invited to assume full ownership and responsibility. Chances are you're at least partly complicit in blocking the dynamic exchange of these qualities.

Dare to inquire on the source of these feelings. Reclaim your land titles. Place precedent on your own self-definition. And assume full responsibility for your own sense of worth and appreciation. Do not put the responsibility of such core pillars of psychological wellness in the hands of anyone but yourself. You are not defined by her abilities, capacities or even willingness to view or treat you in a certain way. And if you grant her the responsibility and power to define you, she'll inevitably shirk away at the pressure you've unconsciously placed on her.

So begin by offering yourself the love, appreciation and compassion you desire, and from that place of sheer overflow, offer it to all those around you. Especially your partner. The call is to become so abundant and unconditional in your offering of these gifts that they become the signature of your relationship— and one that your partner feels a deep call to harmonize with.

Just like a tuning fork will automatically resonate at the same frequency as the one previously struck, you have the power and opportunity to initiate that first strike at all times. It's simply the burden of balance that insists on the other making the first move. The greatest cure to the burden of balance and its stinging undertones of rage and resentment is to come from a place of simply *wanting* to gift your love. Not a half-hearted "wanting" but a generous, full-bodied desire.

What experiences do you *want* to gift your partner? What do you want them to feel? What do you want them to enjoy in your presence? How can you make her life with you more powerful, healing, and restorative than life without you?

Most importantly, does the prospect of gifting your partner these things excite you and fill you with life and energy? Or does it feel like an undue burden?

So many people ask, *"when should a relationship come to an end?"* The answer is far simpler than many relationship experts make it out to be.

Whether induced by a verbal death punch or by decades of suppressed pain, a relationship will have reached its natural end when either partner no longer desires gifting their partner the love, patience, reverence, compassion, intimacy, experiences, and encouragement to evolve in his or her chosen path.

When this gifting becomes a compromise, a burden or a constant struggle, it may very well be time to release yourselves from that dynamic and enter a period of self-renewal before re-entering this fire.

Until then, the invitation is to be that gift.

To be the first striking of the match.

To be the torch that lights all others.

And to dance and play and relish in the shared flames that only you and your partner can create.

King's Log

1. In what ways do you and your partner fall victim to the burden of balance?
2. Where do you feel like your partner isn't "pulling her weight" or "doing her part" in the relationship?
3. In what ways do you withhold aspects of your love and generosity? Why?
4. In what other ways are you subtly (or overtly) antagonistic towards your partner? How do you truly feel about them?
5. What are you most excited and blessed to be able to gift your partner?
6. When you think about gifting your partner love, patience and reverence, what resistance or rebuttals show up? In what ways do you feel like she's undeserving or unworthy? And who is it that *believes* so? Are they absolutely true?

King's Word

1. I forgive myself fully and completely for any and all patterns that have arisen from this burden of balance. Acknowledging where I've weaponized my own love and generosity.
2. I am in the fullest and most effortless enjoyment and expression of my love, compassion and reverence for my partner.
3. I reclaim full sovereignty over my own self-perception, fully independent of my partner's conditioned actions or limited viewpoints towards me.

4. For as long as I consciously choose to remain partnered, it is my highest will and intent to gift my partner the greatest love, compassion and reverence I'm capable of offering at this time. I do so out of sheer joy, pleasure, and sacred duty.

Embodied Inquiry

While thinking about your partner, and placing your attention in your heart area, ask:

1. What would it be like to be totally generous in gifting my partner the qualities of love, compassion and reverence?
2. How is it that I became so willing and desiring to gift my partner what she desires to feel safe, loved, and empowered in her fullest expression?

Shadow 2: The Denial of Interdependence

For something as common as intimate relationship, so few of us ever come to appreciate just how challenging and soul-expanding they can be. Even fewer of us tap into the most fundamental of truths that a relationship offers. That our relationships aren't these tidy, fixed things that we can control. That they are in fact living, breathing, ever-shifting dynamics that we can surely influence, but never achieve absolute control or certainty over.

This triggers our defenses. Our insecurities. Our fears. Our resistance. Most men will spend the majority of their lives in staunch resistance to this dynamic exchange. They'll feel unsafe and burdened by an environment that they don't have absolute control or authority over. And in turn, they'll make self-sabotage a welcome guest in their hearts so that they may exile themselves back to a place of forced solitude. For when we're alone, we feel safe.

Independence, for most men, is easy. We can control our environment, and we can control the temperature of our lives. Our movements are unimpeded. Our decisions are direct. Linear. Immediate. Relationships can never offer the same level of predictability or control. This is the plight of the man who feels that he can't be devoted to his purpose and his relationship at the same time. Robbed of the speed and simplicity of the single man, mission and relationship feel mutually exclusive.

For to be in an intimate relationship is to discard that simplicity. It's to invite a powerful exchange of energy, intention and influence that at times can feel more limiting than expansive. One may feel intensely burdened by a relaxing Sunday afternoon that could, with the wrong combination of words, rip the stitching off an old unhealed wound and ignite an epic, eight-hour emotional thrill ride. An enigmatic dance, shifting between combustion, catharsis, and eventual reconciliation. When we try to force this powerful flow into a safe and predictable pattern, we deny it of its very essence. A relationship should never be confused with warfare, but there are many steps to the dance.

Within this dynamic dance, it's our rigidity and denial of interdependence that leads to an insurmountable clumsiness. It takes a nearly unattainable degree of groundedness and open heartedness to hold the container for interdependence to naturally operate without resistance. But to do otherwise, is to be in denial of its very nature. For relationship, like life itself, is in constant flux.

And when we aggressively react to our partner's perceived "intrusion" on our ideals and independence, we send the implicit message that it's not okay for them to appear in their truth and fullness. In doing so, we resist the interdependent nature of relationship itself. We inadvertently wound by communicating the message that they're "too much." That they're a burden or obstacle. Something to be overcome.

But no matter *what* your partner is experiencing or expressing—they're not a burden. They can only ever be an inconvenience, threat or disruption to an unhealed or lesser-matured aspect of you. But when you act from your depth, there's no longer a need to overcome. Instead, there's a natural willingness, even a joy, in oversaturating both you and them in pure presence and acceptance. This is where the skills you adopted as the *Alchemist* in the previous chapter come into play.

This is not the same as allowing yourself to be an emotional punching bag. Nor a scapegoat for their own unchecked or projected fears and traumas. Boundaries remain vital. Respect, especially so. You're not called to tolerate and withstand toxic behavior, abusive tendencies and endless blame. Nor are you called to forcibly endure a relationship where the predominant notes are disharmonious to the song your soul wishes to partake in.

This is simply to propose that as long as you're committed to loving and remaining with your partner, you're called to infuse that love with the greatest degree of unwavering presence and acceptance as you can open up to. Her transformation through this presence may be blindingly fast or painfully slow. But your *own* will be undeniably accelerated.

So many books on relationship and masculine/feminine polarity will point to this steady, "unwavering presence" as the pinnacle of masculinity. Which is not entirely incorrect. But for most, it will set an unrealistic standard that makes it even harder for men (and their partners) to accept anything less than perfection, creating even greater shame and inadvertent, self-induced stoicism as a result. Remember that this is far from easy. And you're allowed your own missteps. Yet we have to consciously build our capacity to "hold" our partner's entire range of experience without judgment or a sense of being burdened, or being so easily knocked off our own center.

Strive to grow each day in your ability to hold your partner in her fullness. Acknowledge, and be compassionate with the parts of you who still scream, *"What about me?"* And allow evolution to proceed at the speed available to you both. This is the core of intimacy and trust. The hidden gift in this process is that as we expand our capacity to stand unwavering in our presence and compassion for our partner's moods, states, emotions and actions, we in turn learn how to give ourselves the same presence.

We stop resisting our own shadows. Our own fears. Our own trapped emotions or old identities. All of which we are *also* in deep, intimate relationship with. Let the truth of this soak in. If you're actively resisting aspects of your partner, you're undoubtedly resisting aspects of yourself. This is where the opportunity for growth and healing becomes circular and self-reinforcing.

The magic of relationship—particularly in the gut-lined trenches of transformation—is that healing can become circular. Your partner's growth becomes your growth and vice versa. They become intertwined. When you drop an old identity that resists her emotional expression, you in turn expand your capacity to hold, accept and deeply love *all* of her. This, of course, opens her into a feeling of greater trust and safety that naturally, without effort, expands her desire to gift you the warmth now radiating off her heart.

This is tremendously healing. Likewise, when she drops an old belief around how she's unlovable, she in turn becomes more receptive to your touch. She becomes available to receive the gift of your affection and, in turn, gives you the pleasure and sheer joy of offering it and having it received. You become spared the pain of a rejected offering from the depths of your heart.

The paradox of this is that this luscious, effortless exchange of healing, love, and growth takes effort to get to. This effort begins in the acknowledgment of interdependence, and the choice to value its gifts and teachings rather than condemn or deny its demands. It's a choice you're of course free to make.

On a final note, interdependence isn't the same as dependence or codependence. You're not waiting at the reckless whims of your partner unless you allow yourself to be. While you don't have total control, you *do* have will, choice, and influence. In most cases, you're not honoring these capacities nearly as much as you ought to. This is where following your mission and being in a relationship *aren't* mutually exclusive. Far from it.

Instead, you're called to gift her the opportunity to orient around your mission. Speak your truth and follow your purpose before they atrophy, metastasize and turn into resentment. There's a bitter betrayal that comes with not doing so. The momentary compromise may get you to the dinner table with her friends, but the rotting mass of resentment in your heart will only ferment and seep out in other ways. You don't "free" her with your compromise. You liberate her with your truth. For today's suppressed truths become tomorrow's stinging resentments. The dance is not yours alone. You don't choose all the steps. But your leadership and influence within the dance are both the gift she yearns for and the freedom you crave.

King's Log

1. In what ways has the denial of interdependence shaped or influenced your view of relationships?

2. Do you often feel burdened or inconvenienced by your partner's emotional states, desires or wishes? Why?

3. In what ways do you feel frustration over the lack of "control" you have of your relational environment?

4. In what subtle ways do you seek to control or manipulate your partner's behavior or actions, rather than positively inspire them?

5. Who is it that insists on controlling your partner and why?

6. Is part of you "'waiting' for your partner to change? How? Why?

7. In what ways do you currently compromise where you'd be better off boldly (and compassionately) taking a leadership stance and inviting your partner to orient around that declaration? What fears or resistance arise when you imagine yourself doing so?

8. Do you trust your partner's ability to follow your leadership? Why or why not?

9. What reasons might she have for not yet trusting your leadership?

10. In moments you do assert, follow a "mission", and claim a need for yourself; are you doing so out of self-love or out of subtle punishment for an unhealed hurt?

King's Word

1. It is my highest will and intent to come into deep appreciation and acceptance of the interdependent nature of my relationship, and positively shape and influence them with my love, power and mission.

2. I hereby withdraw all energy and intent from the subtle and toxic manipulations or passive-aggressiveness I've previously used in an attempt to control my partner.

Embodied Inquiry

While thinking about your partner, and placing your attention in your heart area, ask:

1. What would it be like to fully and compassionately accept and hold space for my partner's entire range of emotions and desires?

2. How did I become so strong and courageous in declaring my mission and intent, and inviting my partner to orient around them with love and power?

3. I am unwavering in my ability to compassionately hold my partner's full range of beingness.

Shadow 3: The Illusion of Ownership (Re-Relating vs. Relationship)

Relationship itself is a misnomer. For in truth, all marriages and relationships end.

Statistically, maybe 10% of relationships lead to marriage or committed partnerships. Of those, maybe 50% last. Of the ones that last, an even smaller fraction does so out of genuine love and connection, while the majority are simply "maintained" out of fear.

Fear of loneliness. Fear of shame. Fear of "starting over." Fear of messing up the kids. They're maintained mostly through suppression. Suppression of our hurts, suppression of our desires and the suppression of our truth.

How many times have we watched some clip of that old couple celebrating their 60th wedding anniversary, and heard the question, *"What's the secret to your long marriage?"* and you'll almost always hear the guy mutter something like:

"Easy. I always let her be right."

Beyond the pursed-lip veil, he's essentially confessing: *"I suppress my deepest truth and betray my boundaries to maintain this "thing" called marriage that I've been conditioned to hold onto at all costs."*

In our matured view, we don't seek to "maintain" anything. Instead, we seek to continuously dissolve and build anew. To evolve and re-relate. When partners are truly committed to growth, healing, and expression of truth, the context called "relationship" is ever-shifting.

We consciously "let go" of any locked ideas of what our relationship is or must be. We let the container be fluid and ever-expanding. We grant one another the sovereignty we each need.

In a year-long relationship, your goal should be to fully embrace 365 different versions of your partner. To not demand or feel entitled to any specific version—but to encourage, welcome and acquaint to whichever wishes to arise next. That encouragement isn't a timidly vocalized utterance of support, but the felt force of your unconditional love and reverence. Understand that your deepest love is the sun that nourishes all life. Even unspoken, her heart feeds off it like a plant feeds off photosynthesis.

The result, an unfathomable blossoming that you each get to ravish in. Your commitment shouldn't be to "everlasting" love, but to your daringness to allow what's already been to gently dissolve and give way to the next.

The paradox is that the healthiest and longest-lasting relationships aren't bound by undying and self-sacrificing commitment—but in allowing your relationship to die as often as is natural and necessary. For to be in a healthy relationship is to be in constant re-relating. In a world where nearly every traditional marriage vow is broken, should we really continue relying on the well-trodden "till death do us part?"

Commitment is an exquisite and precious thing. It conjures up a degree of endurance and effort that would be far too easy to bypass when things get challenging. But we have to be realistic about that which we're committing to.

It's perhaps less alluring as a vow, but all I can personally commit to is:

1. To always honor, embrace and appreciate you as an ever-evolving soul and being.
2. To encourage and support that growth through a commitment to unconditional love, reverence and compassion.
3. To continue re-relating in this way so long as it inspires and empowers a desire and capacity to continue gifting you these things.

Your own vows may look and feel different. The point is to commit to what is life-affirming and expansive. Not possessive or stifling.

Resist making *any* commitments that can only lead to a compromised or half-hearted expression. For the second you subject yourself to an unattainable agreement, you step out of integrity. Instead, commit to loving her fully for as long as you're consciously choosing to remain partnered.

Commit to radical honesty—with yourself and with her. To speaking your truth and following your genuine desires—while in turn, honoring and inspiring the same in her. For denying yourself and your partner this gift of constant expansion and re-relating is a grave disservice with devastating consequences.

This shadow quickly darkens when our unwillingness to re-relate turns into a false entitlement of ownership. It's easy to miss as it's so deeply entrenched in our culture. It's become almost normal to treat each other as fixed objects incapable or undeserving of growth or evolution.

Control and ownership are synonymous. And sadly, we seek to control those whose actions, behaviors, and decisions have the greatest influence over us and our lives. But in doing so, we become in relationship to something dead—a previous version of our partner that simply ceases to exist.

You can't hit pause on your partner's growth when the coordinates of their journey happen to be inconvenient and incompatible with your disposition. Growth can be messy. At times, it can feel like an unlubricated tussle between one another's sharpest edges. It can only wound and slash until you coat the sharp edges with love, compassion and pure allowance for her expansion.

Let it be clear, you don't own your partner's sexuality. You don't own their choices. As such, give up seeking control over them. Ironically, we have far more influence when we truly lead with love and compassionate power—not fearful control and false entitlement. Likewise, reclaim the land titles of your own personal real estate. You are sovereign, and there are few things more dangerous than a man who falsely assumes himself to be caged and oppressed. No relationship worth participating in should ever feel that way.

It's for this reason that all healthy relationships, at their very core, are "open." Not as carte blanche to break the sacred and defined agreements within the relationship, but to have such agreements be subject to constant re-evaluation and re-configuration, rather than a dreadfully binding force. For no one can truly express and expand while feeling encased within the narrow, previously agreed upon walls of permission and acceptability.

The golden rule prevails: Grant your partner the same freedom of expression and expansion that you yearn for. Commit to re-relating and reorienting around that expansion, not resisting or condemning it. The greatest gift of a relationship is to spark and support mutual growth and evolution, not impede it.

Yet this is only made possible when you've earned your crown and chosen to powerfully display the virtues it represents. This is now within reach. You're at the doorstep of this transformation, and the thunderous knocks at the door have been heard.

Together, let's awaken the *Fearless Lover*.

King's Log

1. What can I truly and authentically commit to in my relationship? What have I committed to in the past that can't be maintained with complete integrity?

2. What are the unspoken agreements or entitlements that are "running" my relationship at this time? Do they truly work for me? For my partner? Can they be re-evaluated?

3. What are the expectations or entitlements I feel my partner has of me that feel stifling and/or no longer appropriate? Can I communicate this with compassion?

4. What are the expectations or entitlements I have of my partner? Have they actually consented to them?

King's Word

1. It is my highest will and intent to gift my partner the sovereignty and freedom of expression that I desire for myself—dropping any and all sense of ownership and entitlement, and instead encouraging and empowering each step of their evolution while reimagining our relationship to best suit it.

2. It is my highest will and intent to know and honor myself as free and sovereign within my relationship, inviting my partner to re-relate to me as I evolve.

Embodied Inquiry

While thinking about your partner, and placing your attention in your heart area, ask:

1. What would it be like to see, honor, appreciate, and encourage my partner for the ever-evolving person they are?

2. How did our relationship become such a safe and powerful container for encouraging and supporting one another's growth, healing, and evolution?

Awakening The Fearless Lover

As you confront these shadows within the fires of your intimate relationship, you begin to give rise to *The Fearless Lover.*

And in truth, a lover can only be considered fully awake and in his power when he's become free of the fears that would otherwise have his love diluted, bent or compromised. Fear is a constriction of love and power. It's where they both get choked off from authentic expression.

Such is the fear exhibited by the man who keeps an "emotional bank account," reducing his love to a quickly depreciating currency while tracking withdrawals and deposits like a devoted accountant.

Such is the fear exhibited by the man who refuses to hold court for the natural and ever-shifting states of his lover. The man who fears the torrential downpour of her emotional upheaval, choosing to board the windows to his own heart and soul.

Such is the fear of the man committed to the safe and sanitized. The man who'd prefer the predictable erosion of his own lover's heart than dance and relish in the awe-filled combustion of her upward ascent.

The long overdue dissolution of these fears and shadows is one of the most rewarding transformations you'll enjoy as a man. You'll become more energized, for it requires massive amounts of energy to maintain and uphold that chokehold. All the force you've been unconsciously using to choke love out of your relationship becomes available to redirect towards more noble cause. All the energy misallocated to the patterns of closure, constriction and petty vengeance become liberated for higher purpose and deeper presence.

The Fearless Lover isn't an effort to embody. It's one of the greatest joys. It's self-regenerating. For every moment spent acting from the place of *The Fearless Lover* invites more energy back to you. *The Fearless Lover* is compassion, acceptance, love, power and passion in action. It's where the inner king animates into your intimate relationship, and where you get to *truly* be the gift she's been silently waiting for her entire life.

What you're about to embark on is both rare and precious. Sacred. Something that only you and your partner can ever share. Your invitation then is to be completely devoted and totally willing to allow the shadows we've confronted to continue to unravel and unwind. Maybe they'll all dissolve in one shot, or perhaps it'll take months or years to continue undoing the knots they've created in your mind and body. What's important isn't the amount of time it takes, but the choice you get to make right now to continue confronting them, while continuously seeking to embody and express yourself as *The Fearless Lover.*

With your inner king as a witness, make this commitment and be totally ready and willing to step into this initiation, knowing full well that what arises on the other side, can and will be beyond anything you've ever experienced before. With that sacredness and intention, it's time to move into the initiation. It's time to dethrone the lower aspects of your relational self, and its impulses towards petty vengeance and selfish pride.

It's time to crown *The Fearless Lover.*

Crowning The Fearless Lover

The guided initiation into *The Fearless Lover*
is available to stream at:

www.iseeyouking.com/relationship

Evolutionary Accelerators

Evolutionary Accelerator #1: Make the First Move

Practice Duration: Constantly.
Practice Frequency: Indefinitely.

Description:

In their seminal *King, Warrior, Lover, Magician,* Robert Moore and Doug Gillette describe the king as someone who possesses the power to generously acknowledge and appreciate his constituents. Simply put, it takes a king to crown.

Within your relationship, you're invited to be the king rather than the beggar. A man who's so grounded in his own being and positive power, that he doesn't need others to validate it. He's his own source. It's derived from his rightful reign, and his knowledge of such.

To live in alignment with this power is to give *without* the need or expectation of reciprocity or balance. To be generous in our offerings of love and appreciation is to reaffirm our power and capacity to do so. This is the difference between a beggar and a king.

An "emotional bank account" is reflective of the transactional relationship. It's the basis of codependency and conditional love. It's reaffirming a place of inner poverty where your sustenance and place in life is based on what your partner can or can't provide.

With this shadow now in the active process of dissolution and transmutation, a cornerstone of our work will be to simply honor the reign of our *Fearless Lover* by granting him providence over our intimate relationship.

The practice is simple. For the next 24 hours, and for as often as you can remember to do so beyond that, you're invited to "make the first move."

Drop the need for "balance" or to be seen, heard, loved or appreciated *first*. Instead, give from a place of overflowing abundance. Even if presumed.

By no means should this be taken to mean that you deny yourself from receiving the gifts from your partner, nor place your partner's needs above your own. As we mentioned in this chapter, an intimate relationship is maintained on the premise that both partners genuinely desire gifting one another the love, reverence, connection and intimacy that encourages one another's growth, healing and evolution; and are actively expanding their capacities to do so.

In this practice, we simply initiate this gifting as often as we're called, dropping the need for any perceived balance or reciprocity. It's an unconditional flow and expression of who we are as *The Fearless Lover.*

1. Show appreciation first.
2. Offer safety and acceptance first.
3. Forgive first.
4. Apologize first.
5. Listen first.
6. Acknowledge first.
7. Express love first.
8. Express intimate desire first.

In doing so, drop the need for constant relational balance, or the unspoken quid pro quo. Likewise, be mindful to not silently insist on a specific response or a reaction.

Instead, as you make the first move, sense an overwhelming enjoyment. Feel awe and gratitude over your sheer capacity to offer these things, and do so from a genuine desire of enriching the life of your partner. There is an aspect of unconditionality we're endeavoring to achieve.

If you notice any inflamed or agitated objections arise within you, especially ones that are bitter, resentful or judge her to be undeserving, these are likely remnants of the dethroned shadow. Acknowledge them and saturate them in your own compassionate embrace and loving stance. In all cases, however, make it your honor, your duty, and your right as *The Fearless Lover* to make the first move.

Evolutionary Accelerator #2: Pickup lines

Practice Duration: 2-5 minutes.

Practice Frequency: As often as you're inspired to.

Description:

Ultimately, there are no universal magic words that can transform a relationship. It's the "place" from which the words come from that truly makes a difference. Emotionality and energetic intent will always speak louder than the words themselves. While inspired actions taken from that same place of pure intent will always speak loudest.

The following words, however, require you to reach into that place within you where *The Fearless Lover* dwells. It's nearly impossible for these words to be authentically spoken from any of those shadow aspects. While these words are powerful and healing in of themselves, the magic here lies in *who* you'll be accessing within to speak them.

When spoken with sincerity, these "pickup lines" will offer healing over past hurts, bring wholeness where there's still disconnection and, most importantly, create a context for deeper connection, intimacy, and mutual gifting to flourish. You're invited to create your own. But as a starting point, you may work with:

1. There's no part of you that I'm not completely in love with.
2. There's no one you can't be in my presence. All of you is welcome and safe here.

3. Loving you, *all* of you, is a privilege that I cherish.
4. What can I gift you right now to make you feel safe, heard, and fully seen?
5. You're my partner / woman / person. There's no one I'd rather do this with.

The first stage of this practice is done solo as a self-healing practice. To begin, simply visualize yourself saying each one to your partner. As soon as you declare each one, notice what defenses or rebuttals show up for you.

Endeavor to trace back to their source. Feel its energy signature. The totality of the mental/emotional construct that's animating (and giving energy) to the negative reaction. Peel back the layers through deeper inquiry:

Who is it that feels (partner's name) is unworthy/undeserving of my love?

Who is it that's unwilling to let (partner's name) show up in their fullness?

Who is it that resists (partner's name) negativity/sadness / victimhood?

Who is it that's unwilling to forgive (partner's name) and why?

Who is it that finds it unbearably hard to love the totality of my partner?

Who is it that is angry with/hates/dislikes/is repulsed by (partner's name)?

Once again, this is first used as a self-healing and clearing process to dissolve constraint and negative intent. When you arrive at a place where they can be said authentically without resistance, you're invited to offer your partner this greatest of gifts.

Likewise, hold no expectation over how she receives it. Let your gift be the joy and power of the offering. For your ability to offer it is a power worth rejoicing in. She may receive it in a thousand different ways. It may be a master key in unlocking her heart and giving her the healing and resolution she needs. She may be shocked and not know how to hold it, or she may even be skeptical and unable to receive it at this time.

Her reaction and capacity to receive it is not personal, nor is it for you to judge, condemn or feel victimized by. It's simply a product of whatever wounding is still alive in her.

These "pickup lines" are about putting down our defenses. In working with them, we see what those defenses are. We witness the past hurts. The past resentments and betrayals. The remaining guards and servants of the nearly overthrown shadows who remain steadfast in disallowing *The Fearless Lover* to claim his reign.

Gift them as often as you feel called, for each one is as much in service of her healing and growth as it is your own.

Evolutionary Accelerator #3: Evoke. Evolve. Arouse. Awaken.

Practice Duration: 3-5 minutes.

Practice Frequency: At least once per week.

Description:

Most conversations between partners are flat, benign, and mostly in service of the status quo. Remember, as king, we don't use our voice to fill the silence; we use it to speak law and truth into the air. We use it as an evolutionary accelerator, engineering moments of insight, healing, and revelation.

The power of our word is immense. In this practice, we'll use our words to arouse insight and revelation, and ultimately encourage or evoke the "next version" of our partner that she's yearning to become. This is where you practically get to play a supporting part in her evolution—and the fullest expression of it.

You can make this a weekly practice. However, skillfulness and spontaneity may be your best allies in offering them.

Questions to gift your partner:

1. What would you like me to honor?
2. Where do you need to be seen or heard right now?
3. Who are you working on becoming?
4. What's more important to you than anything else right now?
5. What can I gift you?
6. What would you like to experience more than anything else?

Evolutionary Accelerator #4: The King's Gaze: 9-Phase Eye Gazing:

Practice Duration: 25-35 minutes.

Practice Frequency: At least once per week (but as often as you'd like).

Description:

This is a complete couple's practice that encompasses and integrates everything we've discussed throughout this chapter.

Through this practice, you'll experience authentic re-relating, perhaps truly *seeing* your partner for the first time. You'll also tap into the reservoir of deep, unyielding compassion and unconditional love—while recognizing the constant interdependence that creates the "signature" of your relationship.

Performing this practice just once can yield life-changing transformation in your relationship. Done with consistency, you elevate your relationship to one of unconstrained love, connection, and intimacy.

> You may practice using the instructions below, recording your own version. Alternatively, for a full recording and deeper focus on the "Relationship Fire", you're invited to join the *Awakening The Fearless Lover* program at
>
> www.iseeyouking.com/afl

Instructions:

1. Sit comfortably, face to face with your partner, ideally in dim candlelight.

2. Take 3 deep, centering breaths from your heart space. Almost as if it's your heart that's breathing in and out—internally affirming, *"It is my highest will and intent to see and receive you fully."*

3. During each stage of this practice, you're going to gaze into each other's eyes while generating a certain shared state. This requires deep trust and vulnerability. Start off by stating the following to one another:

4. Anything you experience is perfect. Any reaction you have is exquisite, and it is my privilege and honor to share it with you.

5. Declare this vow to one another and affirm one another's trust in the other.

6. **Phase 1 (Connect):** For two minutes, simply gaze into each other's eyes with equal parts giving and receiving. Use this as a moment to simply

melt into one another's awareness—and open the gates for total intimacy and connection.

7. Now, with nothing but your gaze, thank each other for sharing this connection, and gently close your eyes for a moment.

8. **Phase 2 (Innocence):** When you open them again, you're going to see each other's innocence. See nothing but someone who is totally and completely innocent. See one another's inner child. See one another's struggles and challenges. See and acknowledge how each of you has been shaped and influenced by so many fears and hurts in this life. See one another's deep desire to do good. To be happy. To be whole. Just like you. Open your eyes and connect totally and completely to each other's humanness and pure innocence. Hold this gaze for 1-2 minutes.

9. Now, with nothing but your gaze, thank each other for sharing this moment and gently close your eyes once again.

10. **Phase 3 (Apology):** When you open your eyes again, you'll gaze at each other with nothing but pure apology towards the other. Offer the tone, energy and feeling of apology for all the hurts you've caused or participated in—consciously or unconsciously. All the subtle forms of attack or micro-aggression, be it emotional or energetic, with your words or with your silent thoughts. With your actions or inactions. Silently own and offer that apology for any negative intent—no matter how it's been presented. Offer it not from a place of guilt or shame, but from a place of acknowledgment and ownership, and most importantly, from a place of wanting *only* the best for them, and genuinely not wanting to ever inflict harm in any way. Open your eyes now, generously offering your apology while fully receiving theirs for the next two minutes.

11. With nothing but your gaze, thank each other for their acknowledgement and apology. Affirm that you've received it, and gently close your eyes once again.

12. **Phase 4 (Forgiveness):** When you open your eyes, offer your total forgiveness through your gaze. Once again, acknowledge their innocence. Acknowledge that they've only been acting out of their own hurts, fears, traumas, conditionings, or negative influences. That they've done their

best. In this, feel resentment and bitterness transform into compassion—and offer that forgiveness and compassion fully. Open your eyes now and for the next two minutes offer and receive this pure forgiveness and compassion.

13. For one more minute, see if you can turn it up: Melt any resistance. Melt any thoughts of undeservingness. Drop any stream of thought, any stories that have been revisited in your mind, and simply put your full attention on the underlying energy of compassion that you now share. Continue dialing this up and offering it to one another through your gaze.

14. With nothing but your gaze, thank each other for their forgiveness. Affirm that you've both granted it and received it, and will commit to continue doing so beyond this practice. Gently close your eyes once again.

15. **Phase 5 (Awe/Reverence):** When you open your eyes again, you'll look at your partner with complete awe and reverence. You'll dare to see beyond your fixed ideas of them. You'll look beyond any stories you've held onto about who they are. Instead, you'll take them in fully. You'll ask: "Who *is* this human before me"—who are you *really* looking at? Acknowledge the possibility that maybe you've only ever known or seen or felt 10% of who they truly are—and that the rest has been projections and incomplete ideas and perceptions filtered through your own lens of what you can or can't receive. But now, open your eyes again, and for two minutes gaze at them with complete *awe* and *reverence* of their exquisite fullness, their deep mystery, and their endless potential. Offering this complete awe and reverence. A complete desire to *know* them and *see* them fully as they are beyond all stories and perceptions. Likewise, allow yourself to be fully seen and revered for who you are.

16. For one more minute, see if you can turn it up: Melt any resistance. Melt any thoughts of undeservingness. Dropping any stream of thought—any stories that have been revisited in your mind—and simply put your full attention on the underlying energy of awe and reverence that you now share. Continue dialing this up and offering it to one another through your gaze.

17. With nothing but your gaze, thank each other for their awe and reverence. Affirm that you've both offered it and received it as fully as you can at this time. Gently close your eyes.

18. **Phase 6 (Gratitude and Endless Appreciation):** When you open your eyes again, you'll offer complete gratitude and appreciation to your partner through your gaze. Not for anything they've done—but for their innate value as a human // an exquisite soul who's chosen to share a part of their existence with you. Open your eyes now, and both offer and receive this deep appreciation for two minutes, honoring how precious a gift you truly are to one another.

19. For one more minute, see if you can turn it up. Drop the thought of each other. Drop all thoughts, and simply dwell in the *feeling* of appreciation you've created together. See no beginning or end to it. Just an endless field of appreciation. Let your focus and attention on that feeling naturally strengthen and amplify it.

20. With nothing but your gaze, thank each other for their appreciation. Affirm that you've both offered it and received it as fully as you can at this time. And again, gently close your eyes.

21. **Phase 7 (Self-Love):** When you open your eyes again, you'll generate self-love, self-acceptance and self-appreciation. While mirroring that back to one another. Give the other the gift of witnessing you in full appreciation and love towards yourself. Open your eyes now and for two minutes, generate complete self-love and self-appreciation. Let the self-love you each generate mirror each other's, making it grow stronger and stronger. Now gently close your eyes.

22. **Phase 8 (Love for them):** When you open your eyes again, you'll offer your complete, unconditional love to them through your gaze. Be gentle but unyielding in this offering. Open your eyes now, and both offer and receive unconditional love to your partner.

23. Continue offering this unconditional love for another minute, amplifying it by feeling into your deep heartfelt desire for them to be safe, healthy, happy and in their fullest expression of love and truth at all times. Be totally unconditional in this offering—while receiving it back.

Feel any conditions or resistance melt in this field of pure, unconditional love. Offer this now for a few more moments.

24. **Phase 9 (Love):** Now keeping your eyes open, let the love for the other drop and let it just become a field of pure love that you share. Your love merges with her love, and her love merges with your love. Close your eyes and bathe and saturate in that field. Letting it flow however it chooses to at this time; your only job is to enjoy it. The warmth and truth of who and what you are as intimate partners at this time.

25. This is the true signature of your relationship today. This *is* your relationship in its purest state at this moment. Melt deeper and deeper into it. Silently set any intention for your relationship that you wish. Sew it in this field of pure love.

26. When you're ready, slowly open your eyes. Continue sharing and expressing this signature of love, however you each feel called to at this time. That may include physical or emotional intimacy, or sharing the realizations and insights that came through in the practice.

Optional Reflection Questions:

The following questions are available for deeper inquiry and partnered exploration. However, unless you're well-grounded in forms of healthy dialogue and non-violent communication, it's recommended that you explore them with a trusted guide, facilitator, therapist or counselor. Additionally, you can inquire about our private *Awakening the Fearless Lover* program (www.iseeyouking.com/afl).

Please use appropriate discretion, and only proceed if both you and your partner can fully commit to open, non-judgmental, and non-blaming sharing.

1. In the apology process, what did you each apologize for? Share it and receive it with total non-judgment. Liberate each other from the previous unspoken resentments.

2. In the forgiveness process, what did you struggle to forgive each other for? What resentments or bitterness felt too much to forgive at this time?

3. What blocks or resistance did you have with offering appreciation or reverence to the other?

4. What does the signature of your love feel like at this time?

Evolutionary Accelerator #5 - A Kingdom, Shared.

Practice Duration: 15-20 minutes.

Practice Frequency: At least once per week (but as often as you'd like).

Description:

Many long-time partners have struggled to re-relate to their partner. A product of the "fixed object" syndrome that fails to acknowledge the other's ever-evolving nature.

Further, the unconscious refusal to do so is often caused by forms of unchecked resentment. A lingering bitterness that deems your partner "unworthy" of their highest aspirations. Let it be known that even if this doesn't manifest in overt actions, the undertones themselves, and the stench they leave, is a form of sabotage.

Of course, few would readily admit that they're sabotaging their partner's growth and dreams. But if you're not actively and energetically creating "room for it" in your heart and beingness, then you're very much "blocking" a shared reality where your relationship and their aspirations co-exist.

The other "trap" many partners fall into is that of being in their own "silo" of growth. Where they're each "doing their work" and plotting their own individual goals and dreams, without actively involving the other or integrating each other's visions. This could only lead to one of two outcomes:

1. Blocked or delayed attainment of those goals/dreams/outcomes.
2. Having to collapse the relationship altogether since your partner was never included or integrated within the vision.

This final practice attempts to mend this rift. To not only make each partner intellectually "aware" of the other's aspirations; but to actively invest, advocate for, and self-implicate in its manifestation.

Before you begin, it's recommended that you perform the 9-Phase Eye Gazing practice.

When you're ready, begin with this declaration to one another:

Opening Declaration:

1. You deserve to be happy.
2. You deserve to be healthy.
3. You deserve to be cherished and honored.
4. It is my highest will and intent to co-create a shared reality where your highest growth and aspirations, as well as my own, are served and supported with joyful power.

Core Practice:

Partner A asks: *What is it that you most desire to experience in this life?*

Partner B: Speaking in a present tense, describe with richness a reality you wish to bridge into creation. Do so solely in the positive sense (i.e., resist saying "I no longer want to X or Y")

As Partner A gives a "play-by-play" of their desired reality, Partner B holds a visualization (Experiential Embodiment) of *both* partners sharing that reality. In full enjoyment and gratitude. Meaning, Partner A "gifts" Partner B with their highest vision. And Partner B gifts Partner A with their energy and intent to create and share it.

After 2-3 minutes, switch roles, going back and forth as many times as you feel called.

Chapter 6:

FIRE 3 - YOUR SENSE OF PURPOSE

What makes this an initiatory fire?

If you're reading this book, you're part of the first generation of men who can truly even consider what it means to live a life of purpose, let alone have the freedom to pursue it wholeheartedly. At your fingertips alone, you have unprecedented access to teachings, practices, tools, mentors, communities, and outlets for inspiration. All of which can be consciously curated and channeled to support a life of deep meaning and purpose. Through the daring tales of others, you're generously granted overwhelming and unignorable confirmation to the possibility of living one's sacred truth with balance and power.

Yet this freedom of purpose is both a gift and a potential curse. For with this freedom comes an inner, soul-level pressure to pursue and live in alignment with this mysterious, almost mystical thing called purpose—yet an even greater set of outer pressures and obstacles that seemingly obstruct it.

For the challenge in following one's purpose is indeed difficult. It's mentally, emotionally, physically and even spiritually taxing. It often involves betraying the expectations of those we care about. And it nearly always means a swift departure from a sense of perceived safety.

In pursuing one's purpose, we're met with doubt, fear, and even guilt for veering off the beaten path, while the majority of our brothers and sisters choose to remain on it. We're often stigmatized, outcast, and mislabeled for the mere attempt; leaving us isolated and unsupported where we ought to be encouraged and celebrated.

Such is the plight of the budding entrepreneur who feels a sting of shame when sharing his mission on social media, only to have his old friends silently condemn and slander. He feels the sting of the invisible arrows piercing his fragile hopes. The secret seething of those who've yet to claim the reins of their own life—instead, wishing for his demise in some cowardly act of entrepreneurial schadenfreude.

It's the dream-killing impasse of the college student. The one who senses a crippling misalignment in the path he's pursuing, yet can't break free from the shackles of expectation or the sunk costs of that first torturous year.

And finally, it's the death warrant signed by the vacant pawn when he trades a life of purposefulness for a life of predictable decay within his four-by-six prison.

The shadows run deep in this one. Like all these fires, most men won't even come to realize the initiation they've been plunged into, let alone cultivate the power and courage to emerge on the other side. Living purposefully is a slow-burning fire. It's an easy one to miss. Even when caught, it's an easy one to delay and defer. These flames are warm and provide a false sense of comfort and bearability.

But bearability itself is a curse. It's a prison where you're given just enough sustenance to survive. Just enough entertainment to soothe the wounds of the everyday lashings. Just enough well-timed mercy to keep you from rebelling against your inner captors.

In the land of bearability, the suffering is slow and insidious. You're drip-fed the poison over weeks, months, and years. Slowly becoming more and more sedated—losing your capacity to stand up and rise anew—the memory of freedom and purpose becoming ever more distant. And the will to reclaim it, all but gone.

In the land of "bearability," you never quite realize the urgency of your situation until it's too late. Like the frog in boiling water, rising one degree at a time—his organs tragically seared to mush by the time he thinks to move himself to action.

Most men today have trapped themselves in the land of bearability. It's a land where relief is cheap and normalized. Escape, costly and condemned. For it's easier to stay locked up than to break free. Easier to sooth the gag reflex while choking down on a life you never quite signed up for, than it is to spit it out in a fit of brilliant catharsis.

Sunday Night Football and a six-pack of PBR to bring bearability to another week of cubicle malaise is easier than jumping out of the system and confronting the cognitive dissonance that comes from realizing the truth of your condition.

In part, the lie of linearity keeps us stuck here. We accumulate false merit based on where we land on an arbitrary scale of achievement. Seniority and annual pay raises, rising the imagined ranks, and fearing the crash should we courageously let our grip slip off that rung.

We don't want to "give up" what we've spent our lives "building." We don't want to saw off the rusty hook on which we hang our existential hat.

In doing so, we build our kingdoms on that shaky ground of toxic, GMO'd soil; allowing circumstance to hold us hostage, and doing what we can to pacify the subterranean rumblings that compassionately yet unapologetically threaten to pull our fake empire out from underneath our feet.

In this fearful act of self-pacification, we fail to recognize the exponential speed in which a new, more purposeful life can be created. We deny ourselves the power of irrevocable decision, and the immediate reconfiguration of our realities that support it. We mute our own abundant, regenerative force, and deny our vast resourcefulness, creativity, and influence which would be even further sharpened in the pursuit of our authentic truth.

We mistrust our own power of creation, even when we hold the living heart-beat of human life that sprung from our very seed. We misuse our vital energy, auctioning it off to the highest bidder rather than using it to better our inner kingdom, and from it, build a living empire of authentic expression.

Tragically speaking, we fear the sunk costs more than our sinking spirits. The shame in potentially being struck back down in the field of battle, than the imag-ined safety in playing dead within the walls we built.

Indeed, most would prefer playing a rigged game than rejoice in the freedom of flipping the board, and playing a better one of their design.

Here, we fail to recognize that strength and courage aren't marked by one's ability to endure continued hardship and suffering, but in one's capacity to unapologetically pursue the life they truly desire in its place. In the land of bearability, we never seek to overthrow the oppressor—but instead make the oppression more tolerable.

For such a pervasive buzzword, so few men will ever drum up the courage to live a life of true meaning and purpose. If you're reading this, you're tasked with the great responsibility of honoring your ever-evolving purpose, and making it the "norm" for the next generation of men to follow.

Because while the larger opportunity to live one's purpose is relatively new, man's innate drive to live in accordance with it isn't. Purpose is indeed your birthright. It's what breathes life into your inner warrior. It's only the prevailing and overwhelming influence of the three shadows you're about to encounter that limit your capacity to access it.

It's time to leave the prison.

It's time to let its walls crumble.

And from its rubble, let the warrior rise.

Shadow 1: The Seduction of Safety (Fear of the Unknown)

When it comes to activating your sense of purpose, safety is the siren call that makes us stop halfway.

If a man has yet to reconcile his mortal and existential dread, he's forever bound by the seductress of safety. In the sickest irony, he will give up his life under the false premise that, in doing so, he can preserve it. But life cannot be artificially preserved. It can only be *lived*.

Would you rather live one year on your own terms, or a thousand cryogenically frozen inside somebody else's chamber? The price we pay for a false sense of preservation is great.

There's a common story our fathers used to tell us. They'd talk about how they used to stick baseball cards in the spokes of their bike wheels to make it sound like a motorcycle. They'd talk about the regret. How those cards today are now worth five, ten, or fifty thousand dollars.

Willie Mays, Mickey Mantle. Reggie Jackson.

One moment, mint and pristine. The next, bent and broken, sacrificing their temporal cardboard existence to satisfy the untamed imagination and fluttering spirit of a rebellious child. Absorbed by the moment. Overjoyed and in deep connection with his highest excitement. He's lived it fully. Held nothing back.

And then, one day, that same child grows up. He's bred into a system of scarcity, survival and control. His wild imagination and creative spirit collapsed into a narrow box of rationality and logic.

His passion no longer has a place within the rigid, pragmatic shell he's been pushed into. His intimate tussle with life herself a forbidden affair. Too young to defend his first lover, he lets her perish. Soon, he's conditioned into a cheap substitute. No longer intertwined with life, but seeing it as some future, ineffable "thing" that he has to "build," "create," or "control." Only it's no longer his to build, for his brushstrokes are guided by the expectations of others.

Artless and abhorrent. Dull and passionless. He lives his life not as a sacred blessing with the ever-unfolding purpose once offered by his long-lost lover—but with the drudgery that such a false sense of life can only ever provide.

One day, this same man learns about the monetary value of his old baseball cards, and collapses in regret. He condemns his younger, "ignorant" self who instead of keeping that card in mint condition, used it as a motorized sound effect to light up his soul. He shames his inner child. Tells other men about how he had all those cards in his possession and squandered them.

He laments the lost opportunity. Bemoans his calamitous misstep to anyone who will listen. And they'll confirm his sorrow, offering him a moment of feigned sympathy before drawing the next sip from their pint.

But no one will ever stop to ask, who's the fool?

The fearless child, fully expressed and in flow with life?

Or the rigid, fear-based card trader, forever protecting his possession between thick plexiglass, fearing the smallest smudge? The man who'll tote it around the country like a second-rate carnival prize, showing it off to other men of the same delusory disposition. The man who literally refuses to leave his fingerprints on the thing he claims to "own"?

Ask yourself: Who has truly recognized the card's *value*? Who's living with a greater sense of abundance and purpose?

The child, generously merging with the richness before him, letting his spirit expand, pulsate and appreciate with each emphatic clack? Or the man stuck in regret? Failing to recognize that he's literally inches away from untold riches at all times—and that only life herself can ferry him over into such a sensual affair?

But it's a gift she's only welcomed to offer once you relinquish your sense of scarcity. It's a relationship that can only be authentically restored when you overcome the seduction of safety and drop the fear of leaving smudge prints on this thing you call "life." Those smudge prints are sacred. They're yours and yours alone to leave.

But like his most prized baseball card, man will encase himself in thick plexiglass. He'll wall himself off from the dangers "out there." He'll claim to be stuck or oppressed. But that will only ever be a small part of the greater truth. For he is his own warden. And he fears being released back into the untamed embrace of life herself, and what that embrace may inspire in him.

Understand, life's value is only realized when you become inseparable from it. You can't "build" a life from within your prison walls. Only the fictitious idea of one. To be free, and to express freely as a man, is to invite and embrace the mystery of your own unfoldment. It's an interplay with life herself. A dynamic exchange of life and love with everything and everyone that enters your kingdom. There is no room for the illusion of safety.

The price you pay to be admitted into a life of this dynamic, unfiltered unfoldment, is your stubborn insistence on safety and control. And the truth is, you're already paying it. Whether you accept it or not, you're constantly courting the unknown. Yet the promise of safety is a seductive one. A siren's call that can only lead you to the shores of inner captivity.

To desperately grasp at the illusion of control is to expend one's energy in putting up a wall between you and life. This wall cuts you off from life's greatest offerings. It denies the multitude of possibilities that life is placing before you in each and every moment. It shields you from the rays of pure, undiluted potentialities that are here to spark your evolution, and burn down the archaic structures that no longer support it.

In fearing the unknown, you choose a life of artificial sterility and inner entrapment, rather than the openness and receptivity that every moment demands of you. Indeed, to fear the unknown is to put second-grade safety on a faulty pedestal—which is to overvalue the promises of your inner captors and send your sense of purpose to the deathly gallows.

Purposefulness is what drives us beyond the prison walls. It's a powerful impulse constantly seeking expansion. It's one of few forces strong enough to blast through whatever thick bedrock your prison rests on. It penetrates the seemingly impenetrable. And when it does, you come into close contact with the warrior you've had access to all along.

One step at a time, he'll lead you out onto the grassy fields beyond those old prison walls. With each step, you'll grow in courage. Hyper aware. Courting the unknown. Relishing in the freedom you've been all long.

The sun will shine brighter than it ever has. You'll delight in its rays. And in the clearing ahead, you'll hear the clacking of cardboard against spoke, and your once-lost lover—life herself, shall be waiting.

King's Log

1. Where am I holding back from doing what I truly want? Why?
2. Is my current career or business a perfect vehicle for my sense of purposefulness? Why or why not? How can it be?
3. Is my relationship a suitable vehicle for my highest sense of purposefulness? Why or why not? How can it be?
4. How and where do I overvalue maintenance of the familiar/status quo? Why?
5. Who is it that's afraid of purposeful change, expansion and transformation — and why? What's he holding onto?
6. Would I be satisfied with the next 5 years looking more or less the same as the last 5?
7. What do I really desire? Why am I not actively living or pursuing it?
8. What excuses have I been making for not doing so? Are they absolutely true? Whose stories are they?

King's Word

1. It is my highest will and intent to relish in my constant and ever-expanding sense of purposefulness. Overcoming any need, desire or insistence in clinging to the familiar.

2. It is my highest will and intent to know and experience true safety in the vast freedom of my own emerging mission and purposefulness.
3. I courageously open up to a sense of purpose and aliveness in all that I do.
4. I relinquish all stories of scarcity and fear around living purposefully.

Embodied Inquiry

1. What would it feel like to be totally and utterly fearless in receiving and expressing my highest purpose, moment by moment?
2. How did I become so wise, strong and courageous in knowing and expressing my purpose?
3. How did I so easily reclaim my sense of purpose?
4. I am undeterred and unconstrained in my constant expression of purposefulness.
5. How is it that I have constant and complete knowledge of my highest will and how it wishes to express?

Shadow #2: The Vacant & The Grandstander

The next shadow is created within the constant tussle between two polar extremes: *The Vacant* and *The Grandstander*. But while they exist on opposite poles, they're potent enablers of each other's dysfunction.

We'll begin with *The Vacant*. *The Vacant* is present in your tendency to "check-out" detach, or disconnect from your present situation. It's where you withdraw your attention and presence from the moment before you, judging it as unworthy of your full engagement.

There's a sense of coasting. Of going through the motions. Of being half-hearted and limp-wristed as you close your eyes to much of what life is presenting before you.

This subtle condemnation of the present moment is facilitated by *The Grandstander*. *The Grandstander* is the one who falsely equates purpose with a singular goal or mission. He believes his purpose to be one massive, overarching outcome or event and "checks-out" of any moment or situation that isn't directly support-ive of that outcome.

The Grandstander seeks the checkered flag at the *Daytona 500* but curses the practice laps and the tire changes that would get him there. He lives for the final put to clinch The *Masters* but denounces all the "inferior" moments that preceded it, free of fanfare.

The Grandstander wants the glory of victory but denounces the millions of micro moments that contribute to it. He lives for an event, a result, an emergent—none of which are *actually* available as anything but an "idea" in our moment-to-moment awareness.

But beyond the micro moments that correlate with our big mission, *The Grandstander* struggles to remain present and purposeful within all other events that don't correlate to his fixed image of victory.

We may see our grand purpose as building an eight-figure publishing empire, becoming a legendary firefighter, running for congress, or cleaning the plastic out of the ocean, but when faced with soothing a teething infant back to sleep, or acknowledging a lover's hurt, we "check out." We judge these in-the-moment, micro purposes to be unworthy of our fullest attention and engagement. Our skillfulness and strength are reserved only for what our ego judges to be worthy, which, by definition, is always going to be limited and self-serving.

It's the classic case of the "successful businessman," who carves out an envious position within his industry yet loses his standing at home. What matters is not the amount of "time spent" but the quality of that time, the fullness of each moment, and the purpose he awakens to in each passing interaction. The "successful businessman" essentially turns off the fluidity of purposefulness, puts up a dam, and directs it all towards one place.

The Grandstander is also present in the man who "holds out" for a grand purpose. He feels entitled to the grandeur but refuses to engage in anything until some magnificent purpose lands before him. In doing so, he resists the lower rungs of the ladder that would bring him to the mighty purpose he so desires. For even the tallest ladders are rooted and anchored into the ground. This is the man who'll spend his entire life waiting on the sidelines. He wants the glory of the Hail Mary pass but refuses to engage in the dozens of trench battles, and run plays that earn him such an opportunity.

The Grandstander is plagued by a culture obsessed with the highlight reel. Quote card wisdom that reminds him of his limitless nature and capacity to do great things, but fails to mention the inner stance that leads to their expression.

Lofty aspirations are wonderful. A world-changing mission is to be celebrated. But neither is available to *The Grandstander* who judges, condemns, and disconnects from any moment that doesn't match his predefined palette.

Like many of these fires, there's a twisted irony in this. In reserving his presence and attention for a singular, fixed "purpose," man will spend the majority of his life in various degrees of disconnect. What he fails to realize is that, in doing so, the purposefulness he was reserving for his grand mission hasn't been preserved or strengthened. It's been harshly atrophied by his refusal to be nourished and engaged by the world around him.

Nothing rusts and dulls a man's blade faster than his persistent refusal to use it. Checking out and going vacant are the subtle ways in which a man will force himself into premature decay and obsolescence. In standing idle, waiting for the specter of his purpose to reveal itself in the far distance, we allow sand to fill our eyes and blind us from the very thing we're seeking.

In their extremes, *The Vacant* and *The Grandstander* miss an all-important fact. They fail to recognize that purpose isn't so much a "thing" as it is a "way." A *modus operandi*. An inward "stance" he takes within the world regardless of outer circumstance. He fails to realize that purpose isn't a fixed thing, but a transient and spontaneous thrust of life, intermingled and inspired by the moment before him. Like sight or sound, it's a sense through which he connects to the world around him.

Whereas *The Vacant* and *The Grandstander* will spend most of their lives drifting and disconnected, void of intent, *The Warrior* that gets awakened in this fire is always engaged and oriented around the highest good, regardless of the situation that befalls him.

The Warrior doesn't wait for the moment to be "grand" enough to act. He honors it for what it is, and sees himself as implicit in the quality and texture of each moment. For this man, all moments are sacred. Neither more nor less important than the one before, or the one yet to come.

Few men in history had greater reason to "check out" than Victor Frankl.

Subject to the untold horrors of a death camp, disconnecting from the moment would seem to be the only reasonable response. Yet this wasn't Frankl's experience. Instead, he awakened to his sacred relationship to each moment, allowing meaning and purpose to self-renew with each new set of circumstances before him. Whether it was a troubled guard he could help through his work as an analyst, or his own existential survival, purpose was ever unfolding and self-evident through a wakeful eye and an open heart.

And therein lies the hidden truth. It's not that your purpose is elusive. It's that *you* are to it. You are utterly unavailable to that which you seek. In condemning your child's 2:30 AM nightmare, you miss the wellspring of compassion that can awaken your heart and seep out into every dimension of your life. Ever-evolving from one moment to the next, meaning and purpose are inseparable.

Purpose will only ever find its mate in the purposeful. It craves a trusted source. Someone who can listen to her, hold her, and live in co-creative harmony with her. Much of man's inner struggle comes not from a "lack of purpose", but from his inability to accept and express the one knocking at his door.

In our work, we embrace and pursue our mission wholeheartedly. Whether it's a Pulitzer or personal best in the gym, we set lofty goals and take our moonshots. But most importantly, we awaken a constant sense of purposefulness. Never clinging to one fixed thing, but allowing purpose and meaning to reveal themselves with each passing breath. We give ourselves full permission to self-renew. To stop carrying around the carcass of a purpose long dead, and in that lightness, wake up to the one standing before us.

Dear Warrior, it's your time to awaken.

King's Log

1. In what areas of your life do you check out or disengage from? Why?
2. Who is it that believes those moments to be unworthy of your engagement?
3. Who is it that judges most moments to be unimportant and unworthy? Why?
4. What does purposefulness feel like to you? Where is it most accessible? How would it express itself in every moment?
5. If you were to be purposeful in every moment, would you "run out" of purpose or would it be strengthened and ever flowing?
6. What big moment, outcome or result are you holding out for? Can you feel the same connection, appreciation and purposefulness to all the micro-moments that precede it?

King's Word

1. It is my highest will and intent to cultivate and express a sense of purposefulness in all that I do, regardless of how important or unimportant a small part of me judges it to be.

2. It is my highest will and intent to recover a sense of purposefulness to all that life so generously presents.

Embodied Inquiry

1. What would it feel like to be purposeful in all moments, no matter how big or small?

2. What would it feel like to express a sense of strength and purpose all the time?

3. How did I become so constantly and effortlessly purposeful?

4. How is it that I have the superhuman ability to be purposeful with all that life so generously presents before me?

Shadow #3: The Willing Pawn & The Shackles of Expectation

The pursuit of purpose can only begin in earnest once we break free from the shackles of expectation. The task is one of the bloodier we encounter on the path towards authentic kingship.

When we were young, betraying expectation of authority felt like sure annihilation. For when we are dependent on others for survival, unquestioned compliance becomes our greatest strategy to ensure it. But in doing so, we became conditioned to filter every decision through the lens of imagined consequence rather than deep purpose and potential opportunity.

Any movement outside the narrow lines placed before us, would, by definition, separate us from the pack and expose us to danger. As such, we were bred to be pawns on somebody else's chess board. An archetype that most men never quite mature out of.

Indeed, *The Willing Pawn* was born before you ever had a chance to protest his influence. From the moment you came into this world, you've been bred into a life of meeting expectation and appeasing authority. When you were five, the rewards may have been a new toy or the rare praise of your father. Twenty years later, you're still playing the same game. Auctioning off 50+ hours per week for the mere pittance of weekend Costco runs and an annual teeth cleaning.

When purpose is amputated from spirit, life becomes linear and predictable. You can take safety in being surrounded by so many who've chosen the same path. Marching along in single file, scanning ID cards through rusty turnstiles, fearing the economy, leasing a new Toyota every five years. The life of a pawn is relatively simple. It's a well-worn script with only so many moves available to contemplate. For in abdicating self-leadership, you relinquish the need for a constant sense of purposefulness. In being dragged along on a second-hand mission, you get to take your marching orders rather than writing your own, and dodge responsibility for any calamitous end.

It's a tempting trade-off. Your physical survival, at least in the short term, doesn't depend on awakening self-leadership and purpose. A withering soul doesn't light up a CAT scan. An empty heart still beats. And a half-dead man is still technically alive.

Like the pawn on the chessboard, the sacrifice is only evident in the moment before he's knocked off the board. And on the day you perish, you will get no apology from those you've auctioned your purpose off to. You will have no one to blame. Your bravest option will be to feel and express the grief and rage as fully as you can, and let your legacy be one of caution and courage misplaced, lest you be implicit in placing the next pawn on the board.

This tragic tale—the sad story of the purposefully vacant, half-hearted man dragging his feet through the motions is nothing short of a Stockholm-syndrome-of-the-soul. Sure, he may offer a modest protest in the form of a limp-wristed complaint. Maybe three beers deep he finally touches upon the first layer of sorrow, and expresses a fledgling desire to break free and reclaim his life. But sober thoughts in drunken states never lead to skillful action. In the end, this man is more or less destined to rationalize his predicament, and justify his implicit agreement to stay stuck and subjugated. Identifying, and even sympathizing, with his imagined captors.

But you can't learn to love what you do any more than you can learn to love the rival football club. You can't authentically sign off on a mission that isn't dear to your heart any more than you can wed a partner who doesn't light up your soul.

Sure, you can love the confidence that comes from doing something you're good at. Likewise, you can shoot down psychological sorbets all day long, and reframe your situation until you're blue in the face and black in the heart. But do not delude yourself into thinking you've escaped the prison walls. A prison cell well decorated with motivational posters and token rewards is still a prison cell.

So what keeps a man stuck in his cell? What makes him play dead and succumb to this dreaded Stockholm syndrome of the soul?

Once again, we must turn a hard stare to the shackles of expectation he's been born into. The invisible hand of parents, partners, friends, colleagues, culture and country that have imposed their will on him. The invisible hand that would twist and distort his authentic purpose to better suit theirs.

With every expectation imposed on you, you're chained to a rusty anchor that weighs down your every movement. For when expectation is imposed and accepted, you trade in your own spontaneous, authentic expression, and the skill and speed in which you can follow it.

Everything gets filtered through the fear of betraying those expectations. Truth becomes muddied. The pursuit of it infused with fear, guilt and shame. And the friction too coarse and abrasive to generate any momentum in a direction of your authentic choosing. With soul-deep lacerations, life becomes a game of inner pacification and outer appeasement.

This appears in the subtle guilt complex that arises in the twenty-year-old man who wants to take a year off from college to travel through South America, yet feels a greater sense of guilt and shame with each passing semester.

It's the man, four years deep into medical school, who can't honor his genuine awakening to be a poet or a painter, lest he be judged by those around him. Sunk costs, subtle-shaming, and stinging guilt keep him locked into an ill-suited script.

It's the man who's expected to marry—and to have kids—and to stay at his job until he has another one lined up to replace it. It's the man who has countless hurdles and hoops to jump through before stepping into the authentic mission that should've preceded them all.

It's the man who has to satisfy an ever-changing, ever-growing list of conditions and expectations before he's earned the right to taste the sweet nectar flowing out from his own heart.

The unfortunate truth is that most men will only ever escape the chains of expectation long after their hearts have stopped, and their dusty bones have slipped through the iron cracks. But it need not be this way. The escape is always available to the man who places his sense of purpose above all else. The shackles of expectation are not impenetrable. They're vulnerable to the virtues of courage and truth. Melting under the inner flame of the warrior who declares his sovereignty and abides by his word.

Hold no illusion. This is challenging. But you do your loved ones no favors by staying chained to their set of expectations. You mustn't be implicit in creating or perpetuating a situation where only rage and resentment can thrive. For where expectation begins, your authentic pursuit of purpose ends. And where expectation persists, resentment reigns free, eventually stitching itself to every action you take.

Yet resentment is nothing more than a self-inflicted reaction to your perceived powerlessness. A passive aggressive "revenge" taken against those imposing their expectations on you, and "preventing" your movement towards your truest calling. Taken across a long enough timeline, the subjugated can only ever rage against the one subjecting.

You can't truly offer your love to your parents or partner if you inwardly experience them as an oppressive force, subjecting you to a list of soul-crushing expectations. Compromise is the lowest form of expression a relationship can take. It's not sealed with the stamp of trust and love, but in the bloodstained ink of rage and resentment.

The call then is to break free from the chains of expectation. Not as an act of cathartic rage or ill-willed defiance, but as an expression of unconstrained love. Love of self. Love of other. Love of life. Love of mission. Love of the very thing that animates you into physical existence and keeps blood surging through your veins.

Understand that the pawn can never love the queen. He can only die in her service. He can move in one direction—mindlessly, like cattle to the slaughter. Yet the Queen is life herself. She is flow. She is to be honored, revered and protected at all costs. She doesn't want a heartless martyr. She won't mourn the loss of a pawn. She wants a skillful warrior who fully recognizes that service to her, and service to his mission, are inseparable. He's ready to perish in that pursuit, yet he is not resigned to that hopeless fate. He honors life fully, and as long as there's a move to be made and a heart that still beats, he boldly makes it.

This is the man the Queen desires. She will knight the warrior and crown the king. But only if he's first chosen to accept and express as that role.

My brother, it's time to awaken *The Willful Warrior*.

King's Log

1. Where are my actions still guided by the expectations of others?
2. What areas of my life are no longer in accordance with a true calling or sense of purpose? Why do I allow them to persist? What consequences do I fear? How real and likely are those consequences?
3. If I had a hundred million dollars in my account, what expectations would I no longer tolerate being placed upon me? Why do I allow them now? Will ongoing compliance truly free me "someday"?
4. Who is it that feels fear, guilt or shame around forging my own path?
5. Who is it that equates my own purpose or journey with disappointing others?

King's Word

1. It is my highest will and intent to become totally free from the imposition of others' expectations on me.
2. I am totally and completely sovereign in expressing my own will, mission, and sense of purposefulness.
3. I courageously invite and call in a sense of purposefulness to guide my every action and decision, knowing and trusting the rewards that inevitably follow.

Embodied Inquiry

1. What would it feel like to be effortlessly free and sovereign from the expectations of others?

2. How did I become so willing to live in the fullest expression of my purpose in every moment?

3. What would it feel like to be deeply connected to my own power, mission and sense of purpose at all times—embodying it with natural confidence and ease.

The Willful Warrior as Chainbreaker

The Willful Warrior exercises and expresses his personal will with ease and power, while compassionately releasing himself from anyone and anything that would attempt to claim his power as their own, including limited and outdated aspects of his own self. He does so not as a violent rebellion against "other", but a deep-hearted reclamation and honoring of his own power—and the kingdom from which he seeks to build. In more practical terms, it's a movement towards becoming more himself. A simple concept which may unpack a lifetime of laboring as he rips through the masks and superimposed molds through which his most potent and pure energy gets expressed through.

Like a magician summoning the spirits, the "conditioned," "egoic" and "social" selves are evoked, conjured and *given* to the motivations, expectations and influences of those around him; or the culture he's allowed himself to be assimilated within.

This concept need not be esoteric. It's hidden in plain sight and in our everyday languaging. *"She brings out the best (or worst) in me"* and *"I like who I am when I'm with you"* point to fluid, ever shifting personality constructs, or more accurately, manifestation of emotion and behavior that's influenced by those we're in contact with.

In short, we're bundles of intent-infused energy and potentialities that coalesce, and achieve momentary cohesion around whatever ideas or expectations are imposed on us. Most of which are not our own, even if they appear as such.

What brings this out is a bit more complex and mysterious. But what's clear is that until we're authentically who we are, regardless of intermingling influences, we're still being shaped from the outside in.

Expectation is an evoking force. And until we've cultivated our awareness to notice how and where we're being "evoked," or perhaps more accurately "provoked" and triggered, liberation won't be gained. Nor will the steady progress towards an aligned goal, and a sense of purposefulness that precedes it.

While many men blindly believe themselves to be free, *The Willful Warrior* dares to notice where he's still being influenced or shackled to the expectations and subtle commands of others. This is brave and necessary work, for he rightly acknowledges that expectation and external influence, however subtle, are still barriers towards the fullest expression of his truth.

For example, a married father with a young child will never be able to fully rise to the occasion while still hooked into old identities, beliefs and expectations that "life should be easy" or that *"I'm a bachelor whose main goal (and right) is to sleep with as many women as I please without consequence."*

He becomes scattered and dissonant. Perpetually dissatisfied and impaired in his capacity. A prisoner to competing forces and doctrines from both beyond and within himself. It's maddening and tortuous; with no end and no victory to be claimed. For appeasing an endless list of contradicting expectations and influence is the game of fools. For the king, a more noble, yet arduous goal remains.

His end goal is his personal sovereignty, and the free *will* to express it. Yet free will only becomes "free" when it's fully unshackled from the limiting and binding influence and expectations of others.

In our work, "negative influence" is used as a relative term. It's defined as any influence or expectation that runs counter, or non-supportive to your personal truth or consciously chosen purpose. It's the total sum of expectation, influence and agenda that's been both imposed on you, and unconsciously accepted.

It's common to reject parents, partners and "society" as a whole for the expectations they quite naturally try to impose on you—whether overt or subtle. Yet this wholesale rejection is the mark of the fearful man—not the sovereign king, and the willful warrior who serves him. And the violent rebellion, as is so often the case, is too brash and sudden to extract the rich insight that comes through a more gradual peeling of the layers.

At his core, *The Willful Warrior* holds a mature view over reality. To demand the world ceases in its subtle and unconscious manipulations and influences, or worse, self-exile himself from them, is both impractical and unnecessary.

The Willful Warrior, on the other hand, can fully allow those around him to hold opinion or preference over how he lives his life, rules his mind, and builds his kingdom. The difference is, he's become effortlessly immune to that influence. In becoming unshackled to those expectations, he can allow them to be as they are without feeling fused or bound to them in any way.

He feels no obligation. No guilt or shame in pursuing his own path. And no hidden resentment or hatred towards those who'd otherwise suppress him with their agendas. The insight he gleans is that fear, resentment, and rage are in of themselves a binding force. They further entangle oneself to the very subjects he wishes to be liberated from. They maintain and prolong the life of an imagined victim, and the powerlessness he exhibits.

Finally, as *The Willful Warrior* unshackles himself from the world, he also loosens his child-like expectations of the world. He is conscious in wielding his own influence. He's aware of the unspoken expectations and insistences he's placed on others, discarding all those that are limiting, and transforming the useful and necessary ones into consciously crafted and well-stated boundaries and agreements.

For any man whose own expectations of others make him vulnerable to being triggered or flung into an unflattering state, is shackled by his own immaturity. Unshackling will culminate in a deep and unflinching examination of where he shackles others, as well as himself. For in his inquiry, he realizes that they're both one of the same.

Beyond this initiation, this process is ongoing—with more freshness, aliveness and liberation achieved as each subsequent self-limiting chain is broken. Until one day, he realizes himself unshackled completely. Utterly at peace, devoted to his purpose, and expressed fully in his power.

The markings of such a king are undeniable. They are the light under which all men find a glimmer of hope to break free in their own right. They are the flickering flames, generously offering their brilliant light to any man ready to break free in the name of their own fiery purpose.

A king he is, and a king he inspires in all. So too, a king you shall become.

Awakening The Willful Warrior

Sword in hand, ever at the ready, *The Willful Warrior* is what delivers you back to life.

He is the perfect balance between desire and duty. Between Intention and action. He never dwells excessively in what he "might" do. He never lets his dreams or intentions rot and sour in the lockbox of his mind. He moves swiftly and deliberately, recognizing that purpose-driven desire is an erratic and ever-fleeting energy that requires motion to persist. It needs to be swung through his sword, and pierced into the reality presented before him.

In this, *The Willful Warrior* is in full attention, in service to the moment. Neither humble nor noble. Simply a breathtaking display of love and power that weds life in all her radiant forms. He places no judgment on the moment before him, accepting each one as an opportunity to be intentional and purposeful. Accepting each swing of the sword as holy and sacred as the one that preceded it.

The lion doesn't judge his chase. The python will strangle and swallow whatever prey you place before him. And *The Willful Warrior*, awakened and embodied, will never undermine, judge, or delay his own swing. His swing is uninhibited. Sheathed neither by fear nor cowardice. It's not dulled and constrained by a deluge of thought and self-judgment. It's not weighed down by the past nor made too light by his airy thoughts of the future. It's not given too much importance nor too little. Everything is natural—imbued with the same level of grounded reverence.

A million-dollar deal and a five-dollar meal you treat a street beggar to are of equal value. Skillfully birthed from the moment before you, and your naturally arising purposefulness within it. Whether your mind deems it revolting or remarkable, understand that you are inherently worthy of the moment before you. It can be no other way. Likewise, the moment is worthy of you.

In this sacred pact, a constant sense of purposefulness is awakened and expressed. It's where *The Willful Warrior* places himself on the chessboard in service of his Queen—of life *herself*—knowing that doing so is inseparable from his own purpose and mission. He is ever ready to swing his sword and act in his highest good, He's a man of natural, decisive action. It's his honor and blessed duty to act.

And as the chains of expectation are released, the *Willing Pawn* and all he ever stood for is relinquished from your heart and mind. Our warrior assumes his own credo. He doesn't put the past on a faulty pedestal. He isn't swayed by the lives of lesser men. He resists the whirlpool of rage, regret and unchecked resentment that the majority of his brothers remain spiraling down.

It is time for these qualities to become your qualities. In your purest expression of purposefulness, you'll neither self-inflate with importance and superiority, nor become excessively modest, collapsing yourself into self-imposed smallness to better accommodate the aching hearts of lesser men. You'll cease fearing the sunk costs of past decisions. You'll de-credentialize all those you've granted authority over your life to. You'll unshackle from expectation, and release back to the sacred pact with life *herself*—allowing her, and only her, to reveal the mighty, ever-shifting, ever-evolving purpose before you.

Rather than being frozen in time, holding out solely for some grand mission that's yet to appear, your sole focus is on the next swing of your sword, knowing that it will inevitably reshuffle the deck and provide you with a new reality to orient around.

Rather than making ironclad commitments that feel oppressive and burdening, you'll make a few key agreements, allowing yourself to be beholden to them only for as long as you can do so with a generous heart and aroused spirit. You'll recognize all agreements as temporary, subject to change, and only enforceable so long as they remain in service to all parties within them.

In this, you are free. Your sense of purpose is awakened. It's time to breathe the air. Become *The Willful Warrior* you are—and to express the generous gift that at your core, you've always been.

Welcome home, Warrior.

Crowning The Willful Warrior

The guided initiation into *The Willful Warrior*
is available to stream at:

www.iseeyouking.com/purpose

Evolutionary Accelerators

Evolutionary Accelerator #1: Find Purpose in Everything

Practice Duration: Ongoing (start with an hour)

Practice Frequency: As often as possible

Description:

Living with a sense of purposefulness is a muscle that we must start working out. In many cases, it's been completely atrophied from prolonged periods of coasting, checking out, or simply "getting by."

The irony is, so many men will wait for years, tolerating a deadening career or relationship, waiting for "purpose" to swoop in and pull them into a more aligned and favorable reality. But you must meet it halfway. You must resonate with the same frequency that true purpose will find its match in. Failure to do so is akin to attempting to deadlift 1,000 pounds when you haven't even been in the gym for a decade.

To become more readily available to "purpose," begin by finding purpose in the seemingly mundane. Whether that purpose is to make someone feel more love and support in your presence, or to inject creativity, resourcefulness, and insight into every situation, your first step is to simply reclaim an inner orientation around being purposeful.

It's only when you can practice finding purpose in every fleeting moment that you can ready yourself for the grand purpose of your life.

For a full day, and as often as you can, will yourself to do so. Find purpose in everything. Every encounter, every action, every conversation. Make that moment-by-moment purpose soul affirming and enlivening. In service of both yourself and all those around you. Stamp each moment with your own signature, gifting it presence and skillful action.

This is already in line with the inner workings of your body. Every function is purposeful, dynamically awakening to a new purpose as soon as the last one has been completed. Your circulatory system has a purpose, your right ventricle has a purpose, every cell within every organ, bone or tissue has a dynamically shifting purpose that changes with the demands placed upon it. Your goal should be to mirror this dynamically shifting purpose.

As such, every interaction should be purposeful. If you're handing a toddler a bowl of oatmeal, your sense of purpose is to nourish and strengthen him. Imbue that action with such intent.

If your partner is sharing details about her day, your purpose is to exhibit greater non-judgmental presence and compassion, and offer her a chance to feel seen and heard.

If your employee is asking for a raise, other than feeling victimized and burdened by such a demand, your purpose is to tune into the wisdom of where a win-win might exist, and how his skill and sharpened commitment can be more effectively directed towards the "grand" purpose of your business.

If you're struggling to find a purpose in every moment, call on your inner wisdom with a silent, *"I see you, King"* affirmation, and act intuitively with what arises.

At the end of a full day of living purposefully, take some time to journal on how you feel. Was the day more tiring or energizing? Do your inner tools feel sharper or duller? And most of all, do you feel like you've taken a vital step towards a long-lost reclamation of your inner warrior?

Evolutionary Accelerator #2: Unshackling from Expectation

Practice Duration: 1 hour
Practice Frequency: Every 2-3 months

Description:

Most men claim to feel disconnected or blind to their purpose. It's unavailable to them no matter how hard they think. But just like a man in chains can't spread his wings, a man bound by the expectations of others can't soar to higher purpose.

Purpose will only ever find a sovereign man who's ready to live it into existence. To do so, we must first recognize where you're still bound by the expectations, unspoken agreements and influence of others.

Take some time every few months to make an "audit" of what expectations are placed on you from the following sources.

When your list is complete, review each item and consciously revoke that unspoken agreement or expectation. Do so primarily as a solo practice, but you may also compassionately call out and break free from those implied agreements and expectations with others; so long as you feel it can be done without blame or aggression.

1. Parents

What are (or were) your parents' expectations of you? What were their unspoken assumptions, agreements, entitlements or insistences? Around your career, education, partner and lifestyle choices?

List what comes to mind, and for each, ask yourself, *"Am I totally and completely free from this expectation or influence? Have I released myself fully from any subtle guilt, fear or shame in pursuing my own path? From the idea that my personal sovereignty can ever be a source of pain, suffering or disappointment?"*

When your list and contemplation is complete, go through each item and, with full authority, state through the king's word:

I hereby revoke all spoken or unspoken, conscious or unconscious, explicit or implicit, duty, obligation or agreement to continue abiding by this expectation, influence, or insistence. May the energy released return fully to me and be re-channeled for my highest good and purpose.

2. Partners / Spouses

What does your partner (previous or current) expect from you? What are their unspoken assumptions, agreements, entitlements or insistences around your job or career, your lifestyle choices, your sexuality, your body and your care and affection?

List what comes to mind and, for each, repeat the contemplation and release process noted above.

3. Society (or the world as a whole)

What does society or the world as a whole expect from you? What are their unspoken assumptions, agreements, entitlements or insistences around your job or career, the way you conduct yourself, your lifestyle choices and unspoken "moral" codes?

List what comes to mind and, for each, repeat the contemplation and release process noted above.

4. Finally, yourself.

What expectations have been drilled so deeply that you've made them your own?

List what comes to mind and, for each, repeat the contemplation and release process.

Chapter 7:

FIRE 4 - FATHERHOOD

What makes this an initiatory fire?

Of all the initiatory fires you'll confront in your lifetime, fatherhood is perhaps the most challenging and confronting. Unlike the slow burn of all the other fires, fatherhood is a raging inferno you get thrust into without much preparation. You're dropped in and forced to transform.

This process is neither controlled nor self-paced. It's a direct hit. A blunt-force trauma to your previous identity as a man, and the predictable structures it once relied upon. There's very little you can do to prepare for the extreme event of becoming a father. You'll fight. You'll flail. And, in your weakest moments, you'll temporarily succumb to total utter collapse. Collapse of your dreams. Collapse of your mission. Collapse of your relationship. Collapse of every entitlement you've held so dear.

You'll experience the momentary despair and hopelessness of a man being pushed to his absolute edge. Complete and total overwhelm, where many of the tools and strategies you successfully relied upon in your previous life are now rendered useless. Like trying to rip through a thick steel door with a dull hatchet. Yet you'll bang and hack and cry and scream, for you know your freedom is on the other side of that steel door. Overmatched and exhausted, you'll die the necessary death. You'll let this fire consume you. You'll let the man die, and the king rise. For only *he* possesses the key.

Fatherhood is initiation of the highest order. No man survives this fire. And the entirety of your inner and outer kingdom is reconfigured around this monumental force. Let's begin with your relationship. No matter how bulletproof and invincible you once thought your relationship to be, all of a sudden, you *get it*. You get why the statistics are so prophetically dire. You come to see it's not that fifty percent of marriages fail, it's that fifty percent of families collapse under the seemingly insurmountable pressure. And that's if you're only using divorce rates as the measuring stick. If you use true happiness, growth and fulfillment, that number would be excruciatingly higher.

Here's why:

I want you to imagine a scenario for a second that in a single sacred breath, your life will be completely uprooted from its core and shaken up in a new, ultra-challenging configuration. You'll go from playing life on a relative "easy mode" to "hard mode" without the cheat codes or practice reps to fall back on. The demands on you will increase exponentially. Financial demands may double, while productive, focused hours will be slashed by the same factor. You'll be taxed emotionally, mentally, physically and spiritually more than you ever have in your life. Your opportunities for deep renewal and self-care will all but vanish.

You'll be giving more of yourself than ever before—your energy, attention, body and vital resources—and the badge of honor you covet after each successful "conquest" will be replaced by the next list of seemingly insurmountable tasks.

All the small luxuries you thought you needed to perform in your career, business and relationship will be stripped from you—your hour of silence in the morning, your epic morning routine, your spontaneous, mission-driven sojourns into the wilderness, dropping it all and taking your wife to Paris for the weekend.

All gone. At best, filtered through a passion-sucking list of negotiations, planning and compromise. The spontaneity and free-flowing joy extinguished. Inspired plans are no longer immediately pursued. The once life-giving pursuit of one's mission, now subject to an intolerable latency period.

It's an emasculating experience. Yes, logically, you can understand and rationalize it all. You can accept the shared demands and responsibilities. You can "answer the call" and talk about gender roles all day long. You can empathize and understand your partner's potentially lessened capacity for connection and intimacy. But don't confuse tepid acceptance with a merciful ceasefire where the more primal aspects of your inner warrior, provider or business owner aren't being rained down on by a thousand tiny arrows.

Such denial will only prolong a battering sense of false bearability. The truth is, you're going to be called to offer more of yourself than ever before, while feeling woefully under-resourced.

Once again, the survival rate is nil. You can only die in these flames and rise anew. Most men resist stepping into this fire. They may not give voice to it, but the resistance comes from the deep inner knowingness of the ego death that would be necessary to survive. It's a death and a rebirth that still isn't given proper space to occur.

While the initiation into motherhood is more recognized, though admittedly not celebrated, revered and supported nearly as much as it should be, a man's initiation into fatherhood is all but ignored. At best, he's expected to rise with nothing short of unwavering impeccability, with the subtle shaming of any false step along the way. At worst, men are relegated to a support rule. An unreliable, yet occasionally useful prop. Conditioned into believing their own clumsiness instead of trained and encouraged to access their own life-giving strength and capacity.

Fathers simply aren't gifted the "right" to feel the enormity and intensity of what they're stepping into. Instead, they feel the stinging shame when they collapse under the pressures they've been ill-equipped to endure—and the self-hatred that comes with every forced smile and slumped stance along the way.

But it's in this same fire that the unforgiving bleakness is melted under a beacon of inextinguishable light. It's where the king is most easily accessed. It's where he awakens. Not through any conscious effort of your own, but within the guttural screams of your partner's final push and the frantic wails that accompany your child's first breath. The king simply can't stay asleep through such an ordeal. Whether or not he gets accessed and integrated into your experience is another matter.

This fire is designed for both fathers and fathers to be. It's an initiatory fire that moves you from a subtle level of selfishness to the sturdy nobility of kingly selflessness. Some authors will create a tidy metaphor so as to not exclude non-fathers. They'll relate the creative process or a new venture to one where you have to embody the "father energy." This isn't false. It's also a participation medal to the real experience. To create a parallel between *actual* and metaphorical fatherhood is to undermine the intensity that every new father will face.

Yet this chapter isn't to be skipped by non-fathers. For nearly all men, there *is* the latent potential of fatherhood. There's a relationship to this fire, child or not. For even resistance to fatherhood is to be in unhealthy and unbalanced relationship to it. The shadows you confront here lie dormant. Untriggered by the seismic force of child rearing that unceremoniously lands at the epicenter of your experience as a man. Yet dormant and worthy of your attention, healing, and reintegration, nevertheless.

If you've been resisting and fearing fatherhood, these unchecked shadows do indeed have influence and reign over your life and your intimate relationship. If you've been passing subtle judgments on friends or strangers who've taken on the role, once again, can you truly claim to be free of these flames?

Finally, the focus here is on the aftershock of early parenthood. Yes, other challenges arise at different stages of parenthood, and those challenges are every bit as worthy of discussion. That said, this process is not about giving parenting advice—but what must precede it. Anything tactical being expressed from a wounded father will be stained with the blood of his unhealed wounds.

Instead, this is about the inner experience of fatherhood. The shadows it illuminates, and the series of awakenings and evolutionary shifts it's here to generously offer. More so than any fire, the prize of awakening isn't gift-wrapped. It's pulled from the darkness, and is ultimately retrieved by the man who plunges headlong with no assurances of his survival.

Let the man dive in—and the king emerge.

Shadow #1: The Rejection of Your Mother's Love

The first shadow we encounter is both the most subtle and powerful. Its influence has been welded to our hearts and tightly fused to our experience since the very early parts of our own lives. It's unavoidable. For this shadow makes its home in the heart of any man who is a son to a mother. This shadow being the rejection of your mother's love.

It may not be explicit. It may not have culminated in some dramatic display. Yet even in its silence, it slices through countless interactions, leaving a winding trail of sharp triggers and biting lacerations that'll haunt us our entire lives.

This shadow torments us in the moment you shirk away from your mother's nurturance. It's when you grunt and sigh when her name flashes on the iPhone screen. It's when you withdraw your love for her and armor yourself from any onslaught of care and affection she feels compelled to offer. It's when her love goes unreceived, unrequited and forcibly fenced off from reaching your heart.

Nearly all sons will at some point resist or reject their mother's love. It's a nearly unavoidable wounding, and a necessary healing. The time for that healing is most ripe and necessary when you step into parenthood yourself. For in continuing to reject your own mother's love, you'll inevitably resist the love that your partner has for your child. You'll judge and condemn her attachment and nurturance. And you'll unconsciously commit the subtlest yet harshest of abuses. Dismissing and denying the divine mother, who, for even just a moment, expressed through your partner in full force.

For some men, they'll experience intense grief. The real-time display of their partner's love to their child may reveal to them a level of nurturance and care that for one reason or another, was unavailable to them as a child. A grief over having missed his own chance at such life-giving warmth. Through this, a subtle jealousy may arise. A victim-laced "what about me", and an even greater condemnation of the bond your partner shares with your child.

This is a shadow many men won't want to look at, for it attacks one's most cherished ideals and self-perception. No one wants to see himself as "envious" of his own child or resentful over his own partner's love and nurturance towards his child. It's also a topic that can't be safely shared with your partner while she's in the throes of her own initiation. Even shared with courage and vulnerability, its potential to trigger and upset is too great. Thus it metastasizes in silence. The rejection of the mother's love strengthened and seeping out in countless microaggressions that can only prolong a cold, dark cycle.

Understand that the love of the divine mother is boundless—it's the most powerful force in the universe. It's the reason you're here reading these very words. Yet rather than meet it with awe and reverence, this shadow will have one shun it and shy away. Rather than celebrate it for the deep mystery and miracle it is, you'll condemn it within the cold dark corner of your heart that's yet to be healed.

Not because you choose to. Not because you want to. But because you've experienced an entire lifetime of rejecting the very same force in your own mother. This is not a dismissal of the toxic forms of control, codependence and subtle abuses that mothers are fully capable of projecting. But it *is* an acknowledgment that even if it's dormant, distorted, or ill-expressed, all mothers possess the seed of unconditional love for their children.

But even if your mother exhibits qualities of control, clinginess, unhealthy attachment and overbearingness, these often stem from the initial wounding of having her boundless love for you go unreceived or silently condemned by your father. At the very least, they're greatly exacerbated by this merciless rejection.

It's taught in popular mythology that a man must "break free" from the mother in order to follow his path and achieve his purpose. This isn't entirely false, but it's also incomplete. We must be willing to question the myths we hold so dear. Where did they originate from? Did they come from a place of deep power, peace and reverence for all life? Or were they borne from pain themselves?

Myths are a momentary truth. But they mustn't be confused for ambassadors of *the* truth—with all the unquestioned authority we'd falsely give them. And in the prevalent myth of the boy violently breaking free from his mother in order to claim his "manliness," a deep questioning is in order.

A boy's heroic leap into freedom and autonomy is indeed part of his evolutionary path. Yet the deed need not be an act of cold-hearted rebellion. True freedom isn't achieved through bloody withdrawal. Boundaries can be set in compassionate power. Paths can be daringly forged without the sting of spitefulness in each step—or the weight of guilt or expectation that would slow us. Most importantly, the divine mother can be honored, appreciated and revered, even when we consciously create healthy distance from the woman who embodies her spark.

We can still allow the purest form of that love to find a home in our hearts. For in dismissing it, we dismiss the throbs of life herself. We condemn the ground beneath our feet. We lament and decry the source of our very existence. Simply put, we can't deny the mother's love without denying ourselves.

The irony is that boys simply aren't conditioned to be able to receive this love. In some cases, we'll feel guilt and even rage in receiving it while we watch our fathers' hearts sour. We'll experience our mother's love as a finite resource that's been misallocated to us at the expense of our father. In other cases, the intensity is too strong for the small, rigid container of what's acceptable. By the time we're in our teenage years, we'll harshly resist it, distort it and ultimately force it into a compromised and colorless state where we allow ourselves to receive it only in small doses.

A dual wounding occurs. We're wounded by our inability to openly receive this powerful source of love and nurturance. Our mothers are wounded by it going unreceived. And so goes the story, generation after generation, weaving its way through our ancestral bloodline, until this wound is cauterized in the flames of this fire—and the king vows to show his son a better, more life-affirming way.

The healing that awaits is long overdue.

Let your steely gaze melt.

May your embittered heart open.

And may you cry the saintly tears reserved for the king who's awakened to the errors of the men who came before him.

King's Log

1. In what ways do you (or have you) rejected your mother's love? Why?

2. What's your immediate reaction to her embrace? To her words "I love you"? To her call? Why is that?

3. What boundaries has she unknowingly overstepped throughout your life? Have you communicated them with compassion and power?

4. How do you *really* feel about your partner's love and affection for your child / children? What's driving that reaction?

5. Must a man "break free" from his mother to claim his own sovereignty? If such a distancing is necessary, is it a physical, emotional, or energetic one?

King's Word

1. I forgive myself totally and completely for any rejection or resistance I've had of my own mother.

2. I forgive myself totally and completely for any responsibility I've felt over my father feeling unmet or uncherished by my mother.

3. I forgive myself totally and completely for any rejection, resistance or resentment I've had towards my partner over her love of my child.

4. I come into healthy and sovereign relationship with my own mother, regardless of her own personal capacity to be in healthy relationship.

5. I cherish and honor the divine mother through which I came, and celebrate "her" in all her life-giving forms.

Embodied Inquiry

1. What would it feel like to be in natural and effortless appreciation and reception of my mother's purest love?

2. What would it feel like to be in natural and effortless appreciation of my partner's love for my child?

3. How did I become so capable of experiencing and allowing unconditional and unwavering love?

4. What would it feel like to experience the awe and reverence for my partner's initiation into motherhood, and the divinity being expressed through her?

Shadow #2: The Man in Exile & The Martyr

Like the *Black Widow*, who kills her mate after she's been impregnated, men often feel expendable in the weeks, months and years following fatherhood.

Grievously reduced to a resource, his dreams and desires immediately feel sacrificed. Back-burnered to an indefinite someday. His flexibility and threshold for bold action and spontaneous adventure slashed. Metaphorically speaking, men are swallowed whole by the experience. Wounded, bloodied and ultimately martyred for a cause they were never quite privy to. There's a tragic irony in this. How an act that brings life can feel so deadening. Yet in many ways, it is.

The things that once made you feel *alive*—being in the throes of timeless passion with your partner, the blissfulness of inspired action, cracking the code of your craft, triumphing over some foe, merging into blissful silence. All gone, or at the very least, greatly reduced.

The things you once relied on for your sustenance as a man have now been withdrawn, withheld, and ruthlessly drained from the energy pumping through your veins. Freedom now comes at a cost. To "bail" and give yourself the sanctuary or space of creation now comes at a toll to your partner who relies on your presence and support. In very rare cases can you escape for a day or a week or a month without the associated guilt or resentment.

Likewise, you may suddenly feel abandoned by your relationship—exiled from your "place" in life, and desperately trying to restore what can't be restored. For it has to be reimagined and rebirthed within this new context. Date nights replaced with diaper runs. Day trips replaced with doctor visits. A bold daringness replaced with weighty, zero-sum decisions.

Culturally, the depiction of the father is bleak. We see movies and shows of the man who's been emasculated by the experience. Defeated. Succumbed. Worn down and bleary-eyed. Trotting the drug store aisles with a soulless gaze akin to sedated cattle marching to the slaughter. With such an overwhelmingly bleak and impotent depiction of early fatherhood, rarely does a man actually get to define his own experience.

The man has indeed been exiled. His old identity, swallowed whole.

Two options remain:

To continue to be vacant. A mere corpse moving through the motions. Limp-wristed and resigned to his cruel fate, waiting for freedom to somehow return.

Or to succumb to the necessary death and wake up to new levels of leadership. To be the brilliant, inextinguishable light your family can orient around. To speak difficult truths and to exercise extreme and unreasonable levels of love, strength, and compassion. To not go out with a resigned whimper, but return with a mighty roar that reclaims his power, and declares, in no uncertain terms, that this is indeed his rightful kingdom.

While the "man" loses his place—this vacancy exists only for the king to claim. No throne should be left bare. And once claimed, it becomes clear that the man in exile was simply in service to the king. That the black widow, swallowing her partner whole, is *not* the cold-blooded killer that she appears, but the merciful agent of metamorphosis for the man she loves too much to allow him to wither in resigned victimhood.

We learn experientially that the martyred man had a cause all along.
And that the throne has finally called home its rightful heir.
It calls for you, the king. You hear it. You answer it.
So few dare.
As a father in his power, it is yours, and yours alone to claim.
Welcome home, king.

King's Log

1. In what ways do you feel you've lost your "place" in becoming a father?
2. Have you fully accepted your "new life" as a father, or do you still cling to what has long past and will never return?
3. What aspects of your life and relationship have yet to be grieved, mourned and reimagined within your new context?
4. Without this conscious mourning, how and where have you grown resentful or victimized by the situation?
5. In what subtle ways do you "rebel" against this?

King's Word

1. I vow to reclaim my space within my family, honoring my role as a father and partner while rising as the king I know myself to be.
2. I shed any and all bitterness and resentment in my heart. Instead hearing and responding to the deep inner calling to expand my capacity in every way.
3. Within my family, I allow myself to be seen, honored, cherished and celebrated; as I offer the same to them.
4. It is my highest will and intent to reclaim my rightful place as the powerful, wise and compassionate leader of my family.

Embodied Inquiry

1. What would it feel like to be in my fullest expression of love, strength and power within my family?

Shadow #3: The Rageful and the Resigned

The third shadow is the final threshold before being initiated into kingship within your family. It's the most perilous and confronting of the shadows. It bears a strong resemblance to the previous shadow, particularly the aspect of martyrdom, but carries with it the darker undertones of a man rebelling against himself and those around him. There's a foreboding hum. The swan song of the resigned. The man besieged by the weightiness of fatherhood, and its ceaseless demands.

Where his spirit alone could once rip through steel, we now find him, a dull and rusted blade. Detached and dejected. Bled dry and betrayed. Withered and woeful. There are few things more tragic than the man who's succumbed to an advanced state of resignation.

Resignation is nothing but rage turned inwards. It's self-betrayal. The culmination of stepping too far out of love, alignment and purpose. It's the build-up of a thousand soul-crushing compromises, and the hopelessness and despair of not seeing a clear way out. We witness it every day. The sullen face of the new father is only ever partly induced by a sleepless night. The vacant look, deadened posture and hushed voice barely escaping a clenched jaw all point to a more insidious shadow. It's the shadow left by the man who's experienced a sudden disconnection from his will and purpose. A man who's given up his crown, and vacated his throne.

In many ancient traditions, the king would surrender himself to a ceremonial slaughter should he become too old, weak, and incapable of carrying out his duties. For our modern man who feels limited, disconnected, and incapacitated in his purpose and relationship, such death also feels unavoidable. Exhausted, overstretched and under-supported, he's not unreasonable in his view.

In his rare silent moments, he finds neither respite nor renewal, but the inner screams of the victim who feels bled dry, tapped out, and betrayed by both the experience, and the players within it. Yet his view isn't reflective of ultimate truth. It's simply the ghastly wail of his injured self. The "purposeful man," the "spontaneous man," the "supported partner," they lie mangled and maimed in a post-partum battlefield. Front line casualties drafted into a war they never saw coming.

This is indeed the experience of the resigned. You'll feel spiritually battered and beyond repair. You'll crave a warm touch that never seems to come. You'll fight the daily reflex of wanting to give up and burn it all down. Longing for a regressive, infantile fantasy, free of responsibility, that's now impossible to return to without causing irrevocable harm. And, finally, when it all seems a bit "too much," you'll search for the self-eject button. You'll keep it close, ready to be pressed. And maybe, one day, like the men you once judged and condemned, even *you* might press it.

If you pull yourself out of resignation and apathy, it's usually fueled by a slow-simmering rage. A self-righteous rebellion against your imagined captors—your family. You'll begin to rationalize an affair. Or the seductive thought of abandoning your post. With rage so present, it'll all be so easy to justify.

You'll falsely believe yourself to be betrayed by their needs and demands. By their lack of love or concern for you. By their lack of care and support. By their cold-hearted sense of entitlement to you and your gifts. And in the icy fields of betrayal, blame and resentment will take root. Curling around the flowers that once bloomed. Choking out what little love there was left to nourish them.

Years will go by. Dreams already withered. Love a fleeting memory. Flooded with shame and regret, you'll use your family as an excuse for abandoning your dreams. You'll blame them and hold them responsible. In doing so, you'll commit the most damaging and reckless of crimes. For there are few greater crimes than blaming your family for your inability to lead your way out of the dark night.

Your child won't bear the burden of your unlived dreams, nor the life you refused to live. Your child isn't the muzzle on your unexpressed truths. On the contrary, your child is the first person completely willing to see you as king. Even before you've claimed your crown.

Likewise, your partner doesn't want to sink down with a slave. She wants to rise up and stand with a king. She desperately needs to feel you take that stand. To share your truth. And she's ready to support it the moment you drop the victim story—the illusory sacrifice no one asked you to make. Your sacrifice isn't real. It isn't imposed. It's simply the story you tell yourself to absolve yourself of the responsibility to rise in purpose.

"I'm doing it for my family." The issue is less with the phrase itself than with the underlying energy. The resigned whimpers of a self-martyred man. Yes, do it for your family—so long as you're doing it for yourself, your soul, and for the greater good you wish to create in the world.

Man is not a lifeless piece of machinery. Man's worth isn't measured by how much he's willing to endure, but by how little he's willing to hide behind the veil of sacrifice in neglecting his dreams.

No, king. Don't do it *for* your family, do it *with* them. Work towards a shared reality, a shared dream, a shared kingdom. One they're deeply involved and implicated in. One they'll be proud to inherit. Let your legacy be one worth retelling. Let them be steeped with tales of your rise, not of your hopeless collapse within the chokehold of despair. King, your time is now.

It's always darkest before dawn. The king's path home isn't a well-lit journey. It's an unaccompanied gauntlet through the stabbing blows of these untamed shadows. If he survives the night, the blood will dry. The wounds will heal. And the kingdom shall once again be his.

Be steady, king.

Hold strong.

And let the first crack of dawn announce your reign to all.

King's Log

1. In what ways have you already "given up" on a sense of fulfillment within your family life?

2. In what ways has that resignation been accompanied with blame and rage towards their "role" in it?

3. In what ways do you view and experience yourself as a "resource" that's been bled-dry? Is it true? How and where can you experience self-renewal?

King's Word

1. It is my highest will and intent to shed all stories, identities and beliefs that would have me experiencing myself as a "depleted" resource incapable of renewal.

2. I release all feelings of rage and resentment towards my family for the erroneous belief that they're responsible for my struggle.

3. I use this struggle as the source of power for awakening of my inner king; knowing that the only true endpoint is one of revelation and renewed power.

Embodied Inquiry

1. What would it feel like to be totally rejuvenated, renewed and ready to rise as the king within my family?

Awakening The King

With the death of the man comes the rise of *The King*.

The king is mortal. He is neither tyrant nor ruler. Rather, his claim is sealed in service and leadership. He carries the extreme weight of caring for his constituents and himself. He holds his entire realm in proper balance—while responding to threat, both inner and outer, with power and skill.

He possesses foresight and leadership. Discernment and direction. He's aware of his capacities, both active and dormant, and chooses his battles based on the resources available.

He never wages an unwinnable war. He never spreads his resources too thin. While he expands his awareness to include his sense of purpose, his mission, his child, his partner, his tribe, his business, his full-spectrum health, and his creative aspirations, he's ruthless and disciplined in maintaining a narrow focus.

Deliberate and exact, he withdraws his energy and resources from battles and campaigns that no longer serve his highest good. His priorities are drastically trimmed. His empire lines are drawn inwards, closer to home. Narrower but firmer. Defensible. And in his deepest moments of contemplation, the king realizes that the world's greatest empires have fallen not due to lack of power, but in the dilution of that power across extended borders. Borders that became untenable, and ultimately vulnerable to collapse. Empires borne not from true will, but from ego-based expansion. From the conqueror's small, temporal self, seeking to catch up to the "infinite" he'll never know himself as.

In his realization, he comes to see that skipping the football game with the boys is no longer a bloodless sacrifice, but in service to the kingdom he's chosen to nourish and solidify. He no longer mourns the "nice to have" side-hustle that's occupied his weekends. Unless it's a true calling, he allows it to gently slip off the bone. He no longer grieves the perceived loss of his freedom, but celebrates the newfound freedom within his chosen set of constraints.

Half-heartedness dies. Ambivalence and apathy are relinquished. Anything he's been tepid or lukewarm about no longer has a place in his kingdom. For it takes extreme heat for any mission to be forged to the sword he wields. It's a heat that can't be faked. But a concentrated furnace built within the heart of his most genuine longings and desires.

In common parlance, he doesn't engage in anything that doesn't light up every part of his being. He resigns from all unnecessary positions, and fiercely doubles down on the ones that bring greater life and power to his kingdom.

Within his noble position, he dares strive to know his true capacity. He expands beyond the faint murmurs of the victim or an infantile "self" craving collapse at first challenge. He relishes in the opportunity to know just how deep his strength goes and how far his endurance extends. He is not plagued by the demands of strength, focus and endurance, but called up by them. If he was a "high performer" in his pre-fatherhood days, he's now a wide performer. Bringing every bit the focus, energy and effectiveness as he did in a single endeavor, except now across multiple ones. Neither more important nor less important. All occupying a rightful place within his kingdom.

Within the walls of his castle, he commits to complete integrity, never striving for an artificial harmony. He doesn't sheath his truth but wields it with compassionate power. Leadership often requires addressing uncomfortable truths, and dwelling in impossible questions. Questions with no immediately foreseeable answers, yet questions that sour and become fatal when left unexamined. He dares to sit in the unanswerable—to seek council when needed, and to act boldly and skillfully with whatever insights emerge from that space.

Similarly, the king must make decisions that aren't always popular. They are, of course, rooted in loving service and a far-reaching awareness to hold the entire realm in mind. He is careful to examine his intent. The hidden saboteurs of vengeful pride and the rageful victim who would weaponize his decisions. He grows in awareness. Becomes more sensitive to the underlying intent in all he does. And through this all, he resists exile. He maintains his post. He remains centered on his throne even when it's cold and thorny. He speaks uncomfortable truths with care and compassion, and through the discomfort, earns greater levels of resilience, capacity, and vigor.

Yes, practically speaking, fatherhood is a call for you to awaken to extreme, even impossible, levels of leadership. To step into a place where serving your family becomes a genuine blessing. Whether it's celebrated or not. Honored or not. Appreciated or not. It is *your* privilege and duty to rise. Not because it's easy. Not because the rewards are obvious and sugar-packed. Simply because you *can*. It's an innate capacity not rooted in martyrdom and sacrifice, but in the sacred pact between you and your highest power.

Ironically, it's an innate capacity that your *child* will see and acknowledge before you do. Beyond anything you do, the king awakens *within* the act of becoming a father. This is the beauty of initiation. You're forced into this fire the moment your child takes their first breath. No matter how much you protest, resist or recede into old patterns of infantile longing, your reign has been sealed in the moment your child opens their eyes and takes in your face.

Understand this:

No matter how you view yourself, your child sees you as king. Feel him evoke this. See yourself through the eyes that he sees you. Feel that as the holiest of responsibilities, for it is.

All it takes is one person to see you as a king for you to be blessed with a kingdom.

This is the ultimate crowning of fatherhood.

It's not a time to be humble or second-guess your claim.

It's time to exercise it with full right—and full power.

For these flames will tolerate nothing less.

Crowning The King

The guided initiation into *The King* is available to stream at:

www.iseeyouking.com/fatherhood

Evolutionary Accelerators

Evolutionary Accelerator #1: Forgive Your Father

Two of our very first, foundational initiations in life were ones we were immersed in from our very first breath. Being a son to a father; and being a son to a mother.

No matter how admirable our parents were in their roles, there are inevitable wounds that come by mere extension of our less developed (and immature) experience and perception of the world.

At a young age, we naturally held infantile expectations of those around us. From the standards of perfection we may have held them to, to the feelings of fear, abandonment, anger, grief, shame and unworthiness when such impossible standards were inevitably unmet.

Moreover, children tend to "inherit" their parents' experience of the world. A boy will have his orientation or "inner stance" towards relationship, career, life and fatherhood "colored" and "texturized" by what he felt as his father's experience. Rarely is this a wholly positive inheritance—and, as such, one that may inevitably leave a subtle stench of anger or resentment.

There is not a single child-parent relationship that won't require resolution and repair on some level at some point. And the most opportune time to embark on this path towards forgiveness and wholeness, which is really to say, a wider and more mature and compassionate view of reality, is when you're about to become a father yourself. For in having untended and outdated parts of you that are still holding your parents to unrealistic ideals—with the ensuing sense of betrayal from each miss—you condemn yourself to much of the same.

A natural humility arises as you encounter many of the similar challenges (and initiations) that they had. And you may even feel your own sense of guilt or shame for having been so "hard" on them—and being unable or unwilling to offer the warmth, patience or tenderness that such an endeavor would've required.

Either way, at this stage, you must offer your parents forgiveness for their real (or perceived) trespasses and transgressions. You must allow them the humanness and compassion that ultimately you now require. You must re-relate to them in an adult-to-adult way, while still owning the fact that you are inescapably your father's son; with all the loadedness that has come with that territory.

There is no single "right way" to do this. Your present relationship with your father—and whether or not he's still alive in bodily form may dictate what is or isn't available as a method of repair. Rather than being overly prescriptive, I'll propose three options that can be used in isolation or combination.

1. Have a conversation with your father:

If you have a good relationship with your father and can comfortably have a productive and compassionate conversation, propose that you carve out intentional time together. Sit by the fire. Walk in the woods. Be out on the lake. Or simply pull up some dining room chairs if that's what's available.

Your intention should be to offer him, for perhaps the first time, a chance to be honest about his experience of life and fatherhood. Free from the well-patterned "commentary" he's been trained to parrot without piercing into the deeper layers of his actual experience out of fear of being judged or condemned for it.

You're no longer a child needing a whitewashed and sanitized version of what may have been, in actuality, tumultuous and excruciating. He deserves to be witnessed, heard and seen in his fullness—and you deserve a truthful and more complete picture of such a major part of your early life. For what goes unresolved and unaddressed in him, risks going unresolved and unaddressed in you.

The vulnerability you allow in him is ultimately the vulnerability you allow in yourself. Give him space and allowance to have had a less-than-easy experience. Resist a knee-jerk childish instinct to take things personally—or to make yourself a "victim" of his inabilities or incapacities.

Acknowledge that what he has gifted you is infinitely more valuable and powerful than what he's failed to provide. And rest in appreciation for the life you've been provided; and the power you have to shape it.

Ask him about his raw, unfiltered experience in becoming a father:

- How did he feel?
- What were the biggest fears or challenges he confronted in embracing the role?
- What were the sacrifices he made? How did he feel about them?
- How did he feel towards you and your siblings?

- What was he most proud of? (About himself and the way he "rose to the occasion.")
- What would he "do over again" if he had a chance? What does he regret?
- What does he wish was more acknowledged and seen?

Grant him his humanness.

You are neither judge nor jury. In this moment, you are a fellow man, a fellow brother plunged into the initiation of fatherhood, as well as his son. You can hold all perspectives dynamically with an intention towards healing and wholeness for you both.

As simple as it may sound, at some point you must accept that you *are* your father's son. It doesn't have to be experienced with manufactured and forceful pride. But neither should you allow this indisputable fact to exist with shame and contempt. The cleanest way to hold this fact is with infinite gratitude and unconditional compassion.

If your father is no longer physically around, you may still have this "conversation" with him. In an old favorite restaurant of his, or a place he used to take you. A place that still carries his "signature."

2. Write a letter and/or speak to an object

If there's too much "charge" in your relationship to have a productive, honest and healing conversation with your father—or if you truly feel he doesn't have the emotional intelligence or capacity to partake in one—you may engage in this exercise with a letter or via speaking to an object or "stand-in" that represents your father.

The goal is simply to be honest. To express and be seen in where you may be holding onto grudges or unresolved anger of your own. Where you feel like he didn't quite show up for you. Give voice to what may have been locked up for decades—and ultimately move towards resolution and forgiveness. This can be done in a dynamic, free-form kind of way.

If you prefer a more structured process, you may follow these steps:

1. Make a list of the perceived trespasses, transgressions or limitations.
2. For each, ask *"who is it that feels violated, betrayed, resentful or victimized by this?"* and/or *"who is it that's afraid of "becoming this" myself?"*

3. As you do, allow any conglomeration or gestalt of memories, thoughts, emotions, patterns, impressions or "energy signatures" to arise—taking deep breaths with the intention of untangling and processing them out.

4. When you feel complete in this processing stage, ask, "Am I totally and completely incapable of similar transgression?" If the answer is "no," allow a sense of humility, compassion and understanding to arise. A shared ground. Free from the infantile relationship that has been previously upholding the story.

5. And finally, from this place of greater awareness, acceptance and compassion, forgive him fully with the following statement:

6. *I release both you and I from this perceived transgression—and any guilt or shame that's been borne from it. You were doing your best within your capacities. As I am now, within my own role as a father. I love you. I'm sorry. I forgive you. You are my father. I am blessed for the gift of life you've bestowed upon me. This supersedes all inheritances, positive or negative, I've received from you. Likewise, please forgive me for the untenable standards I've held you to. I see you, King.*

7. Conclude by honoring your father: Compile a list of the "positive inheritances" and qualities he's exhibited. List all that you wish to honor, celebrate and acknowledge. Knowing the inherent challenges of fatherhood yourself, you're perhaps in a more aware position to know the strength and endurance many of those positive aspects required.

Evolutionary Accelerator #2: Mend Your Mother Wound

Like the practice above, it would be a tall order to "clear" everything in your parental relationships through a single practice. But you can certainly make great headway—and create enough breathing room and capacity for further work.

The first step to mending a wound is simply noting what's there. Getting a clear idea of its location, depth, size, shape, and scope.

While we already addressed aspects of the "mother wound" in the first shadow of this chapter, you're always invited into deeper and ongoing exploration of what still impedes a compassionate and matured relationship with your mother.

Repeat the process listed above, owning that you are inescapably your mother's son; with all that this entails. Experience tenderness towards you both and ultimately free you both from the unhealed wounds that simply couldn't have been any other way, but now, with expanded awareness and compassion; can be healed and transformed.

Evolutionary Accelerator #3: Claim Your Kingdom

Practice Duration: Seconds

Practice Frequency: Indefinite

Description:

Many men will claim to feel "smallest in their own home." They'll feel an occasional rush of power, recognition, and achievement across their career, business, friendships and hobbies, yet will feel contraction and collapse while stepping through their own front door. An invisible stranger to those he believes are either unable or unwilling to see and know him in his truth and fullness.

His posture will slouch. His voice will crack. His presence will shrink. He'll walk his own halls with muted steps lest he leave a ripple. And in his innermost thoughts, he'll experience the inner torment surrounding the sharp incongruence between how he wishes to be perceived by the world, and who he is within his own four walls.

The invitation is simply to claim the space as *yours*. Neither as petty tyrant nor clumsy fool. But simply because every kingdom needs a king. A child needs his father's most potent and virtuous energies to fill the space. A muted existence serves no one. You are called to step up and leave your signature in the halls you walk and the table you sit. It is not only permitted. It is *needed*.

There's a grave misunderstanding that within a family, "the kids take up all the space." This is only true if the king goes absent. Space is a vacuum that must be filled. You have a duty to fill it with the gifts only you can.

The Practice:

In the moments before you re-enter your home; reaffirm who and what you are within it by repeatedly declaring a silent *"I see you, King."*

Let the power build with each declaration. Knowing that each reaffirmation grants you the power and authority to step into your role as leader, lover, partner, and father. One who gets to be witnessed, honored, and celebrated in his fullness—including his humanness.

As king, this means

1. Crowning your constituents: Gifting them your love, appreciation and generosity.
2. Knowing your worthiness around being seen, witnessed, appreciated.
3. Being fully expressed within your home—leaving no big truths untold or sheathed.
4. Declaring your truths (not to be confused with reactionary aggression).
5. Leading your family with honesty and integrity.
6. Being a trusted steward for the movement and direction of your family (having a vision and plan for actuating it).

This is the home you've made. Failure to take ownership and lay claim to what which you've built isn't only an act of self-betrayal, but a betrayal of those within your kingdom. It's a subtle abandonment.

Abandonment doesn't require physical exile. Most men will self-exile and become a domestic specter far before he is physically removed from his post.

Reclaim your holiest of posts and do so with all the virtues you've already awoken to.

Embodied Inquiry:
1. What would it feel like to reclaim my positive power within my home?
2. What does it feel like to claim my space; and my role as king and leader within it?
3. How did I become so courageous and clear in speaking my truth?

Evolutionary Accelerator #4: Draw Your Empire Lines
Practice Duration: 20 minutes
Practice Frequency: indefinitely

Description:

Many men will fail to recalibrate around the fatherhood experience. They'll see it as a "bolt on" to their past previous life rather than a full reconfiguration.

They'll cling stubbornly to pre-fatherhood ideals, goals and activities. Not because those activities still replenish them or fill them with joy. But because they provide a connection point to a pre-fatherhood state they've yet to properly grieve and mourn.

There is no getting around the fact that the demands on your time, attention and focus will increase exponentially. You would therefore be wise to re-allocate these resources from a place of conscious *choosing*. Otherwise, you risk slipping into victimhood and resentment when "life" forces your hand in these so-called sacrifices.

This exercise is simple:

Create a "not-to-do" list.

One that liberates your resources of energy, presence, attention, focus, etc. to that which is most vital and life-giving to you at this stage of your life.

If a hobby, activity, business or life goal isn't a 9 or 10/10, it's likely *not* an appropriate pursuit for this stage of your life. Let it go, allowing any appropriate sadness and grieving to be experienced, but ultimately feeling the lightness and liberation of having reclaimed a "raw material" far more precious.

Evolutionary Accelerator #5: Duty and Capacity

While freeing up resources in the previous exercise, you must simultaneously accept the new duties placed before you. Because many of the "tasks" you'll now engage with are "new" and replace ones you've held dear (or that have been the basis of a past identity), there may be a knee-jerk reaction to those demands.

Consoling a child at 3 AM. Tending to a grocery store meltdown. Building a Lego castle before bedtime for three hours. They can all feel like undue burdens. But once again, a burden to whom? The king stepping into the holiest of roles. Or a past identity who's yet to be mourned?

When you become a father, a sense of duty is either painstakingly resisted or courageously accepted. Suffering arises from the former, while expanded capacity and self-confidence are the boon from the latter.

In this ongoing exercise, you'll become aware of the knee-jerk resistance to any "fatherhood duty" that's met with resistance or a sense of being a burden.

Instead, you'll gain a renewed sense of purposefulness, choosing to gift yourself to the moment that is fully worthy of your presence by sheer fact of being placed before you. And you'll gradually lean into the possibility that your capacity to be "present" to those moments—and all others that are meaningful to you—is perhaps far greater than you've allowed yourself to know.

As a reminder, you can anchor your fullest capacities with a simple inner repetition of "I see you, king."

Chapter 8

FIRE 5 - YOUR BUSINESS, CAREER AND LIVELIHOOD

What makes this an initiatory fire?

T he average man will spend more than half his waking life physically immersed in this container called "work", and an even greater portion of his life engaged mentally, emotionally and energetically devoted to his craft or livelihood.

Physically, you're likely to spend more time stewing in these flames than any other fire in this program. Half a century of forty-to-fifty-hour workweeks, your business or livelihood *is* the stadium where you get to put your evolutionary growth on full, brilliant display. It's where you get to alchemize all the previous awakenings into a tangible gift that you get to serve the world with, all while attracting the synergistic co-creation and support of your brothers and sisters. Yet for such a pervasive fire, so few will ever awaken to the incredible opportunity before them.

They'll continue to see work as a necessary and unavoidable evil in their lives. An oppressive force that robs them of their happiness, taps out their resources, and ultimately bleeds them dry. And at the crux of man's failed relationship with work are the undertones of powerlessness and defeat that plague the words he uses every day. These constructs are ones that men opt into—knowingly or unknowingly—and reinforce every time they auction off their power for the limited pittance of reward they're temporarily provided.

"I have to work" is the victim-laced tirade of the modern man. How many times have you uttered those words to a lover, friend, or child? How many moments of purpose, adventure and flow have you auctioned off in the name of "work"? How many friendships and relationships have been ruthlessly backburnered—not in the name of intense focus and devotion to craft or mission, but in a resigned whimper packaged into these four words:

"I have to work."

The phrase itself has been laced with the cyanide of resentment and victimhood. It carries with it the bloodless stain of your crippled dreams. The ghastly echoes of a billion deathbed regrets.

"I have to work."

I have to. I have to. I have to.

What about... *"I get to"?*

That's what this fire calls us towards. It calls on us to awaken to the sheer privilege of getting to turn our greatest gifts and learnings into a business or livelihood that's of the highest service to all those around us. It's where we get to be the trusted stewards of our gifts, while taking part in the new, more favorable realities that spring from them.

This fire calls on us to shed the layers of negative conditioning that have plagued our relationship to work and business for decades and centuries. Within these flames, you'll encounter the shadow of the "human resource," a glorified, well-dressed workhorse who's allowed himself to regress into an item on a balance sheet. A cog in the wheel. A raw material ready to be tapped out and left for dead.

We'll then venture into the shadows of *The Rank Riser* and *The Resigned*. Well-played roles, and monumental forces that currently shape how the majority of men will go about their career and livelihood. Both man-made constructs that severely dampen the value you allow yourself to express into the world.

At the core of it all, we've forgotten to be bold and adventurous within the unfoldment of our offerings. When it comes to work and business, we've lost a pioneering spirit that lusts for creation itself—and revels in the post-orgasmic bliss with equal parts terror and awe. We've traded the transcendent for the well-trodden path. We settle for work/life balance as if homeostasis is the highest calling a man can aspire to.

But work life/balance isn't the point. It never *has* been the point. How we approach work—how we engage it like a ravenous lover—and how we find deep alignment within this sacred tussle is. It's one that three weeks off, dental insurance, and state-mandated holidays can never replace.

What you're called to awaken to in these flames is *The Steward*. The one who claims ownership over his greatest gifts, and is relentless is finding the most fruitful and impactful channels for them to express through.

Indeed, you will be harshly challenged as you reclaim sovereignty over your gifts and how they get expressed into a business or livelihood. Fear will never be too far behind—snapping at your heels, trying to knock you back down, and drag your dejected self back to the world you left behind.

But *The Steward* you awaken will continuously propel you forward. For in this new paradigm of business and career, you are a trusted steward of your gifts. Not as a human resource, but as an appreciable asset that soars in value every time your work or mission inspires fruitful collaboration or positively impacts the life of a fellow human.

An empire built upon the broken backs and smoke-filled hearts of man is no empire at all. *The Steward* reminds us of this, and is steadfast in ushering a new paradigm of work and livelihood where all in his empire, be they employees, partners or collaborators, are empowered to grow in their gifts, and their opportunity to generously express them.

When you're ready, the flames are calling.

Shadow #1: The Human Resource

Perhaps the most damaging man-made construct plaguing our work lives is hidden in plain sight. It's our first and last point of contact in any job we take. And from beginning to end, its mandate is simple: Extract as much value and productivity from you as it reasonably can, while coating your fears with *just* enough psychological sorbets to keep you from recognizing the thick lies you've been choking down on.

It's a cunning system that's perfected the art and science of dangling the right carrot at the right time. Token rewards to satisfy your need for significance. Annual pay raises that barely match inflation. Lunch-and-learns that promote further indoctrination and system dependence under the guise of "continued education."

If you've outsourced your personal growth and evolution to the department whose very namesake should give you any and all indications of its true intent, you have in turn, become complicit in your own imprisonment. For the sovereign, self-led man doesn't see himself as a human resource. Something to be milked, mined, and drawn upon until his supposed limited resources run dry. He doesn't see himself as a fixed and finite resource. Dehumanized. Expendable. Separated from machinery and raw materials only by a thin black line on a financial balance sheet.

He sees himself as an *appreciating asset*. One that expands in his capacity to serve, gift, and create every day. Through greater skill, experience, strength, power, resilience and peace, he betters himself each day with focused intent. Not because he's unreasonably disciplined. Not because he's a "high achiever." It's all far simpler than that. It's a matter of self-respect and self-reverence. He appreciates what he is. An ever-evolving, ever-shifting manifestation of his highest intent. Stagnation is his death sentence. Continual growth and aligned service, his birthright.

By all means, contribute to a company with a "Human Resources" department if doing so feels aligned and purposeful. But fully recognize, and more importantly, begin investing in yourself as the ever-evolving, ever-appreciating asset you truly are. Be wary of any person, project, client or organization that would value you solely based on what they can extract. Gift yourself wholeheartedly to those who would honor your contribution, and actively gift you further opportunity to expand in your capacities to do so.

If you're an employer, begin to recognize your employees and team members as ever-appreciating assets. Become intimately attuned with how and where they most aspire to grow—and work to find ways where that growth can be of the highest service to your company's mission and stakeholders. The invitation then is to be a champion of the gifts, talents and aspirations of those you lead, not the slave driver they depend on out of sheer need or survival.

You don't want to fight to "extract" value from your team any more than they want to feel ruthlessly drawn from. This heartless exchange has seen its day. As a leader or business owner, it's your role to cultivate a culture of gifting. One where your team members are eager to share their ever-expanding gifts to the benefit of the company's vision—and the company is equally excited to gift them the appreciation, opportunity and resources needed to let the upward cycle continue.

Much like what we encountered in our fire on intimate relationships, the arrangement between employee and employer should end when either party no longer desires gifting the other what they most need to grow in their respective mission.

There's a vital lesson here that must be heeded. Under no circumstances should a man persist in a job or career that he's unwilling to be generous with the gifting of his skill, genius, and power. When a man "denies" and bitterly withholds his gifts out of resentment (whether to a lover or career), he conditions himself to a life of lessened capacity. He may initially do so out of "punishment" to his boss or partner—a "cold war" in response to their perceived lack of appreciation, generosity, and reciprocity. Yet it is he who suffers most. It's the ultimate self-betrayal, for nothing will "tap him out" or "bleed him dry" faster than his own refusal to continue cultivating and expressing the capacities he's blessed with. Ironically, such a passive aggressive refusal impairs him further, making "escape" even more unlikely.

The Hustler

It's important to note that the shadow of *The Human Resource* isn't exclusive to an employee-employer relationship. Whether you're the overworked CEO of a Fortune 500 or a startup founder, chances are you've seen this shadow show up in the subtle workings of *The Hustler*.

The increasingly pervasive, romanticized ideal of the man working 60-80 hour workweeks, inflating with self-importance, while ironically allowing his physical, mental and emotional faculties to come under unceasing duress.

The Hustler represents nothing more than well-disguised martyrdom. Having a stadium cheer you on as you slowly self-mutilate under the modern-day mantra of "hustle" is *still* the hallmark of reducing oneself to an expendable resource. The mission may be bigger than the average coal miner. The clothes may be sharper. The Instagram pics more glamorous. But if you've given yourself so completely to the role of *The Hustler*, you've become the fast-eroding resource—not the steward of the ever-appreciating asset.

Whether it's the corporate workhorse being bled-dry without protest, or the self-employed hustler who puts his slow death on public display to a chorus of hearts and thumbs, both have unconsciously chosen to derive greater significance from their work than their innate value as humans. *The Human Resource* is more willing to die on his sword of overinflated significance than live without it.

Ultimately, he'll get his wish.

King's Log

1. How would you describe your current relationship to work and business?
2. Do you feel expansive, energized and purposeful? Or collapsed and "bled dry"?
3. In what ways do you "withhold" your skill and contributions at work? Who are you truly punishing in the process?
4. What are all the conditioned beliefs and expectations you have around work or business that you can identify at this time? (i.e., work is a struggle, work is exhausting, etc.)
5. On a scale of 1-10, what's your current level of engagement in your craft/work/career (i.e., 1 being "just collecting a paycheck," 10 being "giving yourself generously with love and power)

King's Word

1. It is my highest will and intent to develop greater integrity, self-respect, and courage within the realms of my craft, livelihood and career.
2. I generously exert myself within my career or business; appreciating the display of power, service, and capacity I've developed.
3. I disallow and disentangle myself from anyone or anything, including my own outdated identities, who would see me solely as a resource to be extracted or drawn on.
4. I un-implicate myself from any disempowering and dehumanizing work or business relationships, reclaiming my full sovereignty and personal power.

5. Even within the realms of work and business, I know myself as a sovereign leader and ever-evolving human, worthy of expressing my genius in peaceful balance.

6. Every day, I take practical steps to become more valuable to self and others.

7. For as long as I choose to remain engaged on a project, business or career, I give myself generously to it.

Embodied Inquiry

1. Who is it that believes work has to be "hard" or a "struggle" Why?

2. What would it feel like to be energized and replenished by my craft and livelihood?

3. What would it feel like to be in the fullest expression of my skill, genius and power within my work and business?

4. What would it feel like to become stronger, more capable and more energized by my work or career every single day?

Shadow #2: The Resigned

We now meet a shadow that's so pervasive in our culture that you're sure to encounter resistance to even recognizing it for the limiting force it is. It's the shadow of retirement.

Once again, the markings of this shadow are most obvious in the language we use every day.

"I can't wait to retire."

Why? What *exactly* are you retiring from?

What have you allowed yourself to stubbornly endure for so long that daytime television and guided tours of crumbling monuments feels so appealing? It's an honest question that warrants an honest answer.

Curious to know why men seem to age ten years in the ten months after retirement? Why the proverbial Rolex ticks ten times faster than the clock hanging above his abode of creation and expression?

It's because he's literally turned his back to the mysterious, ethereal force that flows through him and animates him into existence.

So, if you haven't already done so, ask yourself: what can't you wait to retire from?

Are you retiring from challenge? From adversity? From resilience? From the call to greater capacity? From the fear of expressing your art? From the self-contraction that limits your fullest expression. From the shame or regret of having sold your life short.

What are you retiring from?

At no other time in human history did man long for the day where he can put a dent on a La-Z-Boy and flip through 800 channels while complaining about the weather. Man wasn't made to spend the day mulling between Scottsdale and Salt Lake for his next golf retreat. He wasn't made to run a continuous circuit between flatlining leisure and existential liability to those around him. He wasn't built for the indignity of refreshing his stock or crypto portfolio every five minutes, or the feigning of self-importance through his over-inflated accolades.

Retirement may look different than resignation on an HR or corporate by-law, but the energy is the same. It says, *"I've had enough," "I'm done," "I'm too old for this,"* and *"I'm too tired for the sacrifice that nobody asked me to make in the first place."*

It's an inevitable and tragically-impotent conclusion to a life and career of numbing discontent. One spent chained to self-imposed shackles while the key was hidden in a small crevice of your heart all along. A crevice coated in courage that could only be accessed with bravery in kind.

If you can't wait to retire, you're playing the wrong game. You're selling your presence, and suppressing your spirit for a mere pittance. Instead of desperately longing for your final cycle through the company turnstile, find the courage *right now* to pivot into heightened purpose.

Financially free and done with traditional work and business life? Why not consciously devote yourself to being the best husband, lover, father or grandfather you can be? Shave your head and move to the Himalayas with a single-minded focus on self-realization if that's more fitting. Or look around your community and find new, inspiring ways to be of service to the underserved. I promise you won't have to look too hard to find someone to help. But to retire from the intentional expansion and purposeful expression of your gifts altogether is nothing but a bitter refusal of life herself. Instead, drum up the courage to choose renewal.

Renewal of mission. Renewal of purpose. Renewal of career or livelihood. Renewal of spirit.

As we alluded to in the first shadow, it's quite easy to know when it's time to pivot your career or business. When you no longer have the will, desire or capacity to gift your business, career or occupation your fullest gifts, it's time to *lead* yourself to a new place where you can. Only in the most extreme situations where financial destitution is on the other side of a resignation slip should one persist in his resigned trance. But even in such cases, he must absolutely reframe his current position as a means to a more favorable end, and be steadfast in his intention to realize it.

There is *never* a valid or life-affirming reason to persist in "going through the motions." Such a stance only reinforces a sense of deep-rooted powerlessness and despair. Likewise, "checking out" is in stark contradiction to the courage that must be cultivated to find meaning and purpose in your next business or pursuit.

Simply put, no matter how much you dislike your job or career, spending your day in a self-induced coma severely inhibits creative flow and purposeful expression. Rather, it reinforces a zero-sum game of cold-hearted extraction—one where you feel justified and remorseless in extracting resources and value from your company, colleagues, and clients.

Much like relationships then, the call is to make the first move. As long as you remain in a situation, commit to cultivating your skill and power within it. Give your gifts and offer value even *if* they go unnoticed and unreciprocated. At the very least, you will have reclaimed your power and assumed an inner stance that makes you a worthy match to the business or opportunity you wish to pursue next.

As a leader or employer, place a high value on a team member who's deeply attuned to his mission, and is equally excited to find constant realignment and expression within your company. Likewise, under no circumstances should you tolerate the continued presence of the resigned. Vacate the position for one who'll be ready to fill it with focused power and purpose. For the gift he brings extend far beyond the role he fills.

The woefully resigned will always find a new circumstance or challenge to feel victimized by. The cold refusal of his gifts; and bitter stench within the "bare minimum" he provides, will sabotage the culture of empowerment and purposeful gifting you're desiring to establish and cultivate within your team.

King's Log

1. When I think about "retirement," what specifically am I seeking to "retire" from?
2. In what ways do I "punish" my job / employer by withholding my abilities or efforts? Who's truly suffering from that withdrawal and refusal?

King's Word

1. It is my highest will and intent to continuously experience renewal of service and mission.
2. It is my highest will and intent to effortlessly find the areas or opportunities where my greatest gifts can be further developed and put on fullest display.
3. With courage and power, I offer the greatest skill, creativity, genius and power to any situation before me, knowing that in doing so, I make myself *more* available for a more aligned opportunity to arise.

Embodied Inquiry

1. What would it feel like to be totally and completely inspired and empowered in my work?
2. What would it feel like to experience constant renewal of purpose and passion within my career or livelihood?

Shadow #3: The Rank-Riser

The Rank Riser is a well-played archetype in modern western culture. Its influence is strongest in the man who'll auction off the better part of his life, slowly ascending a metaphorical ladder of success. Each rung coated with a token reward to keep him motivated along his torturous climb. Everything is structured and predictably laid out for him with extremely little variance. Forty-hour workweeks. Monday to Friday. Nine-to-five. Two-weeks paid vacation. A raise or promotion every few years.

At first, the predictability and lack of variance provide a soothing balm to his reptilian brain that still equates the fear of unemployment and financial instability with death and abandonment. But over time, that same monotonous routine will lull him into a subtle coma. While he'll claim to have some wild ambition that he's on the verge of pursuing, he'll rarely be able to cultivate the courage and capacity to do so.

Simply put, when a man doesn't need to exercise his focus, willpower, intent, creativity and courage on a daily basis, these qualities quickly become dormant and inactive. This is the more insidious and oppressive side of *The Rank Riser* shadow. When a man plugs himself into the inner workings of a system based on predictability and control, it's only a matter of time before he becomes swallowed by it.

Within this system, he takes what's inherently exponential—and downregulates it to better match the "rules" of the system and its adherents. This is easy to observe in real time. We see it in the new employee who walks through the company turnstile on day one with an expansive sense of eagerness—ready to learn—ready to channel all his learnings, insights and creativity into something valuable. Only to find a few months later, that that same spirit has been bludgeoned to death by the very system he was eager to serve.

Yet even in this early stage, adherence is easier than escape. Maybe even in this short time, he's oriented his entire life around this new job—moved to be closer, invested in a new car or condo, married, had a child. So he'll persist and convince himself that there will be a "right time" to make a big move. But rarely does this happen, if ever. For the higher one climbs up the ladder, the scarier it is to look down. When faced with the choice between jumping back down into the grand abyss or continuing the climb, it's always easier to grab the next rung—even if you have lingering doubts about where that ladder even leads. As we mentioned earlier, man will often fear the sunk costs more than his sinking spirit.

But the ladder is not real. Just like an actual ladder is basically just two support beams with wooden slabs nailed between them, the ladder that *The Rank Riser* climbs is supported by two unquestioned belief structures.

The first is the lie of linearity. The damaging belief that any meaningful career of contribution and service must be achieved through some so-called career path.

The paying of one's dues. The rising of the ranks. This is simply an arbitrary and adopted belief that we've been force-fed since birth. Ever since we were children, the lie of linearity has served as a superimposed organizing function for our entire experience of the world. Our competency, attainment, and qualification are all assessed based on where we land on a linear path of progression. We experience this in the schooling system with all its arbitrary signposts of intelligence and development—and then once again in our careers where our value is extrinsically linked to seniority, productivity, or the accumulation of certain agreed-upon milestones.

Its dysfunction may be apparent. It's devastation, even more so. Yet its claim as "law," for the most part, goes unquestioned. Unfortunately, when enough people in a closed and concentrated system abide by a false belief, it has the appearance of absolute law to all those within it. At its core, this is what a corporate environment or schooling system is.

But in truth, the market has never rewarded those who've "risen the ranks." The market rewards those who've created a remarkable way of solving painful and persistent problems, or delivering immense value—often in ways that are exponentially faster, better, and more innovative than the alternatives. Ironically, it's in blindly committing to a linear and predictable path, and the lack of variance within it, that prevents one from cultivating the capacity to create that value.

Very few success stories feature a linear, straightforward, and predictable path. You're more likely to read about the tale of the man who won big and lost it all, only to reinvent himself and win again. More billion-dollar tech startups are founded by dropouts, big dreamers, and kids in hoodies than MIT grads who worked their way up the corporate ranks for decades before venturing out on their own. The common denominator here is a greater value judgment on entrepreneurial adventure and the virtues it gives rise to, than in the safe, anesthetized path of annual pay raises and a free parking pass.

Beyond the lie of linearity, *The Rank Riser* entraps us with one final belief: self-importance. Simply put, the man who derives the majority of his significance based on where he lands on an arbitrary scale of achievement will *always* be subject to it.

A title, a nameplate, a degree, a designation, a salary. All of them offer us a seemingly objective, observable and measurable way to stack our sense of importance in relation to others. Even if we don't wholeheartedly align with our role and title, we at least feel oriented. We know where we stand. Sure, there may be some "above" us, but there are also many below. From this, we can derive a sense of safety and self-importance. A position within chaos. A hook to hang our existential hat.

Self-importance is also generated with every rung we climb. We may not feel fulfilled in what we're doing, but the plaque handed out at the Christmas party for best "whatever" is enough to make us puff our chests with pride.

In his unbalanced need for self-importance, the rank-rising man is too prideful to have a gap in perceived significance and authority. He can't bring himself from the slow-drip dopamine rush of having ten "lesser men" responding to his every whim, to being back in the wild, relying on his own drive, skill, and resourcefulness for the next catch.

When you're ruled by self-importance, you have no courage to fall off the ladder and back down into the abyss—even if there's a jetpack waiting for you down at the bottom. Yet this is what the path of exponential growth in business or career demands from us. It's difficult to jump from one ladder to the next. Most times, you need to fall back into the abyss where unlimited possibility dwells. We're absolutely horrified of "rock bottom," when in truth, it's exactly where the gifts of resilience, resourcefulness, and expanded possibility are most abundantly found. While the optics are culturally shamed, the recently laid-off twenty-six-year-old sitting in a coffee shop is far closer to building his dream business than his buddy who's clinking shots of Jack over a new promotion.

Self-importance isn't found in a job title or a list of accolades. It's found in your ability and willingness to harness whatever skills, resources, creativity, power, drive, and focus you have at your disposal—and transform them into something that brings value to whichever market you choose to serve.

Most major business or career successes come as a result of a creative breakthrough, and the focused power to steward it into creation. Both forces, while available to be harnessed and directed by man, are not "his." They are mysterious forces that man can't claim. In inflating with self-importance, you implicitly deny, dismiss or fail to appreciate the mysterious undercurrent of power and inspiration that flows through you at all moments. In his self-importance, man will overestimate his role in his success—and in doing so, cut himself off from the more subtle undercurrent that would bring him exponentially further.

The alternative isn't a false humility, but a recognition that any monumental or "abnormal" success you achieve in any career path or business will be mostly fueled by two things:

1. A unique, innovative and valuable "twist" on what's currently being done.
2. An easeful confidence and fearlessness to share and express it.

Neither of these are accessible to the man who's hitched a ride on the lie of linearity while stapling his sense of significance to the token rewards it yields. For example, if you claim a breakthrough idea to be "yours" and attach your significance to it, it becomes more vulnerable to attack. An attack on the idea becomes an attack on your character and personal identity. You become terrified of scrutiny—and hyper-guarded and rigid in any move you make to execute it.

But is a breakthrough idea truly *yours* to begin with? Or are you simply a trusted, and perhaps temporary steward of it? More importantly, which engenders greater courage and fearlessness? Ultimately, it's not a matter of humility, but one of truth.

Self-importance will always precede self-restriction. And self-restriction is what prevents you from fully expressing the gifts that would contribute to exponential growth in any industry or position of your choosing.

A final rebuttal of *The Rank-Riser* and his lie of linearity may include a reference to the ten-thousand-hour rule popularized by Malcolm Gladwell. It essentially states that to achieve world-class expertise or mastery in any given field, you need to put in around ten thousand hours of practice.

While few would argue with the merit of such sustained dedication to your craft, we're no longer living in a time that demands or even rewards general, overarching mastery. That worked back in 1705 when being named John Blacksmith earned you a lifetime in front of an industrial furnace.

But the ten-thousand-hour rule doesn't work in a world that's moving faster by the day. Playing by those same rules, by the time you've mastered your craft through such myopic focus, you'll have failed to evolve, becoming complicit in your own obsolescence. Instead of the 10,000 hours that total mastery *may* require, we'd be better off striving for outcome-based mastery. Meaning, becoming masterful at generating a specific result or outcome for a specific market in a specific way.

As our roles as men evolve, and as our dignity and self-reverence expands beyond that of the martyred workhorse or "human resource" to be tapped dry, we must shed the illusion of slow, linear progress, and instead embrace a paradigm of exponential growth in any area of our choosing. With unprecedented access to information, technology, skill-enhancing resources, and mentors, linearity is a choice—a reckless one that runs counter to who you truly are, and who you must strive to become.

This is our will. This is our right. This is our rule.

Lead the way, king.

King's Log

1. In what ways have you built a life off the "lie of linearity"?
2. What would happen if you let your grip fall off that rung? What would *truly* happen if you "started from scratch"?
3. Who is it that places so much value on any sunk costs of prior achievements and "slow, incremental growth"?
4. Do I trust myself to create (or contribute to) something amazing and epically aligned if given the time and space to do so?
5. Who is it that feels so dependent on the current career trajectory you're on?

King's Word

1. It is my highest will and intent to know and experience my exponential nature as a creator and leader.
2. With great courage, I withdraw all excessive importance given to past achievements or accomplishments, and redirect that energy to my innate power to create new, exponentially successful outcomes.
3. I tap into my fullest potential and express the insight and actions that arise from it.

Embodied Inquiry

1. What would it feel like to achieve success in my business or career in the fastest, most magical way possible?
2. What would it feel like to be in complete awe and astonishment over how quickly a new reality of better design could be created?

Awakening The Steward

As we allow these shadows and their respective constructs to gently wash away, we create space for *The Steward* to awaken.

The Steward is what awakens regardless of your current outer circumstances. Whether you're the CEO of a Fortune 500 Company or an entry-level hire of some faceless corporation, awakening *The Steward* is fundamental to stepping into your fullest expression across your business or career.

At his core, he recognizes that he's the leader and steward of his resources—not the resource itself. In this knowingness, he sees himself as an *appreciating asset*, gaining in value with every intentionally made upgrade to his skill, capacity, vitality, creative insight, focus and willpower.

If he's an employee of a company with limited mobility, he takes it upon himself to dedicate some time each day to become the self-led man capable of breaking out on his own. Even if on the surface-level he's being led by others and being delegated soul-numbing tasks, he doesn't allow himself to check-out and become completely anesthetized to his situation. He recognizes that if he's to ever regain sovereignty in his career, he must make the first move. If he wants to one day earn $200,000 per year while being his own "boss," he takes it upon himself to show up in his current role, ready to gift the exact same value as he would if he were earning 10x his salary.

He goes above and beyond what his "superior" asks. Not as an act of limp-wristed submission, but one of bold-hearted rebellion. He goes "against" his boss by rising even higher, taking his own orders in doing so. For *The Steward*, the surface-level optics are of lesser concern than the man he's embodying. For he knows that this awakening is a non-negotiable precursor to whatever he wants to achieve on a more observable scale.

The Steward is also sovereign in thought. He doesn't downregulate to match the monotonous tone of the system and its other adherents. While others regress and collapse into the lie of linearity, he digs his heels deeper into his own truth and holds the question: *"Who must I become to achieve the things I want to achieve?"*

In holding this question he activates the latent exponential forces of creativity, resourcefulness, ever-expanding skill, and personal power to achieve it. He doesn't dilute his power by cursing his situation or joining his colleagues in their humdrum tune of victimhood and despair. While he's undoubtedly affected by the same things—the economy, the company rules, the rush-hour traffic, the surge in housing prices—he's not subject to them. He's his own man. Unbound. Untarnished by the stain-filled tears of the lesser men around him. He's the steward of his own will.

And when it's time to finally embark on his own and pursue the business or career of his dreams, he does so swiftly and unapologetically. He doesn't hang his existential hat on the rusted hook of significance, and therefore feels no delay in sawing it off the wall. While the notion of jumping off the ladder and starting at the "bottom" may still bring up some fear and hesitation, *The Steward* ultimately trusts his ability to rise back up with a new vehicle of his choosing.

To him, there's no such thing as "rock bottom" or "starting from scratch." There's only a blank canvas and a wider opportunity to invite his genius and resourcefulness to return. The overplayed and culturally ingrained "rags to riches" story may make for a good Hollywood movie, but is far from the actual truth. For the leader deeply acknowledges that nothing starts from nothing. Alchemy is the transformation of one substance into another of higher value and more life-affirming properties. That's what the steward does.

Even at rock bottom, alone in his flat with five dollars to his name, he has access to his current skill set, the capacity to expand it, the mentorship of those who've walked a similar path before him as well as the more subtle, yet no less powerful qualities of drive, focus, self-belief, will, creativity, and resourcefulness. He relishes in the opportunity to harness and direct all these exponential forces to a rapid and more fruitful end.

Likewise, he is the trusted steward, not the prideful owner of the ideas sparking his next venture or project. So he marshals it forward, free of attachment, with the fluidity, speed, and confidence that few others would possess.

He doesn't bog himself down in achieving a global, overarching mastery in his field of choice before feeling ready to express his greatest gifts. Instead, he seeks to serve his market or field through outcome-based mastery. Meaning, the ability to solve a specific problem for a specific market in a unique, innovative, and more effective way. In this, he radically collapses timelines, and accelerates his speed towards success.

As a leader of other men, he grants them the same hard-won sovereignty that he once battled through, viewing his employees as ever-appreciating assets, and being a rare champion of their greatest gifts. He doesn't seek to extract, but to inspire, elevate, and encourage a mutual gifting. For *The Steward*, business is not a zero-sum game, but a sacred opportunity to harness complimentary gifts into even greater outcomes for the company, its team, and the customers it serves. Seeing all three come into harmony is his highest excitement, and one that solidifies his stance as *The Steward*.

Finally, once he finds alignment in his career path or business, and has become the trusted champion of the inner and outer resources of both himself and his company, *The Steward* will seek to re-introduce elements of predictability and control. However, these are not meant to stifle, but rather to stabilize his foundation as he prepares for even greater growth, impact, and entrepreneurial adventure. They are the safeguards to an accelerated ascent, not the almighty rule from which all else flows.

On a final note, *The Steward* chooses to embody these qualities *before* the rest of the world catches up. Operating with courage, transparency, and with the total welfare of employees, customers and the world at large is *not* always going to be celebrated. It's still mostly a silent victory. *The Steward* doesn't delude himself of this, nor insist on outer recognition to continue leading with integrity. As we addressed in the first fire, we must achieve escape velocity from the gravitational pull of the status quo. Whereas those around him regress to the norm, *The Steward* rises above.

Finally, there's a popular and fluffy myth that your income is always going to be proportional to the value you create in the world. While this belief is soothing to those whose benevolence outweighs his desire to exploit others for his own benefit, we must still refrain from cushy, psychologically satisfying half-truths.

Though we're spiraling quickly into a world of greater transparency and accountability, we still live in a world where the dishonest man can make a king's ransom—and a noble king can struggle for a beggar's pittance. In reality, people who produce far less value than you while exploiting, deceiving, and oppressing others, *can* generate more money than you. Not by rule. But by virtue that the world, as it presently operates, still hasn't fully oriented itself around the higher qualities of honesty, integrity and value exchange.

But for *The Steward*, the call still becomes to create a business or career that delivers more value, while gifting customers and employees on the highest level possible. It's an upward race that he's honored to be at the leading edge of. For that's who he is. That's the essence of his claim. And it's who you'll soon become.

It's time to awaken *The Steward*.

Crowning The Steward

> The guided initiation into *The Steward* is available to stream at:
>
> www.iseeyouking.com/leadership

Evolutionary Accelerators

Evolutionary Accelerator #1: Asset Appreciation
Practice Duration:
Practice Frequency: Ongoing

Description:

This practice simply invites you to explore (and act on) the following question: how are you bettering yourself every day?

When you accept the idea that you're no longer a "resource" to be bled dry, but an asset that gets to appreciate in value every day, your entire approach to "work and career" shifts as a result.

In this first exercise, you're invited to simply take the first steps in adopting this new mindset and sense of self-leadership and stewardship.

The *"regression towards the norm"* we encountered in the first fire is likely to sneak up on us again at this juncture. For it won't be "normal" to not tax your capacities in a "work culture" designed to exhaust and extract.

Yet this is your opportunity to become your own agent. Your own advocate. Your own trusted steward of your own resources. For there is not a single person in the world more qualified and trusted to do so. And when you abdicate such responsibility to someone else, you inevitably submit to their agenda and influence.

If you're self-employed and have autonomy over the projects you take on, practice setting boundaries. A firm boundary set with a client is a compassionate boundary set for oneself. If you're not self-employed (and still subject to a host of responsibilities and tasks beyond your direct control), simply begin with the mental shift of being your own "appreciable asset" and find the windows availability to you for the skillful expression of this new mindset.

Appreciable Question	Appreciable Action
How am I expanding my mental capacity?	i.e., refusing to partake in toxic conversation and instead doing breathwork for 10 minutes on my break.
How am I expanding my physical capacity?	i.e., practicing intermittent fasting and doing an efficient 15-minute HIIT workout.
How am I expanding my sense of possibility?	i.e., reaching out to X for mentorship/advice.
How am I expanding my sense of personal confidence?	i.e., actively practicing courage by setting "hard" boundaries with X client—and/or proposing a new direction?
How am I expanding my creative potential?	i.e., Ideating / Journaling / Brainstorming around solving X problem / opportunity.

Evolutionary Accelerator #2: Make the First Move

Practice Duration: 1 Day

Practice Frequency: As often as you feel called

Description:

Many employees will try to "break out" from their current positions of stagnancy and stuckness without first changing themselves.

Essentially, they'll claim to be "stuck" while unconsciously perpetuating the situation by feeling victimized and/or in refusal of truly participating in any meaningful upward ascent.

As discussed earlier, the greatest inhibitor of your growth is simply refusing to gift your gifts. It's in the conscious withdrawal—and your refusal to show up powerfully within the context you still find yourself in. A disgruntled lover doesn't make themselves more "available" to meet their true soulmate by cooling his heart and withdrawing his gifts in the one he's currently in. He does so by first re-sparking his desire to practice being in the fullest expression of his gifts, primarily for his *own* benefit, knowing that in doing so, he becomes a greater pairing partner for a better, more aligned situation.

You can act on this wisdom however you wish. For a more practical protocol, I invite you to consider this: If you got paid $10,000 this week (or choose a number more closely tied to your goal) in your role or job, how would you show up differently? What initiatives would you take? What conversations would you have with your co-workers or team members? What would your energy be? How would you carry yourself? What would you contribute?

One of the greatest tenets of being a man and manifesting in the world, is simply making the first move. When we conform to title and reward, we in turn, solidify the bars of the cage and lock ourselves in it even longer. But when we show up, acting *as if* our situation has already transformed into the one we desire, we become a more willing partner for that new reality. We meet it halfway. It dissolves a sense of entitlement; and opens us up to a greater sense of personal power and trust.

Evolutionary Accelerator 3: Exponential Activity

Practice Duration: A full day

Practice Frequency: As often as you feel called

The goal:

Many of the activities we perform in work and business have predictable outputs. They are linear—with low value results to show. Whereas exponential thinking, and their corresponding activities are quite the opposite—yet are often discouraged and dismissed as unproductive or a "waste of energy."

Within our work, we tend to fall into predictable patterns and "task lists." There is certainly nothing wrong with routine—providing it yields the results we're aiming for. However, in being a servant to a task list versus a steward of creative input (and our highest potential), we put a hard cap on what's possible for us.

Predictable output has its place. But if your goal is to be fully expressed (and *know* your potential), it's going to require a growing capacity and comfort level with "exponential tasks" that can yield breakthrough or road-opening outputs. The invitation then, is to endeavor to create greater balance between your linear and exponential activities. Get in the habit of "taking swings" and initiating actions that could bring disproportionately large and exciting returns.

In doing so, be aware of (and have a threshold) for an acceptable "miss rate." Meaning, actions that yield no practical results, other than the courage, confidence, and capacity you cultivated in being able to perform them—which is arguably the greatest result of all.

Much like how a venture capitalist will place a hundred bets, knowing that the two or three that "hit" will make up for the rest, be the steward of your exponential actions, knowing that with practice and consistency, one will yield a life-changing return.

In short, linear activities produce linear and predictable results.

Exponential activities produce non-linear and less-predictable results.

Exponential tasks will usually involve:

1. Initiating, strengthening or evolving a relationship.
2. Learning something new / evolving your understanding and practical wisdom
3. A pitch or proposal, which, if accepted, can yield a life-changing result
4. Conceiving something new (a new strategy, solution to a problem, product, offer, etc.)

In practice, these may play out as:

1. Pitching an investor
2. Reaching out so someone you admire for mentorship, coaching or advice
3. Reaching out to someone to express appreciation for their work
4. Taking a course / program / seminar on a special topic in your field
5. Crafting a new business plan or marketing strategy
6. Ideating a new solution to a problem your industry is facing
7. Creating art (writing a book, a song, a screenplay)
8. Attending a conference with speakers / attendees you admire (and wish to meet)
9. Making big "asks" that most would cower from.

If you walked into a coffee shop, performing the action of buying a coffee would yield a predictable and linear outcome. However, let's say that instead of ordering a coffee, and burying your head in your laptop for the next two hours, you asked the guy next to you "what he does."

It may fizzle and yield a slightly negative return. But the reward, if it "hits," could be extraordinary and even life changing.

Take note of what "exponential activities" are available to you in your day-to-day life.

And without disrupting your current activities, simply seek to rebalance the ratio a little bit. Renew a pioneering spirit within your craft or career. Open up to new sources of inspiration—and the innovation that can be borne from it.

Chapter 9

FIRE 6 - THRIVING EMOTIONALLY AND SPIRITUALLY IN AN UNBALANCED WORLD

What makes this an "initiatory fire"?

At this stage, it is my hope that we've built up enough courage and power to brave the flames of this most intense fire.

Thriving emotionally and spiritually in an unbalanced world is indeed an initiation of the highest order—one which the majority of men on this planet will flat out miss. We can point to the 34,000 male suicides every year, or the one-in-ten Americans who chase down their morning coffee with a cocktail of numbing agents. But for those more willing to take a qualitative assessment rather than wait for a lifeless metric to call out our biggest imbalances, the wide-scale emotional and spiritual suffering is raw and naked to anyone with an open heart to feel it.

Nearly all of the world's suffering can be linked back to this failed initiation. All abuses, be them personal or collective, can only be attributed to a destructive emotional imbalance, an unresolved trauma or wounding, an unexamined belief or thought pattern—and ultimately a calamitous fracture from our own spirit—our inner king, who embodies and expresses the qualities of unconditional love, compassion, forgiveness, and positive power.

But we are not helpless in healing these wounds. We have not been plunged so deeply into a cold, dark grave of hopelessness and despair that we can't rise back up into the sun's brilliant light. Fractured spirits can be mended. Wounded hearts can be sewn with grace and compassion. Grudges can be forgiven. And the genuine welfare for all beings can be awakened.

The very first thing we'll encounter in this fire is an ancient shadow at the very source of our imbalanced emotional state. We'll track back to the very essence and function of our emotions—and awaken to a new, more empowering and skillful understanding of them. In this, you'll soon discover that it's not the world itself that's unbalanced—but you, in relationship to it versus your relationship to yourself.

Simply put, you're reactive, allowing the world around you to determine the emotional state you embody in any given moment. You are evoked. You are effect, not cause. This is the first fundamental shift to make. For the opposite of being reactive *isn't* proactivity, but in simply being sovereign.

We all want to thrive emotionally. If given the option, there's not a being on this planet who would consciously choose a life of ceaseless torment and suffering over a haven of peace and power. But to be emotionally free, you only have two options: learn to control nearly 8 billion people, which incidentally, many will attempt to do with varying levels of devastation. Or alternatively, learn how to modulate your own emotional experience and hold it in the infinite, vast, loving presence of that which you already are. There's only one attainable answer. The latter, as demanding as it may sound, is the only one with a successful track record—no matter how short its list of victors.

This is why thriving emotionally and spiritually are one of the same. There's no true emotional healing without spiritual growth and expansion of consciousness. Likewise, one can hardly claim to be spiritually evolved if they're still prisoner to the ever-shifting waves of emotion which overwhelm most of the world's population.

Once we make this foundational shift, we'll encounter the shadows of the suppressed stoic and the inner critic—a gang of thieves that rob you of your joy, and normalize a life of defaulted discontentment. We'll dissolve them all by awakening true intimacy with all that enters your awareness. Intimacy with your emotions is an unavoidable prerequisite to accessing your kingly power. For when your emotions are ignored, suppressed, or left in the dark, they remain overwhelmingly influential over your life. The detached stoic may have the appearance of power, but it's just that—a facade. Here, you'll learn how to rip off the masks, unlock the cell, and let all that's been shamed and suppressed to slowly inch out of the darkness to be witnessed and healed.

Be brave, king. Don't be afraid of what you can see, but be gravely concerned about what you allow to remain locked and hidden. One simply can't imprison aspects of himself while claiming to be free. Even a warden lives in his own prison.

At the heart of it all, to thrive emotionally isn't to become free of emotions, but to become free in your relationship to them. This relies on two basic skills:

1. Intimacy with all that arises. Meaning, to free yourself from the judgment, shame and resistance in feeling what you feel—most of which are old patterns, external influences and crumbling identities that have been suppressed, and are thus still actively being played out on the stage of your everyday dealings. This is where a spiritual groundedness is vital. It allows you to go beyond seeing yourself as those limited identities, and instead as the vast spaciousness (call it consciousness, source, awareness, infinity, God, etc.) that can hold everything without judgment, resistance or aversion.

So much of what we feel contradicts or threatens the self-image we hold for ourselves. We defend tooth and nail a fixed ideal that leaves no room for messiness. Egoic identity and self-obsession, in all its forms, are quite fragile and vulnerable. Emotional resistance is the guard at the gate that denies entry to any that would threaten its well-crafted image.

Befriend yourself. Become emotionally available to yourself. Loosen the rigidities of what your experience "must be." Stop defending ideals and identities that have an innately temporal existence. Become unseduceable by the temptation to project judgment and outrage on others before having first plunged into your own inner crevices. This is a lifelong pursuit, with greater depth of intimacy made more possible with each daring and tender confrontation with self. It's one you'd be wise to embrace in each fleeting moment.

2. Emotional fluency: Meaning, the skill, capacity, and willingness to shift through the emotional spectrum with the same fluidity that a blues guitarist can work up and down the scales. Suffering doesn't arise from our emotions themselves, but in our prolonged stasis and reactivity to them. Emotions are meant to be fluid—rising then returning to a state of equanimity—with a short refractory period between them. We witness this quite readily in young children. They'll go from an outburst of intense anger and frustration to unrestrained joy and elation in minutes or seconds. Later on, they *learn* that sometimes, in order for their parents to grasp the depth of their upset, they need to *force* themselves to stay angry.

Later on, this plays out in the resentful husband who chooses to prolong his folded-arm stance and bitter tongue until his partner can feel the etheric venom burning her skin. We mostly resist natural emotional fluidity as an act of manipulation. It's an immature and weaponized tactic that few mature from. But primarily, this learned resistance to shifting emotional states is simply a by-product of a lack of intimacy with the initial state, and the emotion going unheard, unseen or shamed by those around him.

As you begin this work, you commit to years, decades, or even a lifetime of noticing and transforming old emotional patterns, and your relationship to the world around you. It's your intimacy with these emotions—and the spiritual awareness to hold them that leads to their transformation.

This is courageous work. You will get no gold ribbons. You will not grease the rungs of the corporate ladder. You will not have your arm raised in the victor's circle. All you'll receive is your true freedom and sovereignty. It's my hope that this is enough to encourage you to charge headlong into this most tempestuous storm.

Shadow #1: The Reactor (Cause vs. Effect)

What we currently experience as emotion, is really a distorted, weaponized version of its original function and intent. In truth, emotion was never meant to be solely a reactive force. Yet across our everyday dealings, it's made clear that most of humanity is emotionally enslaved by their reactivity. Every state tends to get attributed to a cause.

I feel angry be-*cause*

I feel loved be-*cause*

I feel hopeless, fearful, enraged or excited be-*cause*

In all these cases, be them positive or negative, our emotions have become the *effect* of some initial event external to us. In this unbalanced relationship, we allow the world around us to evoke who and what we embody and express at any given moment. This is done automatically, without choice and without a moment of conscious awareness. When our experience of life is evoked without our conscious choice, we have essentially traded away our sovereignty.

In everyday speak, it's become popular to talk about how we're triggered by a person or event—and then recounting that story to anyone who will validate our outrage, and confirm our stance as victim. We are so resolute in our self-righteous assault against anyone who dares prod against our open wounds, that we miss the opportunity to dive inwards to heal them.

Instead of rebalancing our relationship to ourselves and the world around us, we seek to control the world—willing it to accommodate and orient around our countless hurts and traumas. When we talk about being triggered, we rarely do so in the context of taking full ownership and responsibility for what we're experiencing. Rarely do we use it as an opportunity to become intimate with the injured part of ourselves desperately seeking healing and resolution. Nor do we seek to find the source of the spell we're under. Instead, we stand in unwavering righteousness, condemning the one who evoked the feeling in the first place. Instead of seeing him or her as the unintended (and even misguided) mirror or "teacher" they are, we see them as traitor. As an unholy obstacle towards our sense of peace—and an oppressive force that must be controlled or conquered.

The game of modern society is to attempt to make the world more accommodating. To try and use blunt force and social pressure to subject nearly 8 billion people to live by a set of arbitrary, ever-shifting rules that nobody can quite agree upon. We're waiting for nearly 8 billion people to come into some form of consensus and abide by a specific code of conduct or moralistic duty, while holding our own peace and freedom hostage for a moment we'll certainly never see in our lifetime.

In allowing emotion to be solely a reactive force, we essentially doom ourselves to tiptoe blindly across an energetic minefield. Indeed, in our current relationship to emotion and the world around us, we are all walking hand grenades with our pins pulled out. On a collective level, a nuclear reactor on the verge of catastrophic meltdown.

A life of constant emotional reactivity is hardly a life at all. When you react to every situation, there's a fragmentation of power and influence. Instead of having influence over your reality, you're being influenced by every passing emotion—and experiencing a learned helplessness in transforming your situation.

Transformation of any kind requires a degree of prolonged attention and influence over your inner and outer environment that's simply not possible when you're being evoked and dragged along. You simply can't claim to be sovereign while still denying responsibility and ownership over your own emotions.

Let it be clear that we don't condone any form of ill-intended abuse or intentional malice—be it spoken or unspoken. Abuse is real. Oppressive paradigms must be replaced by ones rooted in love, sovereignty, and positive power. Outrage and reactive force, in extreme circumstances, can be justified and even temporarily useful. But even in these cases, if you haven't claimed ownership over your own emotional states, and used every opportunity of triggering to awaken to greater depths of intimacy, you're still resisting the reclamation of true sovereignty you're being called towards.

I do believe that *everyone*, at some point, must awaken to an inner stance of peaceful power, emotional equanimity, and compassion. A stance where they feel effortlessly compelled to gift their fellow brother or sister what they most need to feel safe, loved and fully expressed in their gifts. But this is the work of generations to come. And it's a path that must first be forged in the reclamation of emotion for what it truly is.

So, if emotion isn't meant to be solely a reactive force—what *is* its true function?

Simply put, emotion is designed to be both cause *and* effect. Meaning, emotion is meant to be a tool we can use to inspire and elevate states and experiences in ourselves and others, while also being an energetic signature that we can self-generate.

Just like one can utter the words "I love you," one can generate and express an unspoken state of love that can be more readily and powerfully experienced by his intended recipient. In this sense, emotion was, and still is a more potent, pre-verbal language.

Words themselves are the least trustworthy form of communication. Saying "I love you" from a place of simmering rage and resentment doesn't inspire a state of love and trust—yet a more subdued and neutral statement delivered from a place of genuine love and compassion does. Actions may speak louder than words, but the underlying emotion and intent beneath those actions speak loudest.

Few understood this better than Gandhi. He was not evoked by those who would oppress him and his followers. He resisted the unceasing prods and triggers that just about any other man would succumb to. He maintained sovereignty over his emotional states for decades, and lived his life as *cause* rather than effect. He chose to embody and express the emotions of compassion and courage when he had every reason to react with the opposite. It wasn't just a peaceful rebellion. For the most part, it was a wordless one. When we talk about *"being the change you want to see in the world,"* we're in fact pointing to our innate capacity to use emotional energy as a language of pure intent that we get to speak into the world.

Learning to self-generate emotional states is challenging at first. Just like a toddler awkwardly trying to string together his words, it'll require patience and practice to rebalance our relationship to the world around us. But for the man who truly aspires to be at the helm of his own ship, there simply isn't any other way. With every thought and every emotion, you're advocating for a new future. With every silent, wordless expression, you either invite the soft surrender of a lover or the inner clench of closure. These emotional expressions must be modulated and used with the same precision and skillfulness that a powerful speaker would use to inspire his company, nation or tribe.

Emotion is indeed energy in motion. But most importantly, it's the unspoken language you're called to use to express the qualities of the king, and the newly awakened virtues from each fire. It's time to start using your emotions as a gift to all. To consciously create a signature that inspires freedom and trust in those around you—and to let your emotions be the *cause* of a more abundant, loving, and peaceful kingdom for all rather than the *effect* of the one you're desperately trying to leave behind.

King's Log

1. On a scale from 1 to 10, how confident are you in what your emotional state will be in an hour from now? How much of that is within your control, and how much is dependent on an external "event"?

2. Who or what is determining your emotions?

3. When was the last time you experienced joy or elation? What preceded it? Could it be generated without that inciting event? Why or why not?

King's Word

1. It is my highest will and intent to achieve complete sovereignty and control over my emotions.

2. I effortlessly achieve total and complete responsibility over my emotional experience—allowing myself to create or invoke my own states at will.

3. I withdraw all consent from the negative external influences to trigger emotional reactivity in me.

Embodied Inquiry

1. What would it feel like to be emotionally free?

2. What would it feel like to reclaim total sovereignty and control over my emotional states?

3. What would it be like to effortlessly self-generate and express whatever emotion I choose in any given moment?

Shadow #2: The Suppressed Stoic

With the first shadow, we established that emotion isn't meant to be a reactive force, but a powerful, unspoken language that we get to use to inspire wellbeing for all those in our kingdom.

Emotions are impersonal and fluid. Just like a man can't own the words that part from his lips, he's not the "owner" of the emotions that enter his awareness or express through him. They're not meant to be hoarded, claimed, identified with or held onto at all costs. In truth, you can't identify with "anger" any more than a Gibson guitar can identify with a B-chord, or the morning sky can claim ownership over a rain cloud. But we reinforce just the opposite with every verbal affirmation that binds us to "our" emotions

"I am angry."

"I am happy."

"I am depressed."

This isn't just a matter of verbal semantics. Language, and its symbols, are derived from our experience of the world. In this case, our insistent identification with our emotions. Each of these phrases fuses us to an emotional state. Instead of letting a watery current continue to flow downstream and back into the vast ocean, we bottle it up from the riverbank, drink it with gluttonous force, and then allow it to freeze and crystallize within the frigid confines of our icy hearts. We are not a suitable habitat for emotions to dwell in. They are not meant to be domesticated and controlled within our bodies. They're meant to flow.

The wild paradox is that once we claim ownership over these emotions and hoard them in our bodies, we quickly sense how unsuitable this living arrangement is. We domesticate a wild animal—only to ignore and condemn it. It scratches and claws against our walls, pounds against our doors, and screams for freedom at all hours of the night. But we don't know how to free it, so we immediately disown the very thing we initially claimed.

We tranquilize it with any numbing agent we can find. Then we drag its corpse deep into the basement, slap a deadbolt on the door, and pretend it was never there to begin with. We then go on about our days. We put up a new coat of paint on the scratched walls. We pour bleach over the bloodstains. We replace the destroyed furniture with something more aesthetically pleasing. Satisfied, we invite others into our homes. But even with our fake smiles and pretty words, they too, hear and sense the faint, torturous cries beneath the floorboards, and the stench of its rotting corpse.

This is the work of the suppressed stoic. Just as quickly as he identifies with an emotion and takes it in as his own, he'll resist the pain, disown it, and lock it up behind a steely gaze. Ironically, the path back to freedom is the same we took to get locked in this emotional prison to begin with. We must reverse course. You can't release that which you have disowned.

We'll get back to this in a moment, but first we need to get better acquainted with *The Suppressed Stoic*. We have a cultural obsession with this shadow. The archetype gets portrayed in the media as redeeming and desirable. John Wick, Clint Eastwood, Batman—each of them, cold, detached and seemingly imperturbable. But these are not real men. They are fictional caricatures drawn from the minds of men that point to some falsely virtuous ideal. We wish to see ourselves as utterly undisturbed, skillfully slicing our way through life's toughest challenges while taking false refuge in our steely shell.

And in this view of what it means to be powerful, confident and in-control, there exists no room for a man who experiences anything less than what he believes a powerful, confident, and in-control man *should* feel.

But the suppressed stoic isn't the powerful, confident and in-control man he dreams himself up to be. Quite the opposite. Instead, he's born, enlivened and energized by the fear of any fleeting emotion that doesn't line up with how he wishes to view himself. His power is derived from a subtle sense of self-hatred over who he *truly* is—all because it contradicts the lifeless caricature of unwavering poise and unbending stiffness he's placed on a faulty pedestal.

Bred in this is an impossible entitlement over how the world must see and treat him. Being denied the love or intimacy of a partner, *The Suppressed Stoic* reacts with rage and resentment which gets immediately recoiled and stuffed back down lest he lose his straight-faced persona. The agony of rejection goes against the identity of self-importance he's built up—yet the emotions become immediately hoarded and disowned, ready to be reactivated the next time the world fails to accommodate his fragile construct of feigned stoicism.

A clenched fist beneath a closed heart is even *more* capable of inflicting harm to self and other. It takes a true warrior to fully feel what's passing through—and to drop the mandated coolness that *The Suppressed Stoic* ruthlessly demands and depends upon for his survival.

The invitation isn't to participate in unbridled catharsis and emotional sloppiness. And indeed, clumsily expressing your charged emotions to others, who are in turn "reactive," may induce further harm. Especially if you're still in the habit of weaponizing them. There will be many moments where conscious restraint, until you can process in the privacy of your own heart, is the more skillful of options. We are not here to swim in one another's emotional oil spills. The "cleanup efforts" remain predominantly a personal responsibility. Boundaries remain appropriate and necessary safeguards for both self and other.

The final crime we must hold our *Suppressed Stoic* accountable for is the willful neglect of our own inner truth. Just like how emotion can be expressed as an unspoken language between people—it's also the silent transmission between a man and his higher self. When we suppress it, we ignore aspects of ourselves that are begging to be heard. We hit "mute" to the all-important message that would realign our lives in more favorable ways.

This is the dynamic that contributes to things like Stockholm syndrome of the soul. If you're not listening to the whispers beneath the floorboards, you become more prone to accept the surface-level mistruths of others. Whether they represent the suppressed wound or the hushed whisper of your higher self, emotions need to be seen, heard and discerned. The goal then is to melt away the steely gaze, and see every trigger, emotional reaction, and disproportionate response as a messenger of an unhealed hurt or unreceived message.

This is only possible through deep intimacy with your emotional experience. When you can meet every passing emotion with deep presence and attention. When you can stroke them with your awareness—touch them, embrace them, and feel them without fusing or identifying with them. This is not to be confused with self-coddling. It is an act of plain lucidity, and the courage to remain awake to your own experience.

A central teaching you've likely heard before is that you are *not* your emotions. This is true, yet paradoxically, you're inextricably intimate with them. The goal isn't to dismiss them or deny their presence, but to shift your relationship with them. In trying to become "emotionally free," you're creating an adverse relationship with your emotional states. As if they're an oppressive force to be overcome. But it's not your emotions that are unworthy of your presence, it's you, who's yet to become worthy of the persona and identity you aspire to.

What gets built here is your capacity to embody the vast, infinite space to hold anything. For your child, your partner and the collective at large. Your capacity to love and hold space for your child or partner is a direct reflection of your capacity to do so for yourself.

Finally, there's been a wave of teachings in the last few decades suggesting that men should feel okay in sharing their feelings. That it's okay to cry. That it's okay to be vulnerable and have a moment of total breakdown and unrestrained catharsis. This is true—helpful, even. But what these teachings lack is that it's just as okay to feel elated. That you can celebrate, be joyful, and have total reverence and gratitude for everything around you without losing face or giving up your con game of being so unmovable. These teachings miss the fact that emotions are an *experience* that we get to self-generate, and gift to ourselves and those around us.

Being vulnerable is a starting point. Progress only accelerates when we become both deeply intimate with all that arises, and skillful in self-generating the next emotional state we embody and express. This is the work of a true master and a worthy king. As you come into contact with these long-lost aspects of yourself, there will be times where you'll be taken aback. You'll recoil. You'll despise what you see, for it doesn't line up with the cemented image of the strong, confident man you've idealized yourself to be.

The Suppressed Stoic will judge, condemn and resist. Fearing his demise, he'll put on a more "spiritual" guise, using detachment as his sedative of choice. Your job will be to remain so courageous and unwaveringly intimate with your experience that you simply relinquish the need to suppress or bypass anything to begin with. You don't kill the stoic with rageful force so much as you make him redundant through strength and intimacy.

King's Log

1. Imagine watching yourself cry / scream / experience a fleeting moment of defeat or failure? How do you feel? Can you allow it, or is there a part of you that refuses to let that emotional experience be seen?
2. What other emotional experiences or expressions does "he" condemn?
3. Who is it that resists those experiences, and why?
4. Who is it that feels defined by his emotions?

King's Word

1. It is my highest will and intent to come into deep allowance for any emotional experience that enters my awareness without resistance or self-judgment.
2. I liberate myself from my own harsh judgments or disallowance of my emotional experience.
3. I come into complete understanding and acknowledgment that my emotional experience does not define me or my value as a man, regardless of what high ideals I hold myself to.

Embodied Inquiry

1. What would it feel like to be fully capable and willing of holding my entire emotional experience without fear, judgment or resistance?

Shadow #3: The Illusion of Permanence

The final shadow we encounter is the illusion of permanence. It's the very force that keeps us from experiencing the level of intimacy required for deep emotional healing, and spiritual awakening.

Genuine intimacy is only made possible through deep reverence and appreciation. These qualities can only be attributed to something when we approach it with the intention of sensing and experiencing its presence and nature. Fully embodied acknowledgment of the transient, ever-shifting reality of all things is the master key to making intimacy possible. We'll use the analogy of a lover.

If you knew that your lover would perish before sunrise, you'd hold her closer than you ever have. You'd have no restraint in how much love and healing you'd want to gift her. You'd be able to self-generate this state regardless of how many past hurts and silent traumas have plagued your relationship. You'd effortlessly offer the forgiveness, apologies, presence and intimacy she deserves in those final moments to find deep peace and resolution.

Like the example above, most of us will only grasp the notion of impermanence when it's put on physical display. When actual illness, fatality, or crisis befalls us or our loved ones, our temporal reality becomes unavoidable. The spell has been broken, the illusion revealed, and we immediately become intimate with self or other in those final fleeting moments.

Because so many of us experience our emotional states as life itself, it becomes the perfect practice ground for awakening to the truth of impermanence—and, in turn, letting this principle be the entry ticket to unguarded intimacy with all that arises within our awareness.

Emotions may *feel* fixed and solid. As they arise, they're so overwhelmingly charged and convincing that it becomes difficult to envision any other "state." In a fit of anger, peace feels unattainable. In a moment of sheer joy and elation, frustration or rage seem like distant specters incapable of penetrating the walls of your being. Yet, in truth, no state lasts. Emotions are meant to dissolve as quickly as language rolling off the tongue. Our fearful insistence on permanence is what keeps them stuck.

Most of us are so fused and identified to our emotions, experiencing them as "life" itself—that to admit to their temporal, impermanent nature would be to admit to our own. In coming to terms with the rise and fall of every passing state, we have no choice but to confront our own sense of mortality. It's something we're literally deathly afraid of doing. The illusion of permanence, therefore, is a comforting one—and one which we cling onto at all costs, even if it means insisting on the forced continuity of our most agonizing states. Our egos would rather live in permanent torment than in temporary peace. At least the former gives it some ground to stand on.

This shadow has one final trick up his sleeve. It's perhaps the strongest binding force that locks emotions into place even when their natural expiry has passed—leaving a toxic stench that oozes out from our pores, and poisons all those around us. It's a conniving trick we've all fallen subject to. And one that will dramatically increase the quality of our relationships and lives the moment we free ourselves from its spell.

When we dare to look deep into these flames, we notice the truth that's been hidden in plain sight all along. One that's easily missed for it's so pervasive across all human interactions.

Despite how justified and righteous we may feel in doing so, the truth is, we solidify our emotions in order to weaponize them. In this sense, we are all abusers. Anytime you've refused to let some fleeting hurt evaporate back into the ether, you've done so with the sole intent of manipulating or harming the one you feel is responsible for it. It's the silent, bloodless war we all fight with one another. It began as children, when we would force ourselves to preserve a state of anger or frustration in order to have our parents attune to the level of hurt they've caused. It later becomes present in the husband or wife who willingly holds onto anger even when the general mood has shifted, and there's a genuine opportunity for heartfelt connection and repair.

We hold onto lower states of anger, apathy and sadness in order to influence or manipulate the actions or feelings of another. We falsely believe that they must sense our outrage, and *experience* it in order to accommodate our needs and desires—needs and desires which we ourselves are unaware of. This is of course the least productive, and most abusive way to inspire a gift from another human. For instead of using emotion as a temporal and fleeting gift that we get to self-generate for the benefit of self and other—we solidify them into razor-sharp ice picks that we mercilessly stab each other with until someone caves.

On the emotional battlefield that this shadow insists we live our lives on, being wronged gives us an apparent "upper hand." It makes us feel owed. That others are indebted to us. It's an aggressive stance that denies the other their sovereignty—and even the opportunity for reconciliation. Only a small percentage of abuse would ever be objectively verifiable. It's a subtle game of ill-intent that gets played out with our emotional states. Fortunately, this shadow is not a difficult one to spot. It simply requires impeccability of both your word—and the underlying intent and emotional energy behind it. It requires a depth of honesty that most humans aren't capable of having with themselves. It demands that you ask yourself in every interaction: "*Why am I holding onto this anger?*" or "*By saying this / feeling this, what do I want him or her to feel?*"

Initially, you'll be shocked and humbled by how much of your silent emotional transmission is used to wound or to make one feel guilt, shame, remorse, or shared outrage. There is no peace available to one who insists on denying the same in another. And there is *only* suffering for he who would solidify his emotions in order to cause harm—even in the subtlest of ways.

Emotion wasn't meant to be "held onto" with a false sense of permanence. It was meant to flow like water—like chords being struck on a guitar, vibrating for a few seconds, offering their gift to the room, before drifting back into nothingness.

The shadow stance is to catch, bottle up and solidify our states of anger and hurt so that they seep into the room and harm those who we believe have harmed us. The awakened stance is in allowing emotion to be self-generated, and flow out as a gift before passing back into nothingness. As our primary and ongoing "king's log" and "embodied inquiry" for this shadow, we simply examine and relinquish within the flames, the one who would let any state or emotion dwell beyond their natural occurrence. We uncover his motives and his mechanisms. And perhaps, in doing so, release ourselves from an inner contraction and rigidity that's been clamping our life experience for longer than we can remember. At its core, this ongoing inquiry, and living as response it yields, is what it means to be emotionally and spiritually thriving in an unbalanced world.

Such is the work of *The Master.*

That work begins now.

Awakening The Master

As these shadows begin to dissolve within these flames, we awaken *The Master*. More than any other awakened state, *The Master* is a homecoming. It's a return to what you've been all along.

With the master comes a natural ease. He's undisturbed by the emotions of others, for he's deeply attuned to the fleeting ephemeral nature of them, and the unhealed hurts that provoked them in the first place. For this, he responds with compassionate power rather than closure or cold-hearted crossfire. By his own authority, he un-implicates himself from the distorted, fractured, and emotional firings of his so-called counterpart. He de-credentializes others from defining him and his character through their limited viewpoints. In an unbalanced world, he remains sovereign. A generator of his emotional states rather than the reactor. *Cause* of his situation rather than the *effect* of those around him. He's the evoker instead of the evoked. And in this rare simplicity, he becomes a master of his reality.

He isn't a master over others but a master of himself. And by all accounts, he's simply a normal man unclouded by the deluge of emotions. He can sense the future because he's implicit in its creation. He speaks it into existence through the language of his emotions, and the actions they inspire.

For *The Master*, emotional resilience has nothing to do with bullheaded endurance and suppression. Paradoxically, it's a process of release, renewal, and the deep recognition of the transience that underlies every state. In this knowingness, he doesn't cling to any state—yet doesn't suppress or deny any emotion either. He's attuned and intimate. He can hold any passing emotion like a parting lover without feeling the need to possess or weaponize it. His intimacy is deepened by his willingness to see within himself that which would have lesser men recoil in fear or self-hatred. He denies nothing. He is intimate with all. And in doing so, the world soon yields to his unwavering love and power. For his love and power is made genuine in this awakening. There's no longer a fragmentation of influence. His love is no longer compromised by his untended wounds—and his power is no longer diluted and dispersed across countless hurts and their covert agendas. He is indeed his own master.

There's no endpoint to his mastery. Just like a blues guitarist can always slide through the scales more seamlessly—or add a new speed or signature, *The Master* sees no end to his capacity to feel his way through the world.

He goes beyond "emotional intelligence" and strives for emotional mastery—meaning, the ability to slide between emotional states without resistance, self-identification, or solidification. Instead, he embodies and expresses emotion as the silent but potent language it was intended to be. He's fluent and generous in his offering, using it to generate and project love, gratitude, authentic power, and all the qualities associated with the king. This is his enduring gift to the world. This is the signature he joyfully imparts in every interaction.

This is his true, living legacy.

Crowning The Master

The guided initiation into *The Master* is available to stream at:

www.iseeyouking.com/spirituality

Evolutionary Accelerators

Evolutionary Accelerator #1: Prima Materia

Practice Duration: 5-10 minutes
Practice Frequency: daily

Description:

In this practice, you'll cultivate the ability and capacity to self-generate emotional states on demand, using them as a form of unspoken language while developing confidence in your natural ability to shift from one to the other.

The natural realization in this practice is that there's a fluidity between states. Such realization will shorten the "refractory period" between any "charged reactivity" you may experience, and your choice to return back to neutrality, equanimity or non-resistance.

A useful frame for many is to view yourself as a musician playing different chords. A note is played, it reverberates, and then it gently fades back into undifferentiated and choiceless silence.

Be effortless in this "playing." You don't need to "be" happy, which may feel like an undue burden. You simply need to "play" happy with the same ease as any musician can play a B-chord.

Much like a toddler's first words or a musician's first strums, this may feel awkward, clunky or "out of tune" at first. But with consistent practice, both the "fullness" of the emotions you can generate—as well as the fluidity between them will greatly increase.

You can do this practice either standing or sitting. Between each "state," rest in "neutral" or "natural silence" for about 5-10 seconds, noting the tone of your "baseline" at this time. As you continue to practice, pay attention to see if your baseline or "return state' evolves as well.

When you're ready...

Round 1: Two minutes

1. Play "Happy" for 10 seconds.
2. Play "Excited" for 10 seconds.
3. Play "The feeling of being loved" for 10 seconds.
4. Play "Gratitude" for 10 seconds
5. Play "Confidence" for 10 seconds.
6. Play "Courage" for 10 seconds.
7. Play "Love" for 10 seconds.
8. Play "Strength" for 10 seconds.
9. Play "Laughter / Hilarity" for 10 seconds.
10. Play "Peace" for 10 seconds.

Round 2: Two minutes

Similar to Round 1, except this time, you'll put a predominant negative emotional pattern or state between each "positive" note. This could be fear, frustration, anger, sadness, grief, guilt or powerlessness. Anything you feel your body and mind is most reactive to.

The goal of this advanced set is to create easeful and available mental, emotional and even somatic pathways from your reactive patterns back to positive states. This way, when something gets "evoked," you're well practiced in not-dwelling in that state, but finding a familiar rung back to wellness/ neutrality.

1. Play "Happy" for 10 seconds.
2. Play "Anger/grief/shame, etc." for 10 seconds.
3. Play "Excited" for 10 seconds.
4. Play "Anger/grief/shame, etc." for 10 seconds.
5. Play "The feeling of being loved" for 10 seconds.
6. Play "Anger/grief/shame, etc." for 10 seconds.
7. Play "Gratitude" for 10 seconds.
8. Play "Anger/grief/shame, etc." for 10 seconds.
9. Play "Confidence" for 10 seconds.
10. Play "Anger/grief/shame, etc." for 10 seconds.
11. Play "Courage" for 10 seconds.
12. Play "Anger/grief/shame, etc." for 10 seconds.
13. Play "Love" for 10 seconds.
14. Play "Anger/grief/shame, etc." for 10 seconds.
15. Play "Strength" for 10 seconds.
16. Play "Anger/grief/shame, etc." for 10 seconds.
17. Play "Laughter / Hilarity" for 10 seconds.
18. Play "Anger/grief/shame, etc." for 10 seconds.
19. Play "Peace" for 10 seconds.

Evolutionary Accelerator #2: Full Spectrum Emotional Sensing

Practice Duration: whenever non-optimal states / reactivity arises
Practice Frequency: daily

Description:

This practice is a continuation of what we introduced in "Sense Play" earlier on.

Just like there are countless ways to hold a lover; there are countless ways to hold your emotional states or patterns. Most will hold their negative reactivity in resistance, avoidance, impatience or straight up condemnation.

Traditional spiritual practices will often recommend holding your emotions in "presence / allowance / choiceless awareness"—often referred to as simply "witnessing."

This is indeed a worthwhile endeavor. However, dispassionate or detached "witnessing" may not always be readily available for more charged emotional states that have been long repressed. They may need a different form of "presencing" to accelerate their resolution.

You can rotate between as many of the following as you feel called. Typically, after experiencing an emotion through just a few of these aspects, it will begin to automatically fade or transform.

16 ways to be intimate with a feeling state:

1. See it.
2. Touch it.
3. Smell it.
4. Taste it.
5. "Drop into it" (plunging your awareness into the feeling).
6. Surrender to it.
7. Love it.
8. Be in "awe" of it.
9. Celebrate it.
10. Laugh with it (at the absurdity of the "story" that's holding it into place).
11. Mourn it (recognizing its impermanence—ask "where will this be in 1,000 years?)
12. Observe it from above.
13. Observe it from a multitude of distances and angulations.
14. Observe it from the viewpoint of any object in the room.
15. Observe it from the imagined viewpoint of anything or anyone.
16. Observe it from the viewpoint of your higher self / inner king.

Evolutionary Accelerator #3: Emotional Sparring

Practice Duration: weekly

Practice Frequency: 10 minutes

Description:

Many of us have an 80/20 of emotional reactivity. Meaning, there are a few core and recurring "situations" or "patterns" that are responsible for the vast majority of our negative emotional reactions. This may be a "type" of exchange with our lover or partner. Or it could be a recurring dynamic with our boss or manager or employees.

The first step in this exercise is to identify the 2 or 3 core reactive patterns you experience (and recall the feeling states that accompany them). Rather than wait for them to inevitably reoccur, you can practice working with them in the privacy of your own awareness.

Just like an MMA fighter or boxer will spar with a similarly-styled opponent for weeks or months before the "main event," you'd be wise to "spar" with your core negative emotional patterns where there are certain "safeguards" preventing the damage that can be done.

Few people would *choose* to use their rare windows of peaceful solitude to "recreate" their most stressful situations, yet the cost of being beholden to a "triggered" state that can erupt at a moment's notice is far less practical and skillful.

When you've chosen the reactive pattern you want to work with, try to evoke the situation. Imagine the other "players" present. What they're saying, how you're reacting, and how it feels in your mind and body. Chances are, you won't have to "imagine" the reaction. Your bod/mind and nervous system will likely configure into a similar pattern as if the event was happening in real-time.

Now use the tools and skills you've developed in the previous two practices to "hold" the emotional pattern with different types of "intimacy" and/or switch between states (to practice emotional fluency). Let this be dynamic. Allow your own wisdom to dictate "how you hold" the experience—and what you do to "get back" to neutrality or a positive state. You may find that some methods of experiencing the pattern are more effective for your particular makeup or constitution.

But the more you can pattern your way out of reactivity; the less you'll be prone to slipping into the pattern the next time it gets "evoked or triggered." And even when it does, you'll have practiced the steps to come out of it quicker, more confidently, and with less collateral damage.

Evolutionary Accelerator #4: Emotional Ascension

Practice Duration: minutes

Practice Frequency: as needed

Description:

Technically, one can jump from one emotional state to another; no matter how "far" the perceived distance between them. A low note to a high note needn't take much more effort to a skilled musician than scaling up one note at a time.

However, while you're developing this mastery, it may be useful to "play the scales" when trying to climb out of a denser and stickier emotion.

Going from depression to ecstatic joy may be too "big of a leap." Emotional Ascension™ therefore is about pulling yourself out from a hole—one rung at a time.

For example, if you're feeling reactive anger or rage, your pathway to a positive state may look as such:

1. Ange/Rage about X person/situation
2. Anger/Rage about yourself (claiming responsibility)
3. Feeling the raw power / potentiality within the anger
4. Feeling confidence/awe around your ability to own and express that power
5. Determination to express that power to create a more healthy/positive dynamic
6. If you're feeling sadness / grief / despair, that path may look like:
7. Depression
8. The heaviness / sadness / grief within
9. The tenderness towards those feelings
10. Vulnerability
11. Self-compassion and love
12. Celebrating the goodness of your own heart / compassion for all.

You can dynamically create your own "ascension map" for each reactive state you encounter. Or you can proactively create these paths—which may give you greater confidence in your day-to-day life, knowing you have the tools to "climb back" to a state of wellness and empowerment no matter where you've landed.

Chapter 10

FIRE 7 - EXPRESSING FULLY IN A SUPPRESSED WORLD

What makes this an "initiatory fire"?

I welcome you to the final fire, king.

This is where you'll take all of the preceding initiations, and return back to the world with their gifts fully activated and ready to be expressed. The inner king has undoubtedly awakened. It's now time for him to stake his claim and preside over his kingdom.

Yet his claim isn't marked by how loud he screams. It's not secured through baneful threat nor tyrannical rule. Instead, it's confirmed by how strongly he's willing to swing his sword.

Your fullest expression of all the virtues we've awakened throughout this program *is* the force that puts your inner king on his throne. It's what earns you the right to rule—and the trust of both yourself and your constituents that your rule will be seated in deep love, positive power and reverence for all it touches.

But while most men would be sincere in proclaiming their willingness to fully express these gifts, so few will actually develop the courage, commitment, and consistency to do so. For beneath it all, we're met with the sheer terror over our own power. The man in chains may dream of breaking free, but he is terrified of what he'll be called to do with his newfound freedom. With no one left to oppress him, he becomes responsible for his fullest expression.

He lives and dies by his own sword. And that, as counterintuitive as it may seem, is often more terrifying than the oppression itself. Likewise, no matter how noble his intent, a single errant swing of his sword can cause harm to those around him. This is no small thing. Take a moment to check in. Ask yourself: *"Do I really want to be free?... and do I really want to express myself fully as a man?"*

Resist the knee-jerk reaction of "of course" and truly ask yourself if you're ready to be fully responsible for its virtuous expression across all of life's containers? Chances are, the answer becomes less obvious. Any courageous roar is most certainly accompanied by the panicked howls of this fire's shadows. For in these flames, we'll meet the shadow of *The Sheathed Swordsman*—a coward in warrior's garb, terrified of penetrating the world with his sword.

When we talk about suppression, we often think about the suppression of emotions. But there's a deeper, more fundamental suppression that most men encounter. It's the suppression of his fullest expression in each passing moment. A self-imposed constriction and self-censoring over his most aligned actions, and the cascade of outcomes and events that their reverberations would produce.

It's found in the moment where you feel a pounding impulse to say the six words that can thrust your relationship into a completely new direction—a point of no return—but settle for the well-worn smile and passive utterance instead. Its influence is felt when you feel a call to take that big swing in your business. The one that would reconfigure the chess board, and set you and your team up for a massive leap that sends shockwaves throughout your industry—but instead get reined back in by the fear of "messing up a good thing."

It's experienced inwardly when you hear the inner whispers of greater purpose, but suppress it due to the terror of feeling judged by your family or peers, and ultimately failing by your own accord.

If we can overcome *The Sheathed Swordsman*, we'll bravely confront two final shadows: *The Potential Paradox* and *Your Legacy*. Both of which create a tremendous inward pressure to succeed, yet paradoxically, create a form of existential paralysis. One where you can't reconcile your limitless potential with your finite expression of it, and thus remain stuck in the in-between.

Finally, we'll unpack the notion of a man's legacy—stripping it down to the bone, and revealing it for the limiting force it truly is. With these final shadows undone, you'll be free to live your life from your inner throne, living *as* the king you are, and always have been.

Expressing fully in a suppressed world is indeed our final initiation. It's ongoing. Moment by moment until the very second your heart stops and the sword is planted back into the earth. For life itself, and every passing moment within it, is initiatory in of itself. We are all inextricably partaking in the ceremony of our own lives.

Presiding through it as *king* is where you earn your final crown.

Shadow #1: The Sheathed Swordsman

Do you trust yourself enough to be a king? To move boldly. To decide swiftly. To lead with heart, vision and with power. Or do you still doubt your own steadiness?

Do you lack the groundedness to remain firmly planted in your vision? The self-trust to not succumb to the harsh winds of change or the seductive whispers of your remaining shadows.

Do you trust the thrust of your own sword? The rebellion you'll ignite. The position you'll win. The empire you'll create.

Understand that it is only you who is standing in the way of the throne. Most men are their own prisoner. They'll fight for the very thing that they themselves restrict. You're your own captor—and it's all because of how deeply you fear your own freedom and what you'll do with it.

No sane man would deny his own freedom. But to be free, you must own it. You must shed the fear of living with the consequences of what gets expressed with that freedom, for it's the fullest expression of your heart-infused power that invites more of it to flow through you. It's the momentum of the preceding swing of the sword that gives direction and intent to the next.

But most men won't trust themselves enough to fully express the power they have. They'll sheath their swords, de-arm themselves, and ultimately crawl back into their own tiny cell where they can limit their influence and impact on the world.

There's a reason for this. When we have unchecked anger and unconfronted shadows, de-arming ourselves limits the amount of harm we can create. On a subtle level, we sense that our intent isn't as pure as our egos would like to think. And in truth, many of us still act in ways designed to harm. Most of the time, that harm isn't physical but emotional and energetic. We say things to make others feel responsible or guilty, or to share the burdens of our suffering.

Abuse doesn't always require a raised fist or a thunderous voice. Sometimes, it's our silence that cuts deepest. Anytime we say or do anything with the subtle intent of making someone feel anything less than empowered, supported, and cared for, we have committed a form of abuse. I highlight this not to shame, but to shed proper light so that we can free ourselves from the subtle negative intent that most of us carry—and in turn, regain trust in our own fullest expression. Ultimately, in confronting these subtle layers of ill-intent, we develop the trust and capacity to swing our swords powerfully but not recklessly, knowing that as we carve our place in the world, it's made better for it.

This brings us to another paradox. How exactly do we know the world is being made better for it? Every villain believes himself to be the hero of his own story. Few people act with pure malice. In most cases, they feel righteous and noble in their abuses and atrocities.

So, what makes us different? What makes our rule any more altruistic, empowering and compassionate than another man's? And most importantly, how can we ensure that in expressing ourselves fully, we do no harm to others?

The short answer is we can't. We can only continue in our commitment to cultivate the virtues of the king, while developing the self-awareness to confront all remaining shadows of ill-intent that would compromise them.

But even then, we can never guarantee it. For in expressing fully, there will always be those who experience harm from our actions. If we shut down our current business to pursue another one of greater purpose—our clients, collaborators and contractors, at least in the short term, will absorb that blow. If our deep longing to gift our love to another woman requires us to leave behind a stale marriage void of the same mutual gifting, even the most truthful and compassionate exit won't spare your wife from the wounding.

There's an extreme weightiness to this. Through our honest pursuit of truth and our fullest expression of it, it's impossible to not affect others. While some would encourage you to move swiftly and ignore the body count, we're not stoic warriors. We care. Deeply. And this is both honorable and irreconcilable. Afterall, how do we reconcile a life of full expression that *still*, even with its positive intent, still leaves behind a body count?

The truth is, we can't. We can only grow to become comfortable in that paradox. We can only learn to gradually build up the self-trust that we are in fact virtuous in our pursuits. That our dedication to non-harm is sincere and also sometimes unavoidable.

We'd also be wise to acknowledge the truth that most men will overestimate the scope of "collateral damage" they may inflict, and underestimate others' power and capacity to rise through and beyond it. It takes a calcified image of your partner as "powerless" to assume she won't rise anew from the "devastation" of losing you. Be careful to not deprive others of the dignity of rebuilding on more sustainable and fertile ground. Forced continuity may be far more injurious.

Ultimately, our genuine desire to express ourselves fully must outweigh our fear of the unavoidable consequences. The alternative is simply too devastating. It is not your birthright to live a benign existence. It is your birthright to beautifully express every ounce of truth, love, and compassionate power you've been gifted. The chosen withholding of your greatest gifts will always be a greater crime than the perceived collateral damage from your accidental misfirings.

Such is the beautiful, yet at times excruciating experience of walking this earth with others. Even a Buddhist monk will accidentally step on an ant while walking up the monastery stairs. Intend no harm—but don't lock yourself in a self-imposed prison to guarantee it. And when harm is caused, accept full responsibility. Make reparations where necessary. Not in self-shame, but in genuine compassion. Don't let the paradox keep you paralyzed in fear. Let it crack open your heart and reveal to you the true interdependence between all things.

In this paradox, we awaken. In this paradox, we are enlivened, for we see and acknowledge how a single swing of the sword can change the fate of an empire for decades to come. Our expression then becomes sacred. Holy. And we, as king, finally accept our rule, claim our throne, and surrender to the absolute wholeness of all things.

This is your birthright.

Unsheathe your sword, wield it with every drop of love in your body, and swing it with every ounce of power you've been gifted.

Such is your right. Such is your rule.

I see you, King.

King's Log

1. On a scale from 1 to 10, how much would you say you are truly in the fullest expression of your love, power and truth?
2. In what ways do you self-censor, stop short, or "sheathe" your sword? Why?
3. What are you so afraid of "disrupting" by being fully expressed? What evidence do you have that your "disruption" would be as fatal and devastating as you believe it to be?

King's Word

1. It is my highest will and intent to express fully, trusting in the goodness that underlies it all.
2. As an act of self-respect and self-reverence, I am in the constant expression of my highest gifts and virtues.

Embodied Inquiry

1. What would it feel like to be fully expressed in my highest power and truth at all times?

Shadow #2: The Potential Paradox

As we overcome the first shadow in this fire, we're met with another seemingly irreconcilable paradox—your full potential.

Ironically, we live in a time where you have greater access to knowledge, information, and opportunity than ever before. While upward mobility within some arenas is still challenging, sometimes to a debilitating extreme, we still live in an era where just about every individual has greater potential than they would have had just fifteen or twenty years ago.

As such, in the past decade, it's become popular to talk about our "limitless" nature—to be enthralled and utterly awestruck by the sheer possibility of what one can pursue and achieve in a single lifetime. Knowledge that monarchs would have to wait weeks to receive is now available to us in twenty seconds and a few finger taps. Our world is exponentially more connected. These two factors alone have contributed to an immeasurable increase in one's potential. In this, we've become addicted to a form of manic "limitlessness." The sense that we can *do* anything, *be* anything, *achieve* anything.

Fundamentally, this is not wrong. Grounded in reverence, peace, and compassion, these beliefs are empowering, expansive and life-affirming. But this isn't the experience of most people. Rather, we feel an intense burden in achieving our full potential—and a growing sense of discontent and despair as we realize how impossible it actually is.

A droning hum of existential dread seems to pervade all we do. For in choosing one thing over another, we feel both the exaggerated fruits that we missed out on, and the grief for having done so. In short, many of us are haunted by a potential that, by its very definition, can never be fully lived.

For in truth, you can never *achieve* your full potential. You can chase it with every fiber of your being—but you simply can't catch something that's expanding infinitely at a speed far greater than your human capacity to match it.

Every time you connect with a new business contact in the airport lounge or Zoom call, your "potential" explodes into a million new configurations. With will and intent, that same contact could become a partner in a new venture, a supporter of your current one, or a saboteur of your biggest dreams. All these potentials are instantly introduced to your reality. Only an infinitesimally small percentage of them will ever find their way into material existence.

When you make eye contact with the woman sitting across from you in the coffee shop and feel an unspoken resonance with her energy, your potential exponentially broadens into countless new permutations. Statistically, almost none of which will ever be realized.

This creates a form of existential FOMO (fear of missing out). We are bound by a persistent anxiety over our perceived limited nature. We are infinite at our core yet experientially constricted. We can't reconcile an infinitely expanding universe—of which we are—with a limited experience of it. Torturously unsatiated, either a frantic lusting occurs; or a panic-stricken paralysis.

There's an anguish in the paradox between being "limitless" yet only being able to experience and express a small sliver of it within time and space. Mortality isn't a fear of death, it's an inability to reconcile the impossibility of experiencing our fullest potential. Not hearing every song. Not communing with every partner. Not building every business. Not throwing every touchdown. Not painting or singing or writing or dancing every masterpiece.

"Do not go gently into that dark night. Rage against the dying of the light."

And we do. Furiously trying to chase what can't be chased, achieve what can't be achieved, sing what can't be sung, and live what can't be lived. Ironically, it's the very chasing that prevents us from settling into the wholeness of that which we already are.

A part of us simply refuses to be satiated with a small taste of the absolute—not realizing that the absolute is contained within that small taste. As above, so below. As without, so within.

On a larger scale, history shows that a failure to reconcile this existential dilemma leads to a premature destruction. Many great empires, unsatiated, expanded to the point of their own dissolution. Rome, as a collective, fell as its empire lines expanded to a point of being indefensible. Businesses "scale up" to the point of being caved in by complexity, and ultimately being crushed under the weight of its own overhead.

In our own personal empires, we expand our empire lines to compensate for our inner enclosure—frantically attempting to resolve this inner crisis by expanding the borders of our reign—adding layers of complexity to our lives via more relationships, more people to influence, more possessions, more sources of self-aggrandizement. It's an energy of frantic, infantile possession and accumulation that can only lead to premature destruction. Such is the paradox of your full potential.

While the uninitiated man will chase his potential to the edge of the world, and ultimately self-destruct in his pursuit, the king seeks fullness in the finite—and finds freedom within it. The potential paradox is ultimately reconciled by a single shift in perspective. The ultimate paradigm shift, if you will.

Pain exists in the small self only being able to hold a small piece of the whole. In only getting to experience a small sliver of his infinite, and ever-expanding potential. Ecstasy exists in the king's ability to experience fullness in form—

infinity within the finite—and to feel utterly satiated by assimilating the fullness of his experience.

No king worth his crown would willingly engage in an unwinnable war. No compassionate king would put his constituents in harm's way by expanding his empire lines beyond defensibility. In the same vein, your goal is *not* to chase your full potential. It's to have reverence and appreciation for the full spectrum of potentialities before you in every moment—and then to fully express the portion of it you feel most called to bridge into material existence. This is the gift of being human. In a constantly expanding universe with infinite possibilities, you get to consciously coalesce around a single potential—giving it the gift of focus, attention, and material existence. However transient.

In this, you are the ultimate gift to the infinite—and your fullest expression is the mechanism that delivers it.

King's Log

1. What areas of life (and your potential) cause you the most FOMO, regret or anguish around "potentials" that haven't been pursued? (i.e., relationships, business, career, etc.)?
2. Of those "missed" potentials, what causes the biggest sense of anguish? How can you be so certain in that other potential outcome? Even if a "better" outcome was missed, must you suffer for it? Why?

King's Word

1. I find complete fullness and wholeness within every action I take.
2. I am totally and utterly at peace with my potential and the parts of it I choose to experience and express.

Embodied Inquiry

1. What would it feel like to bring full power, attention and presence to all you choose to experience physically?
2. What would it feel like to know, appreciate and revel in your full potential, while only experiencing the expressions within it of your highest calling?

Shadow #3: Your Legacy

About a hundred years ago, one of the most cherished records in all of sports was owned by a man, who today, just over a century later, only the most diehard historians can recall. Within twenty years, when those remaining purists have perished, so too will the name of a man who for three decades owned one of the most lauded records in sport.

Ned Williamson held onto the single-season homerun record for 35 years. He died at 37 years old and was buried in an unmarked grave. One has to wonder if he had been convinced he was immortalized. That he had cemented an undisputed legacy that couldn't be touched. That not even he, the homerun king, could be erased from the annals of time. A man once celebrated by an entire sport tragically reduced to trivia *obscura*. As we embark on this final fire, we're met with two choices. We can weep for Ned Williamson, or we can learn from him.

For in truth, you too will be forgotten. Let this truth not haunt you with insignificance but liberate you from the clench of fear and expectation. For legacy, as you know it, has been a limply dangled carrot. A toxic snake oil with disastrous side effects on the human soul. A manipulative force that most men will spend their entire lives chasing after in a desperate attempt to medicate away their own mortality.

But recognition and appreciation for this ephemerality is also your greatest gift. For mortality, fully felt, is the only *real* motivation one will ever need to live in his fullest expression. It's a permission slip to pursue truth and purpose— not for the sake of having your name etched onto a plaque or to be dipped in bronze—but to be the living embodiment of your highest realized truth in every passing moment.

Living for a legacy is a trapping that most will only ever discover on their deathbed. Cold-limbed, wispy breath, and not a warm hand in the world to console the regret of a heartbeat auctioned off to the highest bidder. Legacy is not the point. Legacy won't be measured. Legacy is little more than a cheap substitute for a man who hasn't realized his limitlessness, and pursued his fullest expression within it.

For once you're gone, people will tell a million different stories about who you were and how you lived. No two eulogies being the same. All will be subjective. None will be accurate. Each retelling filtered through the skewed lens of the particular teller.

Kurt Cobain. Mickey Mantle. Steve Jobs. Leonard Cohen.

Each had their life stories committed to ink hundreds of times over. Each paradoxically portrayed as hero and villain, pious and petty, famous and infamous. Swinging between poles as the aperture of the recounter contracts and dilates around their skewed and limited vision.

In truth, you will never be viewed how you want to be viewed. You will never be fully appreciated for what you've done—and you'll never receive enough compassion and forgiveness for your missteps along the way.

It then begs to reason that to be a slave to legacy is a tragic waste of one's life. A legacy, for all intents and purposes, is not real. It's a subjective experience filtered and ultimately obscured by the trappings, projections and secret agendas of the person recounting it. There is not a single person on the planet more qualified to define who you are and how you lived than you. People's perceptions, beliefs and opinions of you, be them positive or negative, are both largely coated in falsehood, and beyond your control. In this, "fearing what people think" is a closely linked shadow that finds its root in the same core pattern.

Inaccuracies aside, in truth you *will* be forgotten. If not by the next generation, then the generation after that. Think of everything you've created and will create. With your hands, with your mind, and with your will. Where will those things be in 10 years from now? In 50, in 100, in 1,000, in 10,000, in 100,000?

Even if you did something *truly* monumental and world-changing, you'll be but a footnote in whatever they use as history books—and in 300 years, those books will have been burnt or digitally erased and replaced by new books where your great-grandkids will have become footnotes. Statues crumble. Empires get forgotten. Entire civilizations get swallowed up by the cataclysmic impulses of a force far greater than the human mind can ever comprehend.

Most men will spend a lifetime trying not to be forgotten while forgetting about the very things that truly immortalize him. For man isn't immortalized by a bronze statue, but in shaving the rust off his own beating heart.

A man will spend decades "building" a legacy in the boardroom while his son goes virtually unfathered, and in turn, spends the next forty years bleeding out from the wound of an absent father who prioritized a balance sheet over a ballgame.

It is said that there's nothing a child needs more than to observe his or her father in the daily pursuit of his truth. The child doesn't want the reins to the "family business" or the trip to Disneyland that those extra hours supposedly provide. He wants to see the king in his power—and to know that such lofty aspirations aren't of lore or legend, but in the living heartbeat and moment-by-moment actions of he who's claimed his throne.

Yet in frantically avoiding being forgotten, we resist the fullest expression of our love, creativity, and impact. In tiptoeing across the crosswalk we call life, we slip into the abyss of our own existence. The point isn't to be remembered. The point isn't to avoid being forgotten. Legacy is not the point. For a legacy is not left. It is *lived*.

It is *lived* into creation moment by moment. And it's never too early nor too late to live it. To do so requires both intense commitment and absolute reverence for the moment by moment unfolding of your fullest expression—and a devaluing of some stagnant legacy that's both unreal and beyond your control.

It requires you to be a humble servant to the unfoldment of your own innate gifts. For in truth, being true to what wishes to express through you—to stamp itself onto reality— will be a daring and thankless endeavor. Freedom comes in the process and in the lightness in shedding the need to live for a legacy.

Mickey Mantle drank himself to death.

Kurt Cobain ravaged himself with heroin-filled needles, until a shotgun shell ripped through his skull.

Steve Jobs played host to a pancreatic tumor that overstayed its welcome and overtook the entire house.

In those final moments, we wonder if legacy was something they were concerned about. Or perhaps their final freedom came in no longer having to *be* Kurt Cobain, Mickey Mantle, Steve Jobs, and the pressures of legacy that came with such.

I can't speak for them, and I won't speak for you. I can only invite you to *live* your legacy. An invitation that can't help but ignite any man who still has a gift to give, and an awakened heart that simply sees no other way.

Your greatest mourning will not be in the perishing of a loved one, but in the moment you come face-to-face and heart-to-heart with the reality of having never really lived.

It will rip you apart. It will swallow you whole. You'll feel a greater sense of remorse than you've felt your entire life.

And as the sorrow sweeps through the inner sanctum of your soul, you'll lift your head up.

Agony will transform into astonishment. You'll become intertwined with the pulsation of life herself.

And your fullest expression will no longer be an aborted pipe dream—but a birthright, finally realized.

King, it is time to be born.

Awakening _____

This final chapter isn't mine to write.

It is for the world to witness.

For what awakens is simply the fullest expression of *you*. In all its truth and perfection.

Beyond definition. Beyond legacy. Beyond anything that one can ever put word or title to.

It's the constant, ever-shifting mark you leave on the world around you— gifting yourself to the moment, and daring to express all the qualities and virtues you've already, and will continue to awaken.

For there is no end point. Only a deepening.

Life is your throne room.

Your initiation is ongoing and ever-unfolding.

I shall step out of the way.

For, king, this chapter is yours to write.

Grip the quill with awe, love and reverence. Never too loose. Never too tight. Always with full awareness of who you truly are within this great interplay.

May the ink spill with the unique brilliance that only your rule can provide.

For your rule now begins.

Long live, the King.

Afterword:

THE PATHLESS PATH

What preceded has been a modern path towards personal and spiritual development.

Yet it's important to recognize that all paths are temporary.

They provide an additional level of safety and structure to an otherwise arduous and unpredictable ascent.

But we must acknowledge that the mountain predates the path.

The path is superimposed on the natural terrain before you.

And ultimately, it too, must vanish.

Paths are useful up until the point when you've developed the sensitivity and perceptive capacities of a skilled tracker or hunter.

Likewise, there will be a time in your own development, perhaps now, where you can ditch the blazed trail and allow your instincts and expanded sense of perception to lead the way.

A guide (in the form of a skilled coach, mentor or ally) can also be a useful companion on the trek up. But even with assistance, you must be careful to not abdicate responsibility in your own healing, refinement and development.

You must remain empowered, and at the edge of your capacities at all times. No one can do the work for you. No one can claim the throne in your name. And be wary of any coach or teacher who insists on establishing a spiritually-clothed dependence for a moment longer than its natural utility.

Your ever-sharpening discernment shall be a key inner guide. And the ever-growing brightness of your heart, the torch that lights all. I see you, king.

If you wish to be supported personally by the author; he will occasionally open up opportunities for either individual or group counsel. You may inquire on such availabilities at:

www.iseeyouking.com/coaching

Next Steps & Bonus Resources

1. If you've benefitted from this book in any way (whether from a single insight; or the complete practice), please consider leaving an honest rating and written review from the site you purchased from.

2. Once published, screenshot your review and send it to **hello@iseeyouking.com** for complimentary access to a bonus training.

3. Stay up to date by joining the private "I see you, king" newsletter at iseeyouking.com

About the Author

Hendrix Black is a coach, guide, and pioneering voice in the modern men's space, having authored a series of widely shared essays that have inspired tens of thousands of men to find greater wholeness, healing and positive power across the major "fires" of their daily lives. He is the co-founder and chief editor of the widely-read newsletter "I see you, king" (iseeyouking.com), which serves thousands of men every year through its various partnerships, programs and experiences. He can be contacted at hendrix@iseeyouking.com

A free ebook edition is available with the purchase of this book.

To claim your free ebook edition:

1. Visit MorganJamesBOGO.com
2. Sign your name CLEARLY in the space
3. Complete the form and submit a photo of the entire copyright page
4. You or your friend can download the ebook to your preferred device

Print & Digital Together Forever.

Snap a photo

Free ebook

Read anywhere